Every Day in
TUSCANY

SEASONS OF AN ITALIAN LIFE

Every Day in
TUSCANY

FRANCES
MAYES

BANTAM

SYDNEY AUCKLAND TORONTO NEW YORK LONDON

A Bantam book
Published by Random House Australia Pty Ltd
Level 3, 100 Pacific Highway, North Sydney NSW 2060
www.randomhouse.com.au

First published in the United States by Broadway Books in 2010
First published in Australia by Bantam in 2010

Addresses for companies within the Random House Group can be found at
www.randomhouse.com.au/offices

National Library of Australia
Cataloguing-in-Publication Entry

Mayes, Frances.
Every day in Tuscany.

ISBN 978 1 86325 676 6 (pbk.)

Americans – Italy – Tuscany – Biography.
Tuscany (Italy) – Biography.
Tuscany (Italy) – Description and travel.
Tuscany (Italy) – Social life and customs.

945.5092

Cover photograph by Albert Hurley
Design by Lauren Dong
Map by Jackie Aher
Printed in Australia by Griffin Press, an accredited ISO AS/NZS 14001:2004
Environmental Management System printer

10 9 8 7 6 5 4 3 2 1

FSC
Mixed Sources
Product group from well-managed
forests and other controlled sources
Cert no. SGS-COC-005088
www.fsc.org
© 1996 Forest Stewardship Council

The paper this book is printed on is certified by the © 1996 Forest
Stewardship Council A.C. (FSC). Griffin Press holds FSC chain
of custody SGS-COC-005088. FSC promotes environmentally
responsible, socially beneficial and economically viable management of the world's forests.

FOR WILLIE

Acknowledgments

FOR SO MUCH PLEASURE along the way, my love and thanks to Ed, Ashley, and Willie. Ed's adventures and fun in the kitchen stand behind many of the recipes, and our passion for Italy is so entwined that these pages are as much his as mine. Ashley's acute and perceptive reading and Willie's *gusto di vivere* contributed to the joy of writing these pages.

Due baci to: Alberto, Tony, Carlos and the whole Alfonso family, Melva and Jim Pante, Sheryl and Rob Turping, Catherine and Jim McLaughlin, all Cortona natives by now. My Italian friends are portrayed in these pages, but no words can capture their grace and warmth. Special love to the Di Rosas, the Cardinali, the Baracchi, and the Calicchia families. Gilda Di Vizio, Albano Fabrizi, Giorgio Zappini, Domenica Castelli, and Ivan Italiani—many thanks. Architect Walter Petrucci and master-builder Rosanno Checcarelli showed me just how easy a building project can be and enhanced my knowledge of Tuscan vernacular architecture.

Throughout the writing of seven books, I've had the luck to work with Peter Ginsberg of Curtis Brown Ltd. He's a paradigm of his profession and a good friend. And with us all the way has been Charlie Conrad of Broadway Books, extraordinary editor and Italophile. Thank you, Rachel Rokicki, my publicist at Broadway, and the whole team, especially Jenna

Ciongoli and Julie Sills. My gratitude to Dave Barbor, my foreign rights agent, to Nathan Bransford and Grace Wherry of Curtis Brown, to Fiona Inglis of Curtis Brown Australia, and to Nikki Christer of Random House, also in Australia. *Mille grazie,* Albert (Secondo) Hurley. I happened to be around when he climbed the bell tower and took the cover photograph that so nicely fit the end of my book. My thanks to Becky Cabaza and to the book designer, Lauren Dong. Photographer Steven Rothfeld and I have worked on many projects together with wonderful synergy. *Grazie,* Stefano. Also a big thank-you to Linda Pastonchi and Elizabeth Shestak for manuscript assistance.

I was honored to receive the Premio Internazionale Casato Prime Donne. My great appreciation to the jury and to Donatella Cinelli Colombini for this award and for placing lines from this book on a vineyard path.

Our kitchen has benefited from knowing many chefs. I especially thank Silvia Regi, Marco Bistarelli, Nicola Borbui, Eva Seferi, and Andrea Quagliarella for sharing their talents and recipes. Also I would like to pour a glass of Brunello for Marco Molesini, Junas Moncada Cancogni, Silvio Ariani, Giuseppe Frangieh, Mario Ponticelli, and Lapo Salvadori.

My special thanks to the editors of publications and producers of lecture venues where I first tried out much of the material in this book:

El Pais (Madrid), *Town and Country Travel, Waterstone* (England), *Signature, Inside Borders, Real Simple, Taiwan Vogue, Powell's Q & A, Casa Claudia* (São Paulo), *Elle Brazil, O Estado de São Paulo, Financial Times, Metro, Toronto Star, Gainesville Magazine, Inspire* (Singapore), *The Sun Times* (Singapore), *The Straits Times* (Singapore), *Silver Kris* (Singapore), *The Durham News and Observer, Journal News,* and *Points North Magazine.*

The Smithsonian Program, Detroit Institute of Art, Nashville Antiques and Garden Show, Dallas Museum of Art, New York University at La Pietra in Florence, Cortona Wine Consortium, Tuscan Sun Festival, Florida Southern College, Hillsborough Literary Society, the Junior League of San Diego, Chapel Hill Historical Society, Impact Programs for Excellence–El Paso, University of Nebraska–Omaha, Salt Lake City Public Library, Campbell Foods, Lane Public Library, Fayetteville Public Library, Denver Post Pen and Podium, Northeastern University, Society for the Performing Arts–Houston, Suffolk University, Vero Beach Museum of Art, Palace Theatre–Waterbury, Atlanta Girls School, St. John's University, Indiana University, Los Angeles Times Book Festival, Sacramento Bee Book Club, Denver Press Club, and Seeds (South Eastern Efforts Developing Sustainable Spaces). For arranging many of these events, where I met so many great people, I thank everyone at the Steven Barclay Agency—Catherine, Eliza, Sara, and my friend for many years, Steven Barclay.

I deeply appreciate my new literary friendships at home in North Carolina and am sending special *saluti* to Lee Smith, Michael Malone, Maureen Quilligan, Oscar Hijuelos, Lori Carlson, Alan Gurganus, and, farther south in Alabama, the painter Rena Williams, a lifelong friend.

Contents

The White Road

"I AM ABOUT TO BUY A HOUSE IN A FOREIGN country," I wrote as I began my memoir, *Under the Tuscan Sun.* A simple declarative sentence— but for me, crux and crucible. From such easy words, fate branches and transforms. Bramasole, an abandoned country house beneath the Etruscan city wall of Cortona, became home. And more than home—bull's eye, heart's needle, center of my private universe.

At the moment I turned the heavy iron key in the door and stepped into my Italian life, I could not have pictured myself here two decades later, could not have foreseen the pleasure, complexity, hassle, frustration, joy, or my intense love for Bramasole, a place-in-time that took over my life.

In Juan Rulfo's novel, *Pedro Páramo,* his character on a hot bus ride carries a photograph of his mother in his breast pocket. "I could feel her beginning to sweat," Pedro thinks. Bramasole seems like that for me. I can sense its life within my life, separate and integral.

The house became my icon. The luminous apricot-rose facade, shuttered windows open to the

southern sun, profuse geraniums, clematis, lemons, and lavender burgeoning in the garden—all this exuberant beauty symbolizes not the life I was *given* but the life I made with my own
two hands. Opening my study window and leaning out into
the bright air, I can see the garden below, even greet each rose
by name. I watch for the jasmine to overwhelm the iron arch
with blooms. I listen to the four musical notes of water cascad-
ing in the ancient cistern. I see all the overlays of the years,
from when the walls were tumbled and the blackberries
choked the land, until now, when the garden rhymes roses,
lilacs, dahlias, and lilies with secret reading spots among the
olives. The only traces of the house's original formal garden
still reign: five wise topiary trees rising from a boxwood hedge.

Across the top terrace hundreds of giant sunflowers hold
court in July, my little marching band of glorious faces. By
August, they bow, like too many rusty showerheads. At that
moment, pheasants arrive. How do they know? The seeds are
a feast and their cranky cries of gluttony sound more like noise
at a car repair shop than the orgy of regally feathered fowl.

INSIDE THE HOUSE, I have my books, my collections of religious folk art, ceramic platters, old linens, and, by now,
boxes of manuscripts in innumerable, crossed-out, underlined, scrawled drafts. My rooms are fingerprints. My husband's wild study, where a painting of Dante looks down on
the poetry-strewn, chaotic desk; our bedroom with the
romantic iron bed draped in white linen; the kitchen where
all my pottery hangs on white walls; the house's original
bathroom with the hip tub; the dining room where wineglasses are always half full and chairs have scraped the brick
floors at so many feasts under the faded blue and apricot
fresco we discovered long ago—the house lives powerfully

on its own and I feel powerfully alive within its thick stone walls.

~

IN A DREAM I was given an ultimatum. I had a choice. Sell Bramasole or lose an arm. The power broker of this dilemma had the face of the academic dean, who told me sophomore year that I could buckle down and take the required courses—economics, she insisted, physiology—or leave the college. No more Roman drama, no Greek etymology.

Now she stood in front of my best-beloved, golden, peach, claret house, waving a hacksaw. House or arm. *Make a choice.* I woke clutching my right wrist (writing hand!).

I'd fully experienced the fact that for me the choice was impossible. So deep in love am I with that symmetrical set of simple rooms overlooking a tender valley, where stars smear the night sky and dawn duplicates what Renaissance artists painted as they passionately re-created such scenes beyond their Annunciation angels or martyrs riddled with arrows. I'm attached to the broad-faced purple clematis clambering around the rusty iron railing of the upstairs patio, bolting through the potted surfinias and the summer-scented climbing honeysuckle that I planted to remind me of country roads in Georgia. I'm devoted to tumbling geraniums and a long bank of white hydrangeas. I admire the iron fence our blacksmith friend, Egisto, made last year. Now every time my grandson runs out the door I don't have to follow, fearing he'll tumble over the low stone wall and fall downhill.

Ed spent half a year overseeing the reconstruction of three long stone terrace walls brought down by landslides during a winter of record rain. We walk sometimes before dinner in my reinstated herb garden and admire the stonework, while still cursing the mud and money. Those walls cost Ed at least two books of poems. They're tied with steel rods into bedrock but appear just as they used to when built by farmers centuries ago. I lost my herb garden to the landslide that engendered the project, but the new garden looks prettier than the original. The santolina, rosemary, nepeta, borage, and rue along the edge blur with bloom and bees and hot scent. My rose kingdom expanded and now the gorgeous Gloire de Dijon, Reine des Violettes, Rita Levi-Montalcini, and Pierre de Ronsard blooms yield to my scissors every day in summer. I love the rousing chorus of birdsong in the spring dawn, the inland sea of whipped-cream fog that fills the valley on winter mornings, and the people who call up a greeting from the road below when I'm watering my strawberry pots.

⁓

A FEW YEARS BACK, while picking the sweet blackberries on Monte Sant'Egidio, I spotted a ruin on a rugged slope. Ed, our friend Chiara, and I clambered through the brush and found ourselves at a partially collapsed stone-roofed cottage surrounded by chestnut and oak trees. We were fatally attracted. What a lonesome beauty.

Originally, we told ourselves, the purchase was an investment. Should we have been more prescient? Over the course of restoration, both Ed and I began to love the remote house. It seemed to have storybook qualities: *The Three Bears, Little Red Riding Hood.* No site planner needed; the builders instinctively placed the house to face the rising sun and to back up to the slope for protection from winter's *tramontana* wind. In the afternoon the stones are warmed by angled western rays that grow longer and longer, finally raking the yard with golden tines. Looking out of the window at dawn, I'm presented with the gift of nacreous light and a thousand shades of green layering down the hillsides. So much for investment. The restoration has occupied me—saturated me, haunted me, and dogged me—completely. Ed perhaps even more. The place is without price. I could no more sell it than I could place my firstborn in a basket in the bulrushes.

Houses are so mysterious to me, especially architectural beauties that seem so fully themselves. How could anything ever go wrong inside? I'm intrigued by classic vernacular types—bungalows, dog-trot cottages, Federal farmhouses— even fifties brick with carport, seventies raised ranch, and the generic megadevelopment houses of the boom time. Small ranches remind me of visiting childhood friends. Two bedrooms, one bath, living room, dining nook and kitchen—all tidy and new. How I admired the close families and the shiny blond floors, the picture window looking out at identical houses, also for close families, so unlike my own riot-prone parents around the home fire in what my mother called the "honeymoon cottage." Even empty houses exude a force field, the potential charge of all that may happen within the walls.

When I saw the mountain house, I felt a molten energy. I hoped it came from the humble Franciscan brothers who roamed this mountain in the 1200s, joyously reveling in silence. Some stayed and lived in caves or built huts of reed and stone. Feng shui doesn't have a name in Tuscany, but the principles must be universal. Our little stone cottage takes power from the raucous discussions among five kinds of owls in the dark, the torrent's wet music in winter, charging herds of wild boar, the old-growth chestnut forest, the squawks of pheasants, spontaneous springs, and Roman roads cresting the mountain.

I have the joy and the hell of having restored to itself

something so ancient, and the luck to become friends with deep-country Tuscans. Now we spend part of the year on Monte Sant'Egidio, one of St. Francis's holy spots. A few of his hermit followers, who lived in caves along the spur of the mountain, turned domestic and built stone houses so solid that they endure eight centuries later. My Fonte delle Foglie (Font of Leaves) is one. Because St. Francis spent a winter at Le Celle, a monastery below us, the hills rising behind Cortona remain a sacred place. Or, at least, a cool place of respite, especially for those sweltering summer weekends when the stone streets of Cortona cook. Local people picnic in the woods, often spending the day.

A pagan ritual of the year is San Lorenzo's night of the shooting stars (August 10). Like many Cortonesi, we take blankets and a watermelon outside and lie on the ground, marveling at the meteor showers.

If I were alone, I might be overcome by the primitive experience of my back against the earth and all the ferocious lights hurtling through the sky. A night so grand, dew dampening my shirt, the Milky Way's pavé diamond path, all the constellations so brilliant that a voice from the sky might begin speaking the Greek myths of bears and seven sisters and intrepid hunters. I might imagine the dark celestial tarp as poked with millions of holes, revealing a powerful heavenly light behind our atmosphere's darkness. I might let my mind spin out to follow the orbit of the smallest asteroid. I might think my spine could send down roots, seeking earth like a sprawling grape tendril.

However, friends pass binoculars back and forth and shout out wishes at each streak across the sky. *No more war!* and *Let them find water here before they drill down to hell*, and *May Ed go inside for another bottle of wine*. As all Tuscans know, on this night wishes are granted. And so I remain firmly in the moment. So close are the stars that I could reach up and touch the burning center of Venus with my forefinger.

⌒

ONE GLORIOUS SUMMER evening at Bramasole, something unexpected intruded on this paradise. The event and, most of all, what it implied, almost ripped my halcyon-blown silky sails. This third memoir of my Italian life revisits that time of change—internal and external—and allows me to explore what I learned about myself and about this green place where I made my home.

Prima le radici, poi le ali, an Italian friend writes to me today. First roots, then wings. Have I sometimes sought wings first?

⌒

THE YEAR 2010 marks the twentieth anniversary of what I still think of as my new life in Italy. Ed and I have the celebration planned for July 5.

When I first drove up to Bramasole with the real estate agent, I jokingly said, "This is it."

This is it. I was oblivious to the phenomenal changes I was entering as that rusted gate opened, and I saw the sunrise tints of the house's facade, colors that have delivered a shiver of wonder every time I have looked up since then. I went to Italy for the cypress-lined lanes, the vibrancy of the piazzas, the pure Romanesque churches in the country, the cuisine, the history. I stayed for the never-ending *festa* of everyday life among the most hospitable people on earth. I made a home here, without really meaning to—the place took hold of me and shaped me in its image.

How did I let this happen? There are many crux marks in one's life, small ones and large. To *take* a decision, my friend

Fulvio says, his usage much more precise than the grammatical *make*. To take a decision also takes you. Even though when I stepped out of that car I did not know how my life would change, I did sense something at that moment. I wanted an aperture, an opportunity to merge with something limitless. I, in the fullness of my ignorance, was willing.

And Italy has proven to be inexhaustible. To *take* the gift of a new and very old country—a whole other sphere of language, literature, history, architecture, art: it falls over me like a shower of gold. It is paradoxical but true that something that takes you out of yourself also restores you to yourself with a greater freedom. A passionate interest also has a true-north needle that keeps you focused. The excitement of exploration sprang me from a life I knew how to live into a challenging space where I was forced—and overjoyed—to invent each day.

The coming twentieth anniversary offers a time to reflect and pore over possibilities for the years coming quickly toward me. I'm old enough to lay claim to owning some wisdom; I fully believe Basho's pithy sentence, passed on from the seventeenth century: *The journey itself is home.*

The second twenty years. Transition feels sweet. I'm balanced between worlds and can roam forward and backward along that *strada bianca,* that white road of the innermost journey. Moments of change. A chance to say yes, or possibly, no. A day like no other. A week straight out of a horoscope. Someone standing on the other side of an abyss, holding out a hand. A new life plan. Forty trees to plant. A journey back. A ticket sent. A fountain to build. A swim with dolphins. A gift to give. A mirror reflecting another era. A blue glass heart under my pillow.

1

Winter into Spring

Buongiorno, Luca

IN WINTER-COLD BLUE LIGHT, THE BELLS OF Cortona ring louder. The cold iron clapper hitting the frozen bell produces clear, shocked, hard gongs that reverberate in the heads of us frozen ones in the piazza, ringing in our skulls and down to our heels, striking the paving stones. In leafy summer, when softened air diffuses the bells, the clarion call accompanies but does not insist; the bells remind, punctuate, inspire. As a benison to the day, the reverberations settle on those nursing cappuccino in the piazza, then fade, sending last vibrations out to the circling swallows. But in winter, the solitary sounds feel more personal, as though they ring especially for you. I even can feel the sound waves in my teeth as I smile my umpteenth greeting of the morning.

Returning in early March, I'm thrilled to see my friends in the piazza. We greet each other as though I have been gone for a year instead of four months. I love the first trip back into town after an absence. I walk every street, assessing the state of the union. What has changed, who has traveled to Brazil, what's on display at the vegetable market, who has married, died, moved to the country? What's on exhibit at the museum? Half of an enormous cow hangs by a hook in the butcher's, a square of paper towel on the floor to catch the last three splats of blood. Under neon, red meat in the cases reflects a lavender light on the faces of two venerable signoras leaning in to inspect today's veal cheeks and pork roasts. Orange lilies against the glass steam the flower shop window with their hot-house breath, and there's Mario, a blur among them, arranging a row of primroses.

Winter returns Cortona to its original self. The merchants along the main street complain that all winter long the town feels dead. *Non c'è nessuno.* There's no one. They wonder if the tourists will return this year. "The dollar is broken, the euro like a hot air balloon," Fabrizio says as he whooshes the imaginary balloon into the sky, then spirals his hands. I visualize a striped balloon heading toward Mars. In Italian, part of every conversation takes place without words. A woman on her cell phone in the piazza paces, gestures, stops, slings back her head, paces again. She says *grazie* fifteen times, laughs. She's on stage, a monologue actor. When she hangs up, she snaps shut the phone, shoves it in her enormous *borsa,* and charges ahead toward her shopping.

I pause to look at shoes, then sweaters. "That war of yours. It's costing the whole world," Daria scolds, as though I personally have bombed Iraq. She's sweeping off her already clean threshold. They forget that when the lira converted to the euro, almost everyone abruptly raised their prices; some simply started charging in euros the same amount they'd charged in lire, effectively doubling the cost of their pizza, shirts, coffee, albums, and pasta. Since Italian wages hardly have moved, most people today are feeling more than a pinch. "Not to worry," our friend Arturo says. "There are two Italys. One economy in sight and another whole economy out of sight.

Everyone has their own ways never revealed to the statisticians. You get paid in cash—nobody knows." This, I think, applies more to independent work and less to the shop owners, who have to give receipts. If I walk out of the bar with no receipt for my *panino,* the Guardia di Finanzia could fine the owner and me. When I buy a chicken, I am astonished—14.65 euros—twenty-three dollars at the current exchange rate. I think of the reconstruction South prices after the Civil War. What is happening to our country? Our dollar is *debole,* weak, shockingly so.

With the wind that must have originated in the snowy Alps, thirty-five degrees feels like zero. *"Che bello,* you have returned before the swallows," Lina says. Because it is Women's Day, three people give me sprays of mimosa, which I love for its brilliant yellow in the stony gray air. Massimo offers coffee, and later, so does Claudio. Roberto at the *frutta e verdura* gives me an extra-large sack of *odori,* the vegetables and herbs used for seasoning. I see that Marco has closed his art gallery and expanded his *enoteca* into the adjoining space. There are two tables for wine tastings and the new display cases are handsome. Still, it's sad to lose the gallery, where many regulars exhibited by the week, hanging their own work and sitting out in the piazza with friends or making friends, while people wandered in and out. But then I see Marco in the post office and he says he's starting a new gallery around the corner. The museum will expand to accommodate recent archaeological discoveries at the Etruscan sites and the Roman villa our friends Maurizio and Helena have excavated. A new chocolate shop has appeared in my absence. It looks as though it landed from Belgium. The hot chocolate tastes creamy and unctuous. An instant hit. The two restaurants that opened last fall are doing well. One already has the reputation for making one of the best coffees in town. It was there, when I stood at the bar sipping my *macchiato,* that

I overheard two tourists. One said, "I saw Frances Mayes's husband, Ed, driving a Fiat. A Fiat—and one of those tiny ones. Wouldn't you think they'd have something better than that?" I turned away so they would not recognize me and become mortified. I love my yellow Panda.

To everything its season, and this is the season to replaster, repair hinges, revise menus, clean courtyards and stairways. From the corner table at Bar Signorelli, I watch this spirited activity along the street. Everyone prepares for the spring and summer that they hope will bring back those innocents with a passion for shoes, leather books, dining, ceramics, peaches, Super Tuscans, and all the good things on offer in this lively hill town.

~

As I STIR my cappuccino, I greet the charcoal self-portrait of Renaissance painter Luca Signorelli above the soft-drink fridge. I'm on a Signorelli quest. He was born here, and spent his life painting all over Tuscany, the Marche, and in Rome. Famous, yes, but in my opinion, internationally undervalued. He always presides over my morning-coffee libations. In the local building superintendent's office, I've signed documents under another copy of Signorelli's self-portrait, which shows my man to be blond as an angel, with direct blue eyes and a strong jaw. A main piazza is named for Signorelli. The local museum features his work. Everyone believes that his fall from scaffolding in the chapel of the Palazzo Passerini caused his death.

Without doubt, he spent charmed parts of his life centered on the piazza, where he most likely ran into a friend one rainy morning and heard the news that da Vinci, what a fantasist, has conceived of a flying machine. Someone tells him that Michelangelo has obtained a great piece of marble (destined to become the *David*), and maybe even that far away a German named Gutenberg just invented a machine to print books. It's easy to see Signorelli in gold-trimmed green velvet, sun glazing his light hair, intent as his neighbor mentions that the Pope has excommunicated Venice, and, has he heard, an ancient statue called the Laocoön has been excavated in Rome. In his spotted painter's smock, he raises a glass in his dim studio and listens as his cousin, just back from Rome, describes the newly invented flush toilet. Going home at night, he bumps into Giovanni, the friar at the Dominican convent, whose sweet ways later earned him the name Fra Beato Angelico. His was a heady era. I know that as a local magistrate he was stopped constantly and asked for favors, just as Andrea, our mayor, is this morning. Signorelli, as a preeminent artist and also as a *genius loci* presence, continues to rise up through layers of time. He's an old friend by now.

~

THE PIAZZA, for a Roman, for Signorelli, for me, for that baby in the red stroller, exists as a great old savings bank of memory. It *is* a body; it *is* a book to read, if you are alive to its language. I could offer Luca a *caffè* if he would just open the door and with a toss of his yellow hair, stride in. He's here; he never left.

Campanilismo, a condition of being: When you live within the sound of the *campanile,* church bell, you belong to the place. Command central, carnival ride, conference center, living room, forum—the piazza also is fun. Never dull. Today the *barista* flourishes my cappuccino to the table. He has formed a chocolate heart in the foam. He shouts to me, "Americans don't drink coffee; they drink stained water."

"Sporca miseria!" I reply, attempting a pun on a mild curse, *porca miseria,* which eloquently means "pig misery." My wordplay means "dirty misery." I'm gratified with laughs from both *bariste.*

Lorenzo is just back from Florida. He buys my coffee and I ask about his trip. "Very nice." And then, staring out at the piazza, he adds, *"Meglio qui a Cortona."* Better here in Cortona. "America," he sighs. "Either empty and there is nothing, or there is too much."

At home in the U.S. of A., I play a CD of the Cortona bells when I feel homesick. Old photos around town show the Allies whizzing in on tanks, liberating Cortona. So familiar is this image, I almost think I was there. The oldest memories, of the Roman forum lying layers below the cobbles, and the even earlier, deeper Etruscan streets, continue to inform the spirit of the place. Memory steams through the baked crust. Old people still call Piazza Garibaldi *carbonaia,* recalling the place where men brought their charcoal to sell. Via Nazionale to some is still the rough and rustic Rugapiana, flat street.

～

THE RHYTHMS OF the piazza are an ancient folk dance. In summer, the doors of the town hall open and the bride and groom descend the steps into the piazza, where we all gather, even for the weddings of strangers from the Netherlands or England. This is where the new life begins. The newborn is strolled up and down. Boys learn soccer by kicking the ball up against the Etruscan Museum. I've been in the piazza at three A.M. in February. Someone with a cell phone wedged between his ear and shoulder leans against the crumbling Ghibelline lion and gestures with both hands. A young man crosses on the diagonal, whistling, or two people are talking, their breath wreathing their heads. The piazza is never empty. And if it were, it still would not be empty. Luca would be there.

The piazza speaks pure Italian—speaks of who lives here and why. Alberto, my architect friend, and I once tried to quantify the meaning of the piazza in purely practical terms.

We measured and analyzed piazzas all over Tuscany, looking at their numbers of entrances, the kinds of buildings and businesses that contribute to the liveliness of a piazza, those that are dead spaces, the patterns of entrances and exits, and still there was something mysterious.

~

THIS MORNING A lone tourist appears, guidebook in hand, bundled in down. In the gelid light, she looks like a just-hatched bird, mouth open as she stares at the town hall clock and the surrounding buildings. She removes her knitted hat and her wispy hair, damp against her head, looks as though a little albumen still sticks to her. She glances toward the antiques in a just-polished window. Two shop owners stand in their doorways, eyeing her movements: the hawks and the fledgling.

I'm done. *Buongiorno, Luca.* See you tomorrow. My rounds: groceries, bookstore, post office, many stops to say hello, flower shop for a few yellow roses for my desk. I shouldn't have bothered. En route home, another Claudio gives me a pot of pansies; Gilda drops off camellias, mimosas, and pink hyacinths at Bramasole; and Fabio leaves on the step a handsome creamy cymbidium. Vittoria brings a bouquet of viburnums to our shrine. I've never before heard of Women's Day, a national holiday in Italy, which commemorates lives lost in a New York factory fire in 1911, but I'm overwhelmed by the gifts of so many flowers. By the end of my first day back, flowers ignite every room of my house, giving the impression of warmth to stony rooms that have absorbed the brunt of winter.

~

THE NIGHT FINISHES at Corys, down the road from us at the Torreone crossroad. Renato and Giuseppe, the co-managers of the hotel-restaurant, are busy serving a table of twenty teenagers who now and then break into song. Ah, no, "Volare"—oh, oh, oh, oh. Papa-bear Giuseppe envelops Ed and me together in a grand hug. Of Lebanese background, he was raised in Rome and has brought to Cortona an unerring good taste in food and wine. He always tells us exactly what we are to eat and drink. He brings over a bloodstone red wine we've never seen, from just around the bend near Lago Trasimeno. Renato catches us up on the news. He is building a "beauty farm" in the old stone parish house attached to the church across the road. He is a wiry man with lank black curls and intense eyes, a consummate Italian cynic with a wild humor. He talks with his whole body. Electrical charges run through his veins. I love to watch him, especially when he's furious with the hunters who are parking in his spaces. He almost levitates with anger. I expect him to tear out his hair at any moment or go up in a puff of smoke. Then the anger dissolves and he's joking again.

"A spa and a church together? The body and the spirit?" Ed asks.

"Yes, finally, and the graveyard is there, too, so everything can be taken care of."

Seems surreal, but I can see us heading there for the massages, manicures, and steam bath. "Are we invited?"

"*Certo, cara*"—certainly, darling. "I am building it for you."

After the antipasto table with fifty tastes, and a big plate of ravioli stuffed with pecorino and speck, and chicken cooked under a brick, Giuseppe brings over five boxes of Amedei chocolates for tasting. The beans come from Madagascar, Trinidad, Jamaica, all over the chocolate map. Then with a diabolical grin, he puts down a plate of *gorgonzola cremosa* so delicious that I'm wanting to lick the scoop. Just as we are about to push back, he pours a *digestivo* we've never tried, a Barolo Chinato, aged Barolo with what we finally figure out is quinine. It's complex and meditative, unlike many *digestivi* that bring to mind being force-fed cough syrup as a child, my mother prying the spoon between my clenched teeth. We are mellow and *commossi,* emotionally moved, by the largesse of our friends. As we leave, Giuseppe's young daughter, Leda, brings me a branch of mimosa.

THE GIVING, the fun, and the spontaneity of everyday life here shock me and return me immediately to a munificent state of being that gradually starts to feel normal. I begin to notice, here at Bramasole, that my skin fits perfectly over my body, just as this house sits so serenely and naturally on this hillside.

At last, to bed. Seems like days ago that I pushed up the plane window shade at dawn, and looked down on silver-edged snowy billows. Think of all the centuries when that view was impossible. Signorelli's point of view, like most Renaissance artists', was straight frontal. I almost see him in his green cloak, flying out of Florence and over the white Alps. How strangely immune we are to the beauty of the clouds from above. The bed is made up with apricot sheets, airy white comforter, and soft pillows. Sliding under the covers, I feel as though I'm sinking through the paradisiacal sky I flew through—when?—only last night. For an instant, I relive descending through flocculent clouds, when all direction seems lost, then the skeins of wispy veils, then the sudden breakthrough, when the green fields, immortal Roman farmhouses, and clumps of sheep appear. Just as he falls asleep, Ed says, "This was a Renaissance day . . ."

RAVIOLI RIPIENI DI PATATE CON ZUCCHINE E SPECK AL PECORINO
Potato Ravioli with Zucchini, Speck, and Pecorino

At Corys, the hotel-restaurant down the road from Bramasole, this outstanding ravioli is always on the menu. Corys's chef, Eva, shares her secret recipe.

Speck (smoked prosciutto) can be used in all the ways prosciutto is used. You can substitute *parmigiano* if you can't locate aged pecorino.

Serves 4

FOR THE FILLING
½ pound Yukon Gold potatoes, peeled
1 cup milk
1 cup water
1 tablespoon parmigiano
1 egg yolk
½ teaspoon salt
Pinch of nutmeg

FOR THE PASTA
2 cups flour
½ teaspoon salt
2 eggs, plus one yolk beaten for egg wash
1 tablespoon extra-virgin olive oil

FOR THE SAUCE
2 tablespoons olive oil
2 slices speck or smoked bacon, diced

1 zucchini, chopped
2 tomatoes, chopped
1 shallot, minced
1 tablespoon butter
½ teaspoon pepper

Pecorino, shaved, as needed

Cook the peeled potatoes in the milk and water for 20 minutes, put through a ricer, and add the *parmigiano,* the egg yolk, salt, and nutmeg. Let cool.

For the ravioli: You can use store-bought fresh sheets of pasta to make your ravioli or you can make your own. For the latter, do the following:

Mound the flour on a countertop, make a well, and add the salt and 2 whole eggs and oil, mix gently at first with a fork or your fingertips, and shortly you'll have formed a rather sticky dough. Knead for 10 minutes, adding more flour as needed. Shape into a mound, cover with a dishtowel, and let rest for 30 minutes to an hour, and then divide into quarters. Roll out each quarter with a rolling pin until the sheets are quite thin— hold them up to the window and they should be translucent. If you have a pasta machine, run the quartered pasta dough through lower and lower settings.

Next, place one sheet, about 6 inches by 12 inches, on the countertop, and in the lower half of the sheet, place 1 teaspoon of the potato filling at 1-inch intervals. Brush an egg yolk wash on the top half of the sheet, then fold over the sheet lengthwise, covering the filling. Gently press out any air in the ravioli, and then cut them into equal squares. Pinch edges together.

Put a pot of water on high heat, adding 2 tablespoons of salt when it has reached a boil.

For the sauce: In a sauté pan, heat the oil, then add the next

4 ingredients and sauté for 5 minutes, then add the butter and pepper and cook for 3 minutes. Add 4 ounces of water and cook for another 4 minutes.

Cook the ravioli in the boiling water for 3 to 5 minutes, then drain. Arrange on a plate and pour the sauce over them. Finish by scattering shavings of an aged pecorino or *parmigiano*.

⌒ ～ ⌒

Pollo al Mattone
Chicken Under a Brick

Weighing down a chicken with bricks seems so ancient. Did the advisors to Roman emperors hatch the slogan, "A chicken under every brick," to go along with the bread and circus motif?

Brick morphed so naturally from the good earth—add water and high heat (*ecco fatto, terracotta*) and civilization started to build in a big way.

Roman bricks were longer and narrower than present-day bricks, but any brick will do. If you have a few handy, you should wash them, let them air-dry, and wrap them in a few sheets of aluminum foil. Otherwise, you can use a heavy pan of some sort. I've used an 8-quart Le Creuset, covering the bottom with aluminum foil.

Serves 4

2 garlic cloves
1 handful of parsley
Zest from 1 orange
4 tablespoons extra-virgin olive oil
½ teaspoon salt

½ teaspoon pepper
1 chicken, 3 to 4 pounds

MARINADE
   2 tablespoons red wine vinegar
   ½ cup extra-virgin olive oil
   ½ cup white wine

Preheat oven to 400 degrees F.

Mince the garlic and parsley and combine with the zest, 2 tablespoons of olive oil, and salt and pepper. Set aside.

Wash the chicken under cold running water and dry. With poultry shears, remove the wing tips, any excess fat, and cut out the backbone. Put them aside for stock. You may want to remove the ribs and breastbone, too.

Mix together the marinade ingedients. Lay the chicken flat, skin side up. Stuff the garlic mixture under the skin, place in the marinade, then cover and marinate for a few hours or, even better, overnight. Turn two or three times.

Heat 2 tablespoons olive oil in a cast-iron pan large enough to hold the chicken (I use a 12-inch cast-iron skillet). Place the chicken skin side down and weigh it down with the two clean bricks wrapped in foil. Cook over medium heat for 5 minutes, then place the skillet and bricks in the oven for 15 to 20 minutes, after which you'll remove the weights and turn the chicken over, cooking another 10 minutes or so, until done. Cut into serving-sized pieces.

Andiamo a Casa—
Let's Go Home

MARZO È PAZZO. YES, MARCH IS TOTALLY CRAZY. The wind could pick me up and set me down in another world. The rain slants sideways, turns back, forward, and almost rains upside down. From a duffle under the bed, I dig out an old alpaca-lined coat and some scruffy black boots lined with fake fur. The sleek black coat, pale green twinset, and silk pants I brought with me go back in the suitcase. March can be balmy but, instead, out come the cotton undershirt, big sweaters, and corduroy pants.

Between bouts of driving rain, we dash out for walks in waterlogged air. Hawthorn blooms in white drifts and a few beaten-down daffodils lean off the terraces. Prune trees let off a pinkish, pre-blossom glow, and lush, long grasses slush under our boots. We've lost a plum tree to the *tramontana* winds. Several garden chairs have blown into each other and flowerpots have tumped over and cracked open. We roam the countryside, huddling under trees when the rain doubles back, checking on the wild asparagus (not yet), and our neighbor Alberto's pool, where we find the weighted cover blown into the water.

"Should we bother him?" Ed asks. Alberto is thousands of miles away in Tampa. "Or just let it sink quietly?"

"We'll tell his gardener. I saw him in the piazza this morning."

The sixty cypresses we donated for our road are thriving. Only one lies on its side. Each new tree is planted near a mammoth old one. Along this Strada della Memoria, Road of Memory, the original cypresses, planted after World War I, commemorated each soldier from Cortona who lost his life. Over the century, many of the six hundred trees had died. When I was given an award by Barilla (no, not for being the biggest pasta eater in Italy), I passed the money on to the comune to reinstate these memorials. I watch over each. The small trees near the old giants thrill me. They seem anthropomorphized, like children with their tall parents. We see that the comune gardeners have trimmed dead limbs from the nearly centenarian soldiers and treated them in spots with some blue medicine.

Each time we return, we comb our land, as we do the town, to see changes—how much have the hedges grown, what pool has been dug in the valley below, if the Castellis have finished building their house, and if all the stone walls survived the storms. Although winter still reigns, she's an old queen by now; soon all the pastel princesses of primavera will return. We're reconnecting with our house, too, in the fastest ways we know. Unpack, visit the neighbors, stock the kitchen, buy summer lily bulbs, plant bare-root roses, wash the dusty wineglasses, reboot the computers, stack the books we intend to read on top of the bookcase—there, we're home.

The first person to see is Placido, our nearest neighbor and, with his wife, Fiorella, and daughter, Chiara, our Italian family. Last year, on September 23, in America, Ed answered the phone and heard sobbing. Chiara's voice broke, spoke, broke again, "Zucchero slipped on the hill they paved at Torreone and skidded backward. He was falling and throwing Babbo to the ground."

"No! Plari's horse skidded?"

"His skull hit hard," she continued slowly. "He immediately went into seizures."

Always looking toward the positive, she said he was fortunate that Carlo, the friend on horseback just behind him, was a highly trained police officer, who managed to keep Placido from swallowing his tongue—and simultaneously to call a helicopter. Within the hour, Placido was in the good care of the Siena hospital. The messages we received from Chiara over the weeks said *the situation is grave* and *three large hematomas* and *I'm afraid.* He lay in a coma for a month, gradually emerging to the shock of what had happened to him. We lived with the image of him sliding backward, falling, falling off the horse like St. Paul in Caravaggio's painting in Rome.

We visited him in October when we were back for the olive harvest and found our friend, this robust, joking, vital man, deeply compromised, weakened, alternately agitated and distant. The tubes down his throat, which he jerked out several times, left him hardly able to speak. He did not want to be in the hospital room with three near-death men, one of whom seemed already over the divide. Placido kept repeating *Andiamo a casa,* let's go home, why were they keeping him, *Andiamo a casa,* it was only a slight accident.

We worried, his family worried, the whole town worried. Everywhere we went people said, "How is Placido today?" Droves of friends visited him, taking over soups and tarts. He began to improve as soon as he was released to his falcon, garden, dog, and the bountiful love and table at home.

Before we get to his house, we see him out walking arm in arm with Fiorella. He looks like himself! Ed's eyes brim as he embraces his friend. Fiorella, looking relaxed at last, says Placido is "Almost ready." He's thinner, with a crease on either side of his smile, but he's Placido. We're oddly flattered when he says we are the only visitors he remembers from his hospital stint. He lost his zest for smoking cigars and drinking grappa, in fact has lost some sense of taste but expects it back. He's not yet riding. Zucchero has gone to visit a friend's horses for an extended stay. The image of Placido placing his foot in the stirrup ever again makes my stomach flip.

In the months of his illness, we faced how unbearable it was to imagine Cortona without Placido. For us, he's a great love and the essence of Tuscan life. Every morning all year, he's having coffee at Banchelli's, often a second with another group of friends. He's a husband, in the old sense, to his land and animals, tending his falcon, horse, chickens, rabbits, and guinea hens. With his friend Lucio, he combs secret areas to find more porcini mushrooms than anyone. He makes archery shields and pouches out of leather. In summer he works without a shirt and I've seen the fading tattoo of Pegasus, the winged horse, on his shoulder. One day he came over and gave us two napkin rings carved from olive wood, our names and the date burned into the wood. Always on his porch there's a bird or owl he's rescued. The cages he makes for their recoveries are works of folk art. A *merlo,* blackbird, with a crushed wing has lived in a jolly yellow and red house for fifteen years. It whistles as Placido passes. The Cardinali family hospitality is legendary. When we first bought Bramasole, we'd hear their parties, the singing long into the night, hoots of laughter. From the window I could smell smoke rising from the grill, count cars parked all along the road. We'd wonder if ever two foreigners might be included in such an evening. Hundreds of shared dinners later, the Cardinali family still symbolizes the most profound reasons we love this place. Telling us about the fall, Placido casually mentions that the name of the helicopter was Pegasus.

⁓

THOSE EARLY VISITS, when we had solitude and endless time to work our land and write poems and chapters and articles, long ago disappeared. Returning in winter restores some of the time for privacy, and for visiting friends outside the glorious but busy summer season, when our kitchen fills with pasta steam and sounds of chopping, when spare beds are often filled with guests who must be shown Pienza, who develop bronchitis, or graze their rented fenders on a stone wall. Also, winter may be the best time to travel. What's a bit of Arctic breeze compared to no problems with parking, reservations, or crowds?

Next week we will take the train up to Florence for the pleasure of experiencing the city restored to an atmosphere of intimacy and discovery. In this season, I can walk into all the churches and galleries, exhilarated to find myself alone, or almost, with the art. The security guard dozes by his space heater. The locals reclaim their city, walking out in the stony twilight in their well-cut wools and flowing scarves, greeting each other. In the *trattorie,* cooks are grilling sausages and pigeons. The fried rabbit with fennel, the pots of *ribollita,* the pastas with *funghi porcini* are served forth. In cold rain, the architecture suddenly seems more foregrounded. My camera responds to the washed air and gives back the soapy gloss of marble, etched shadows of statues, puddles like foxed mirrors, the Ponte Vecchio's reflection in the old green river.

At six A.M., taking a warm *cornetto* from the just-opened bakery to a bridge over the Arno, you see Dante's Firenze in the water, the fresh light sliding downstream. This is the season of thickest hot chocolate in elegant pastry shops and bars, the season of delicate truffle sandwiches with afternoon tea. Florence in winter sets me dreaming as Florence in summer cannot.

The secret of winter travel revealed to me by Ed: Plan on *weather*. Dress for it. As one who grew up in a warm climate, I'm always forgetting to put on my coat. But he's Minnesota born and bred and reminds me: Layers. Socks. Waterproof soles. Gloves. Then we're prepared for short trips to off-track places such as beautiful Mantova, where the fog can hide all the bicyclists, or Bagno di Romagna, where the wind may be frigid but the air is so deeply fresh you'd think they invented it.

⁓

RED WINE IN winter works a spell that I don't fall under in hot weather. The gorgeous, profound Vino Nobiles, Brunellos, and Super Tuscans can overwhelm summer food. Though Tuscans almost never order white wine, even when it's one hundred degrees, local makers are undermining that prejudice with some fulsome and spicy whites. I keep my own stash in summer, especially our winemaker friend Riccardo Baracchi's Astore and some of our recent local whites from D'Alessandro. But when the cold comes down, and in the spirited autumn weather, our biggest Brunello glasses are on the table every night, the decanters filled by six for dinner at eight. The Baracchis, Silvia and Riccardo, the most hospitable people on earth, love to bring over bottles for a vertical tasting of their Ardito. As we go through the courses and vintages, I can taste the concentrated elixir of the dry, scorching summer of '04, the loose juiciness from the spring rains of '05, and the tart edges of the April flash freeze of '06. I love to hear vintners talk about their wines. Like parents, they see the nuanced qualities of their children that others usually don't notice.

In town, Marco, whose *enoteca* faces the piazza, and Arnaldo, who owns Pane e Vino, sponsor cozy winter dinners with a winemaker. Tonight we meet the smiling Paolo de Marchi in his cherry red sweater. His Chianti estates produce Isole e Olena, so he has much to smile about. He's a third-generation winemaker whose family began in the north. Recently Paolo has acquired again the old family property up in Piemonte, where his son now makes wine. Among those who own vineyards, family ties seem especially strong. Many sons and daughters follow the tradition and often take the business into new directions.

The cozy, arched-brick trattoria can't hold another wine lover. The room is filled with, it seems, glasses. Every place setting has seven. Low lighting picks up the crystal sparkle, charging the room with energy. Paolo moves us through his chardonnay, chianti, his two cepparellos (a pure Sangiovese grape content), and two syrahs. With the chardonnay, we start with *crostini neri,* the Tuscan classic made from chicken livers, and *mostarda di peperoni,* a condiment of peppers, and a small cannellini bean salad with sopressata. Because Paolo talks about each wine in Italian and then in English for the benefit of a sprinkling of expats, the dinner extends way into the night. Unlike many tastings I've attended in America, wine flows. Arnaldo doesn't limit us to a taste of each wine, but keeps pouring as people ask questions. By the time we are served the *secondo,* my attention has mellowed. I remember a California friend whose mantra was, "They *all* taste good to me."

For the racy chianti, Arnaldo selected a tasty gnocchi with ragù made from local Chianina beef. The combination could not be more *genuino.* I'd like to stand up and quote Cesare Pavese: "A gulp of my drink," he wrote, "and my body can taste the life / of plants and of rivers."

For the four heavy-hitter reds, we're served stuffed guinea hen and roasted potatoes. We're supposed to guess—which is the aged cepparello, which is the aged syrah? I get them all wrong. Never mind, most of us do, though Ed scores well. The fruit *torta* I pass by, but I do try a sip of the Isole e Olena Vin Santo, 2000. It tastes like late Thanksgiving afternoon by the fire, a cashmere throw over my legs, lines of a poem running through my head. I'd like to make a walnut cake, just to serve with this smooth elixir. Just as I imagine this vin santo held up to the flames and sloshed around for the play of toast and topaz colors, I feel a surge of homesickness for my daughter, my grandson Willie, my writer neighbors, even for Willie's goofy labradoodle. Isn't this the best response to a wine, that *taste* provokes a fierce emotion? And maybe surreal associations? The ginger-curled, bouncing labradoodle is exactly the color of this elegant vin santo.

We fall in bed after one, dreading the alarm set for an early departure tomorrow. Falling asleep, I catch an iconic image from a Fellini movie, a helicopter dangling a crucifix over Rome. But I see it angling through the skies toward Siena, spiriting Placido away. As the blades tilt, Placido waves from the window.

A House Flying

ED'S THEORY CONFIRMED: GOOD WINE CAUSES no problems the next day. By nine, we manage to back out of the driveway, both feeling quite fine. We're off to the Marche. Often our most memorable travels are short car trips, with a map, a book bag, and a change of clothes.

If I were moving to Italy today, I might choose to live in the Marche. The region is studded with unspoiled villages and luscious countryside. There may not be a more divine piazza than in Ascoli Piceno. Drinking cold tea in the retro café, watching the daily bustle of shopping and visiting, meanwhile marking my map with other hidden towns to visit, is a fine way to spend a summer morning. I especially like the town of Macerata, where an opera festival is held every summer. The noble Urbino may be the magnetic star in the crown, but simply drifting around lost on back roads in that region defines an earthly heaven.

I keep reading that the Marche is "the next Tuscany." That's not likely because, with the exception of the coastal road, navigating this province is rough. Traversing the Marche, en route from

Tuscany, you always seem to find yourself behind a truck, winding slowly, slowly to your destination. A particularly rugged stretch of the Apennines sawtooths all the way down the region, just inland, so that narrow lateral roads run up into the mountains. The map looks like a fish skeleton when you pull it out all at once. But few of the rib roads connect with each other. This keeps the inland area quite unspoiled and remote. We speed along, ready for a two-day visit to Urbino and Loreto, homes to major Signorelli paintings.

FROM A DISTANCE, turreted Urbino looks like a town created by a clever six-year-old from architectural blocks bought by indulgent grandparents. Dome, towers, *campanile,* and stacked buildings of golden brick layer and rise as you approach by an upwardly swooping road. Some fairy with wand might fly out of an arch, inviting you to a ball. Or boys of the local, famed Montefeltro clan might thunder out of gates, looking for a dust-up with some longtime foes.

We drive too far into town and immediately find ourselves in the no-car zone, facing a *vigile.* All glittering brass buttons and ribbons, he leans from on high into the window—oh no, we'll be thrown into a Montefeltro oubliette—and suddenly laughs. *"Ogni dieci minuti, gli stranieri senza occhi,"* he says. Every ten minutes, foreigners without eyes. He draws circles in the air with his forefinger, directing us back downhill and around several loops. We slink down the hill and never see the sign we should have seen but somehow land at our hotel right in front of the immense treasure trove, the Palazzo Ducale— *casa dolce casa,* home sweet home of the aforementioned Montefeltros.

Soon we are ordering coffee in the *centro.* University students jam the piazza. What's happening? If this were the university where I taught, a major political demonstration would be starting. But no, they're just nipping into the bar for espresso and talking, talking like their parents in piazzas all over Italy. Several wear laurel crowns trailing with red ribbons. They must be graduating with their laureate degrees, even though it is March. On one boy, I spot a Dante nose. The red-gold hair of one girl falls in Botticelli curls. They look so charming, classical poets reincarnated and walking among us. The lovely La Primavera's friend suddenly laughs, mouth wide open, head back. I can see his molars. How they talk with their bodies! They bend, gesture, smack each other on the back. Their responsive faces are lit. What's that spark in the DNA and why don't other cultures have it? If I had another life, I'd definitely want to be an Italian student with that Renaissance hair.

Classes seem to happen all over town, including the palace. Destiny serves the enlightened Federico da Montefeltro well. He gathered the major artists of the last half of the fifteenth century into his orbit, making Urbino, way out in the Marche, a little Florence. Surely the genes of some of them still crop up in these parts. Perhaps there's a potential Piero della Francesca or a Raffaello among these students.

"I don't get that *'ogni dieci minuti'* at all." Ed looks around us. "We're the only foreigners in town, with or without eyes."

"I see a few guidebooks, but in Italian." The weekends before and after Easter are favored times for Italians to travel. They live by the expression *Natale con i tuoi, Pasqua con chi vuoi*—Christmas with your own, Easter with whomever you wish.

At lunch, a group of professors attending a conference and a couple from Milan are the only other diners. My former colleagues would have been in tweed, khaki ("baggy-butt Americans" a chic Cortona friend says), or sweaters. These

academics come in wearing leather jackets, scarves tied just
so, and well-cut jeans. But like my colleagues, professors
everywhere *really* eat. These are running through all the
courses and several bottles of wine. After such feasting, the
wordy afternoon sessions they face would put me to sleep, but
somehow Italians can manage the stupendous *pranzo* and
charge forth.

The Milanese diners are hardly less ambitious. The waiter
brings them the full antipasto platter, risotto, then steaks.
They consult the city map and their books. Those are delicious
moments for the traveler—a fine lunch with someone you
love, poring over *The Blue Guide* and *Gambero Rosso,* a weekend to explore a new place and each other.

We have our meager scaloppini and salad and a tiny *quarto*
of local wine. The restaurant—the back room of a popular
bar—looks like a provincial hotel from fifty years back—raspberry tablecloths washed many times, majolica plates on the
walls, and scraggly plants madly seeking light. Their sparse
tendrils have been encouraged to climb around the windows.
Literally creepy. The waiter, concerned that we don't have
enough to eat, brings over a plate of what looks like fried flat
bread. "*Cresce sfogliate,* try it."

"Um, looks good. What is this?" Ed passes the plate.
"*Sfogliate* means what, no leaves? Looks kind of like *piadini.*"

"It's like that Indian bread with onions. Nan?" Ed tears off
a piece of delicious layered flat bread with cheese melted in the
middle. Whatever foolish abstemiousness we were practicing
flies out the big windows.

"Or quesadilla." Mine has a layer of chopped chard. "Or,
flattened puff pastry."

We ask the waiter about it, but he just shrugs. "No, not a
specialty, just local. You find it everywhere." We tear through
the whole plate and ask for more. And since we've gone that

far, we order a lemon tart and linger as long as the ravenous
professors.

We have the rest of the afternoon to lavish our attention
on open courtyards, two Egyptian obelisks, golden stones,
and on the endless rooms of the Palazzo Ducale. Piero della
Francesca's famous profile portraits of the duke and his wife
rightfully should be here, since this is home, but belong
instead to the Uffizi in Florence. I remember them from the
first time I came to Italy. The duke in his red, red hat and
clothes stares forever at his second wife, who bore him seven
children and died at twenty-six. You can't see his lost eye on
the right, though you can see the missing wedge at the top of
his nose, both disasters the result of jousting. Too bad his
striking visage doesn't hang near his small and curious *studiolo.* How amazing that this witty room-within-a-room sur-
vives. Was this his hideout? Love nest? The old duke must
have been as passionate for *intarsio,* marquetry, as he was for
painting. The *studiolo* is lined with tromp l'oeil shelves holding musical and astrological instruments, a clock, realistic lattice doors half open. The artists obviously loved playing with
perspective and managed to create vignettes reflecting the
duke's values and desires. Within, you have the feeling that
the images are coded and personal. Maybe no one ever will
parse how each image relates to some aspect of Federico's life,
but as an observer, you sense that the *studiolo* is fraught with
personal symbols.

Of all the palaces I've toured, this one seems the most hab-
itable, with its appealing fireplaces, the variety of decorated
ceilings, and the fanciful doorframes to lure you into rooms
with those magic proportions that make you feel upright and
pleased.

Coming upon two of Tuscany's Piero della Francesca
paintings is like running into an old friend in some remote

airport. We stand before two of his greatest hits—*The Flagel-
lation of Christ* and the somber, archaic *Madonna of Senigallia.*
Though I have come for the two Signorellis this time, I pause
long before the anonymous *La Città Ideale, The Ideal City,* and
then before *La Muta* by Raffaello, an Urbino native. He has
bequeathed us a portrait of a woman more mysterious than the
Mona Lisa. The mute looks as though she has plenty to say,
and hence the tension of the sensitive, reserved face and the
pent emotions behind her enigmatic glance. She was cut out of
her frame and stolen, along with the two della Francescas, in
1975, and found in Switzerland the next year, still mute about
the whole experience.

Ah, my Signor Signorelli! We find his work less promi-
nently displayed than his teacher Piero's. His Virgin sits in a
square room flanked by the apostles. The group could be waiting to see the dentist except that all the apostles have flames
rising from their heads and the Holy Ghost hovers above. I
think they've just been given the gift of languages so that they
can spread the gospels. As a long struggler with Italian, I wish
I had been so visited. The multicolored squares on the floor are
foregrounded, as though Luca really most loved the marble's
abstract designs. The open space of the floor forces you to see
the waiting group as a static tableau. The painting originally
was one side of a standard meant to be hoisted aloft during
processions through the streets. The Crucifixion hanging next
to it was the other face of the banner. Although the crucified
Christ against a muted sky reigns, all the emotional attention
centers on his mother below. She has fainted from grief and
lies on the ground, surrounded by attentive women.

❧

THE ADVANTAGE OF late dining may lie in the three hours
back at the hotel. I've brought my green tea *bagno schiuma,*

bubble bath, and our room has a tub big enough for two to squeeze into, relax, and laugh.

According to Vasari's *Lives of the Most Excellent Painters, Sculptors, and Architects,* Signorelli lived well. As a visitor to the duke's court, he probably dined well. If he were here tonight, maybe he would find his way, as we do, to the Trattoria del Leone, a lively place packed with local academics. We immediately spot *Olive all'Ascolana* on the menu. These fried olives originated in Ascoli Piceno. Served all over the country, they're often prepackaged and therefore diminished—nothing fried should have to travel farther than stove to table. On home turf, they deliver their three taste and texture layers— the crunchy exterior, the hefty olive, and the savory salami (or a mixture of meats) interior. Perfect with a glass of prosecco while you ponder the menu. The *marchigiani* eat well. Their *passatelli in brodo* once cured Ed's migraine. Not exactly a pasta, *passatelli* looks like short fat spaghetti but is made with cheese, bread crumbs, eggs, and nutmeg, then poached in broth—soul food that's also served to children with colds and the elderly. More rousing is the famous fish stew, *brodetto,* made with no more, no less than thirteen kinds of seafood pulled out of the Adriatic. These *marchigiani* are big meat eaters, too. They like their *castrato,* which is lamb verging on mutton, and robust pork liver dishes. In down-home restaurants, sometimes you see various preparations of testicles. I draw a line there. Ed goes for almost every other part of the pig and likes *ciauscolo,* a soft salami to spread on bread.

Ed holds out a bite of his sausage with melted *caciotta,* local sheep's and cow's milk cheese. He likes my baked rabbit just as well, so we swap. At the end, we try a local *di fossa* cheese. *Fossa* means "pit," where the cheese has aged, but unfortunately, I always associate the word with my first horrid knowledge of it—when I confronted the open *fosse biologica,* the

septic tank. The cheese is good anyway—tangy, complex, lingering. Ed asks for a local *digestivo,* after-dinner digestive
drink, and the owner brings over Liquor d'Ulivi. "The very
essence of the olive," he tells us. Pit, leaf, bark, fruit? The old,
old flavors taste like history, and is there a hint of spring sunlight through the branches?

It's easy to project a life teaching in Urbino, having a stim-
ulating career within the confines of the fairy-tale architecture.
As in other great hill towns, you can wander through Urbino
in an hour and see the place or settle in for a decade and not
reach the end.

∽

THOUGH THE WIND still has a honed edge, pears, mimosa,
forsythia, and redbud have been fooled into blooming and the
hills are scrimmed with vivid green. We're driving to Loreto,
home of the house of the Virgin Mary, borne aloft by angels
in 1294, and blown in a storm from Croatia, where it had
paused en route from Nazareth. Believe that and you can
make any leap of faith. I'm dazzled by the idea of a house flying across the sea. Researchers into this phenomenon found
that a shipping family named Angelli brought the masonry
back to Loreto from Palestine when it was in danger of
destruction. Another line, less appealing because there's no
house careening through the air: Crusaders were sometimes
called "angels" and they always returned with holy souvenirs.
These were also days when holy relics were endlessly traded
and stolen. Every church wanted its bony memento or bit of
cloth or hank of saint's hair. The raids and skirmishes and
dealings around these sacred objects make fascinating reading[1] and surely comprise one of the kinkiest chapters in
church history. Loreto, with the touchdown of the holy
dwelling place, hit the jackpot. Carbon dating proves that the

limestone and cedar remnants, not of this locality, are of the period of Mary's life.

Loreto often must be thronged with pilgrims, but today we find the town eerily empty. Along a huddle of open stalls very old women wait for the absent *pellegrini* who may buy their religious souvenirs. The unusual round *campanile* and the proud basilica anchor a broad piazza flanked by arcades on one side and handsome religious buildings along the other. I read that the *campanile*'s bell weighs eleven tons. I'd love to hear its long bongs resounding across the stones; if it began to ring surely the faithful would suddenly materialize and miracles would again occur at the Virgin's house.

"Quiet as the day after judgment day." Ed takes a few pictures. "Where is everybody?"

"All gone to heaven. How did we never know this place was so . . . full of force? And the impression is so *light*. That stone—ivory, but warm."

"Do you think anyone's ever made a study of *campanile*s? Isn't the one in Città di Castello round, too?"

"Ah, that's right! Don't you think that someone has studied every stone in Italy? This one is lovely, like a tall altar candle."

❧

MANY ARTISTS HAVE put their veneration at Loreto: Sansovino, Reni, Borromeo, Lotto, Pomarancio, my guy Signorelli, Sangallo, and others. Inside the church, Mary's Santa Casa, Holy House, may be the magnet, but Bramante's staggering marble surround of the dwelling makes this place worth a detour. The Virgin's house is encased in elaborately carved marble depicting scenes from her life. The best section shows Gabriel, the Annunciation angel, before a Virgin half-turned away and wary. Sansovino, who carved this section, managed the illusion of the angel defying the weight of stone; he appears to have landed with an airy step. A marble bench surrounding the house has twin grooves worn into the stone by the knees of pilgrims who circumnavigate as a penance.

Even a big doubter of the story like me has to feel that the inside of this tiny sacred house transcends legend. Maybe it's the somber black Virgin statue looking down from above the altar. She replaces one supposedly carved by the apostle Thomas, later destroyed in a fire. Maybe it's the humble stacked brick walls, or just that I feel heavily claustrophobic, but the inscription *Hic Verbum Caro Factum Est* gives me a shiver. *Here the Word was made flesh.* Maybe some of the bricks and boards *were* brought back by a monk. *If, if, if* Mary were born here, received the angel, raised the Baby, then this comes as close as one can get to the very taproot of Christianity. A true believer in this site would have to faint or get the gift of tongues from the power of the place. A believer might echo William Sloane Coffin's soaring belief. "I love the recklessness of faith," he said. "First you jump, then you grow wings."

I'm drawn. Powerfully. Even in college, I was fascinated by relics. While walking in a cemetery in New Orleans, I found a vertebra near a collapsed grave. I kept it in a small glass box and carefully labeled it in calligraphic hand, *vertebra of the Virgin.* Soon I had a shelf in my bookcase devoted to my relics. Tooth of St. Mark, shell from the bottom of the Red Sea, splinter of the cross, vial of Mary's tears, a stone from the road to Damascus, small quartz shafts that I called Jesus Wept tears. Faux they were, but I thought that probably ninety-nine percent of those hoisted above altars in gold reliquaries were gathered in the same way. My shelf was a place of devotion, strange as it was, along with books of poetry and Greek plays.

Later, I began to collect *ex votos,* the itinerant paintings on tin or scrap wood to record thanks. I became attracted to them after seeing the Immaculate Conception, a church in Real de

Catorce, a mining ghost town in Mexico. I found, and still do, the impulse of thanks tied to the gesture of making art one of the profound human expressions. Usually an *ex voto* shows an accident, such as a cart turned over, the driver almost crushed but saved by holy intervention from a saint or Mary, shown hovering above in the sky. One of my prizes from 1929 shows a man falling off a rickety chair while screwing in a lightbulb. Fortunately a saint intervened in his fate. Many are scenes of sick children with the parents praying near the bed. Almost always the initials *P.G.R.* and the date appear in the sky. *Per Grazia Ricevuta,* for grace received. As a humanist and a pantheist, I can't not believe in grace received, though the what, where, when, and how of grace remains mysterious to me, and hopelessly entangled with grace *not* received: suffering. But venerating some tiny fragment from the past, yes, I'm stirred by that efficacy. Touch the object and feel time spiral back: That scratchy brown bit of St. Francis's robe in San Francesco in Cortona, the amber necklace of my mother's, that first-cut lock of my grandson's soft blond hair, the crown of thorns I made from brambles, the nineteenth-century wedding dress hanging in my study, the worn handle of the rotary beater that whipped many whites to a froth so many years ago.

⌒

I FIND LUCA's unusually restrained hand in a small octagonal sacristy. The cabinets' fine intarsia represent the robes, censors, and prayer books stored within. Signorelli worked on the Sacrestia di San Giovanni in 1479, covering the ceiling with panels of the apostles, each one of whom is busy writing his gospel; I relish thinking of the apostles not as veteran missionaries but as *writers*. From the dome, luminous musical angels—their muses?—accompany the process. This is a sweet room where nothing dramatic happens except when the incredulous St. Thomas pokes Jesus in his wound. Literalists like him are always crass.

I wonder what Luca thought of the "translation" of the Virgin's house into the Loreto shrine and if he ever considered painting the famous flight. The subject later caught the imagination of Saturnino Gatti, who painted a decorous version in 1510, and later, Tiepolo, who covered the ceiling of a church in Venice (bombed in World War I) with a big passel of angels swimming through the sky holding the house aloft.[2] A house flying through the sky. Outrageous and magnificent! If I leap, will I grow wings? I once tried to fly off a barn with wings made of an old sheet and balsa wood. Lucky, lucky, I only had the wind knocked clean out of me.

I love the idea of a house transported. I buy a metal medallion of the house from one of the souvenir stands. After all, the Apollo astronauts, in their own unlikely flying house, took one of these to the moon.

⌒

I am always energized by the synergy of a writing project. Mysteriously, what you need seems to come to you like a hummingbird to a red hibiscus. As I browsed in the bookstore at the Palazzo Ducale, I picked up a card announcing a Signorelli exhibit opening *today* in the village of Arcevia, not far out of our way home. To reach Arcevia, you wind up and up, arriving at a long narrow street lined with low row houses and widening to a piazza. It seems like a town in Spain: closed and secret. Closed to neighbors, closed to its stupendous view, except for one opening at the back of the piazza.

Three major Signorellis hang in the church of San Medardo, and who is he? The interior, so unlike most Italian churches, has walls, pale as lemon juice, which cast a glaze of transparent light on the paintings. Here's my proof that

Cortona's finest, my *amico* Signorelli, is scandalously under-estimated. These three paintings command the whole church, rendering my initial disappointment—only three works on exhibit?—absurd. Two paintings remained here forever, where they were meant to be. The regal and munificent *Madonna in Trono col Bambino, Madonna Enthroned with Child,* from 1508, has been brought home to Arcevia from the Pina-coteca di Brera in Milan. The grand Madonna, with saints, has long since lost her panels, predella, and side columns to Ger-many, England, and, *mamma mia,* San Diego, so far from home. Nevertheless, the remaining painting stops even the se-verely mentally handicapped boy, whose parents lunge around the church, guiding him, and attempting to enjoy the exhibit though he shouts and farts, creating echoes. He has trouble holding up his head but gazes in wonder at the sublime face of the young Virgin. A veil of peace seems to fall over him from the young Virgin's downcast gaze.

Signorelli often placed a commanding focal point in front of his main subject. In this painting, a cardinal's red hat lies on the floor in the center of the foreground. Maybe Signorelli in-tended a subliminal association with the future crucifixion of the adorable baby held so gently by his heavenly teen mama. Or maybe he just loved the shape and color and wanted to paint *red hat* along with his umpteenth Madonna.

Opposite a della Robbia confection in a side chapel, we find Signorelli's *Baptism of Christ by John the Baptist.* This painting compels attention. Not entirely by the master's brush, the painting showcases one of Signorelli's preoccupations: the male body shown in prime form—and never more so than here, where Jesus stands to midcalf in the river, his legs visible through clear water. Two other splendid male specimens are on view in the background. Signorelli's Christs and saints are physical, manly, and never sentimentalized. God, in a burst of glory, looks down from above as John in his signature animal skins performs the baptism. "The babies of this town get baptized with this to fix their eyes on," Ed says.

Over the altar the church's own Madonna and Bambino preside in the original splendid frame, with all the panels of saints and scenes intact. There's the mysterious Medardo, given top billing along with Saints Sebastian (human dartboard), John, Paul, and several others. One is Roch, and what is he doing down there on the lower right? Spinning? Cutting open his leg? In the pilasters, fourteen smaller portraits frame the magnificent whole. On the steps of the Madonna's throne, the polyptych is signed *Lucas Signorellus Pingebat.* I suppose *Pingebat* must be Latin for "painter," but somehow the word strikes me as funny and, as I try not to laugh, my concentration on the episodes painted on the predellas stops. The faithful of Arcevia have gazed at this polyptych as they made their way to the altar for communion for five hundred years. This thought stops me as I realize I'm one of millions on a long timeline to gaze up at the stories portrayed, to turn and walk back up the aisle and out into the blue day.

Maybe at that moment I was subliminally connected with Medardo. Back at Bramasole, I look him up in a guide to saints and find that he is often portrayed "laughing insanely," or being sheltered from rain by the outspread wings of an eagle. This childhood event gives him the patronage over bad weather. I'll have to remember to watch his feast day, June 8. If it rains, there will be forty wet days to follow. He's a French saint—Medard, who somehow came to be venerated in remote Arcevia. I like his mythic attributes: His horse could leave footprints in stone. The other mysterious saint, Roch (in Italian, Rocco), turns out to be French also. He traveled to Italy, miraculously curing plague victims everywhere he went, including Rimini on the Adriatic. The disease claimed him eventually and he went into the woods to die. He survived because a dog began to bring him bread. I'll guess that the image in Arcevia shows him displaying a plague sore on his thigh, though what the little spindle-looking thing he holds might be, I still don't know. When I read that he's the patron saint of dogs, I'm purely amazed. When my grandson Willie received a dog for Christmas, out of nowhere he named him Rocco. Ed thinks "roch" is onomatopoeic barking—*roch, roch*.

~

WE'RE HAVING OUR forty wet days right now. Ed makes his warm-the-cockles winter soup of kale, white beans, and sausage. I float *bruschette*, toasted with October's oil, on top— and that's dinner.

When I am a hundred, propped in the piazza with a bracing glass of grappa, and think back on the happiest times of my life, these evenings in front of the fire, with our tin trays balanced on our knees, the winter soup's aroma mixing with the fragrant olive wood, the candles lighted, the decanter half full of black wine, with another day to talk about, wind leaking under the door, and the roasted chestnuts after, Ed shaking them over the embers, peeling fast, and handing me one— these nights to recall are paradigms. I eventually pick up a book and go up to bed, leaving Ed by the fire to stare and think what he thinks, take notes on the back of the electric bill, perhaps to doze long enough that eventually I call down the stairs, "It's late. Wake up. Come to bed . . ."

~

THE GOOD FRIDAY procession has to be canceled because of the rain. The participants carry a heavy cross and a statue of Mary to many churches, stopping at each for a blessing. In good weather, the journey is *duro,* hard enough, but on slippery stones with an icy wind—best repair to Paolo's trattoria for a plate of pasta with boar sauce. This weather stays beastly. Should we begin to nail together an ark?

This year my birthday falls on Easter and we are invited to the Cardinali family *pranzo*. I can't think of a place I'd rather be. Placido grills a whole lamb in the fireplace. We are twenty at table. Some of the family is missing the feast. In the fall, Umberto, a nephew, crashed his small plane. His parents and sisters and brothers are still too devastated to appear. My grandson and daughter call during the antipasti and sing "Happy Birthday." Not one to cry, I find this makes two teary bouts for me today. Missing them, and then during the prayer, when everyone stands together and the nephew Umberto is dead and everyone feels his impossible absence . . . and Plari, with his awful accident, now smiling, having roasted meat for all as usual. And another year gathered for me.

Outside, the valley is obscured by rain and *nebbia,* so much more expressive than "fog." Inside we are cozy and familial. Simone's father, who lost his wife last winter, sitting without a word but eating everything in sight. Anna's daughters all smoking at the end of the table. Little Claudia, growing into a beauty, her laugh like a bicycle bell. Fiorella bringing out the ravioli, the mushroom crêpes, everything delicious. Claudio, our head of the *carabinieri*, handsome as a Byzantine icon, telling us that today someone turned over flowerpots in Camucia. Big crime scene! Placido carving. All the women getting up from time to time to clear, reappearing with bowls of *clementini,* the small Sicilian tangerines, and Aurora's chocolate tart. Tuscan cigars lighted, cards snapped on the table. The grappa poured. At the end, other neighbors, friends, cousins begin to drop in, each bringing a huge chocolate egg with a prize inside. The warmth circulating around the table feels like that leap that lets you grow wings.

Those long tables . . . those endless meals. The spit turning in the fireplace and the hens or birds or roasting meats filling the room with savory old-world aromas. I have sat with my back to the hearth a hundred, two hundred times. And the room, as known as my childhood home. Photographs propped all around, an upright piano. At the end, a bookcase, with white sofa and chairs and a round table in the middle stacked with books. But it is the dining table—a long table for twenty, or twenty-five squeezed—that dominates. This, it states, is what's important, a copious arrangement for family and friends, with the fire blazing. The sofa becomes merely a place where coats are piled, sometimes with tired children sprawled on top, dreaming, no doubt, until they are awakened by their parents and stagger out into crisp nights with skies encrusted with stars.

Easter. Is he risen? Has a house flown? Spring is coming. We walk back to Bramasole arm in arm with another fine memory for the future. Our house looms above the road, casting light in golden panels onto the bare garden. How mysterious, a house on its own. We will enter and the rooms will become ours. Right now, Bramasole belongs to itself. I start to sing. *You are lost and gone forever, oh my darlin' Clementine* . . . The rain falls lightly, as though a hand held a gigantic watering can above us, gently dousing us for growth in the coming sunny days.

〜◦〜

ZUPPA DI CAVOLO NERO, CANNELLINI, E SALSICCE
Kale, White Bean, and Sausage Soup

Kale goes by another name, one much more dashing, especially in Italian. *Cavolo Nero,* black cabbage, may not evoke super-hero status, but it's close. Kale does seem invincible and it's known to make the eater more so, too. It's also called dinosaur kale (also called *lacinato*), maybe because its leaves look like the back of a lizard. Those thin knobby leaves squeak. Do not confuse *cavolo,* accent on the first syllable, with *cavallo,* accent on the second, or you'll be ordering black horse, and in certain parts of the world will find it. Hearty and good for the spirit. I like soaked and cooked cannellini better than canned ones.

Serves 12 to 14

2 Italian sausages, skins removed and meat crumbled
4 tablespoons olive oil
2 onions, chopped
2 garlic cloves, minced
2 quarts chicken stock
1 cup white wine
6 thyme sprigs
1 bunch of kale, washed and chopped
4 cups cooked cannellini beans

Sauté the crumbled sausage in the oil until browned, and reserve. Sauté the onions and garlic until translucent. Add to the chicken stock in a big pot. Add the wine and cook until the alcohol has evaporated, then add the thyme and kale. Bring to a boil, then cover and simmer for 15 minutes. Add the cooked sausage and the beans and simmer another 15 minutes.

～❧～

CALDARROSTE
Roasted Chestnuts

We gather baskets of chestnuts in the fall and we have to hurry—we've got competition from every wild boar in the area.

Do we search for the chestnuts or the Chestnuts. The latter are *marrone,* the kind made into *marrons glacés,* that syrupy sweet coated Chestnut. I could eat an entire box, if permitted.

We like to roast either type in the fireplace, as much for the smell as for the taste. Chestnuts must have their skin sliced; otherwise they'll explode. With a short-bladed knife, carefully cut a slit in the flat side. Pile in the chestnut roaster and set it over hot coals (not an open flame) for about 5 minutes and then turn over or shake well to redistribute the chestnuts. After another 5 minutes, pierce one with a knife. It should go in quite easily. Pour them into a bowl, let them cool only long enough to handle, then peel.

In an oven: Preheat to 450 degrees F, and spread prepared chestnuts on a sheet pan. Bake for 20 minutes and then start checking every 5 minutes.

❦

OLIVE ALL'ASCOLANA
Olives from Ascoli Piceno

The fifty thousand *ascolani,* the people who live in the Marche town of Ascoli Piceno, dwell around one of the most beautiful piazzas in Italy, the Piazza del Popolo. At cafés, everyone is nibbling these stuffed, fried olives, a local treat that is famous all over Italy. The olive of choice is their local one, the *tenera ascolana,* quite large, green, with a small pit. The recipe is also called *Ascolane all'ascolana,* that is, the ascolana olive in the manner of the town of Ascoli Piceno.

If you can't find the *ascolana* olive, and you probably can't, use large olives with the pits removed.

Serves 6 to 8 on an antipasto platter

> *Peanut oil for frying*
> *20 large olives, pits removed*
> *½ pound Italian salami, finely chopped*
> *Beaten flour, egg, and bread crumbs on three separate*
> *   plates*
> *Salt and pepper*

Heat oil in a pan until it reaches 375 degrees F or so.

Stuff the olives with the salami. Roll in the flour, then the egg, and then the bread crumbs. Fry until golden, turning when needed. Drain on paper towels, and season with salt and pepper.

ALTERNATIVE FILLING: *With a pastry tube, try piping in a mix of garlic, chopped anchovy, and lemon zest.*

❧

BRODETTO
Seafood Stew

If you look on a topographical map of central Italy, you'll see the Apennines (Appennini), a string of mountains that forms the sturdy and well-articulated spine of Italy, splitting the country in two. On the eastern side, the Cortona side, the mountain range gives to wide fertile plains that end in the waters of the Tyrrhenian, the Tuscan part of the Mediterranean Sea. There's no such landscape on the western side of the Apennines, where the mountains and the sea have a more intimate relationship. Part of the reason the Marche region hasn't been as explored as much as Tuscany is because of mountains, everywhere, making it more difficult to get around. Naturally, the *marchigiani* turn toward the sea for their food. Up and down the Adriatic coast, you'll find everyone who has a stockpot has a recipe for *brodetto*.

If Cole Porter had been Italian, he might have written, "You say *brodetto,* I say *buridda,* you say *cioppino* and I say *cacciucco* . . ." Fish stew by any other name definitely sounds better. Italian for seafood is *frutti di mare,* fruits of the sea or seafruits. Even the Italian word for fish, *pesce,* two syllables, makes the word palatable and musical.

Naturally, a number of regions have their own names for *brodetto,* all made differently. There's *cioppino,* which is all over San Francisco, but I've never seen it in Italy, although it's said to have originated in Liguria, where they eat *buridda;* on the Tuscan coast you'd eat *Cacciucco alla Livornese.*

What Ed suggests: Simply buy what's fresh that day. If the recipe calls for hake and there's no hake, and the flounder

looks good, then buy flounder. Traditionally, cooks used thirteen different kinds of seafood.

Serves 6

> *2 shallots, minced*
> *¼ cup extra-virgin olive oil*
> *4 garlic cloves, minced*
> *3 or 4 strands of saffron*
> *Salt and pepper*
> *2 cups cherry tomatoes, halved*
> *2 cups white wine*
> *½ pound cod, cut into 1-inch pieces*
> *1 pound shrimp, peeled*
> *½ pound small scallops*
> *½ pound flounder, cut into 1-inch pieces*
> *½ cup parsley, chopped*

Sauté the shallots in the oil for 2 or 3 minutes, then add the garlic. Continue sautéing, then add the saffron, salt, pepper, and
tomatoes. After another 5 minutes, add the wine and bring to a
boil. Lower heat to a simmer and cook for 5 minutes.

Raise heat to medium and add the cod, which takes a little
longer than the other seafood, and cook for 3 minutes, then
add the shrimp, scallops, and flounder. Cover and cook on low
for 15 minutes. Add parsley just before serving.

Serve in a bowl on a piece of good toasted bread, or over
spaghetti.

~⁓~

Giusi's Crespelle ai Porcini e Ricotta
Giusi's Porcini and Ricotta Crêpes

For this delicate recipe, try to find bags or jars of Italian dried porcini. Put them in a bowl, cover them with boiling water, and steep them for 15 to 20 minutes, until they've expanded. Drain and chop. You can reserve the liquid to use in other dishes, but be sure to strain it first.

For variety in the *pommarola,* and for a pasta sauce in itself, try using *odori* (minced onion, carrot, celery, parsley) instead of the onion. Also, you can add ½ cup of cream to the sauce. *Pommarola* can be fresh and quick like this, or long simmered for an intense concentrated sauce.

Serves 4 (8 crespelle)

⅓ *cup flour*
1 cup milk
3 eggs, beaten
1 teaspoon salt
4 tablespoons butter, cut in small pieces
1 cup ricotta
1 egg yolk
½ cup parmigiano, *grated*
1 ounce dried porcini mushrooms
Tomato sauce (recipe follows)

Preheat oven to 350 degrees F.

Put the flour in a medium bowl and slowly stir in the milk, forming a paste. Beat eggs separately and add to the mixture, along with half of the salt.

Melt 1 tablespoon of the butter in a 9-inch nonstick skillet to coat it. Ladle ¼ cup of batter into the skillet and cook over medium-high heat. As it's cooking, loosen the edges of the *crespella* with a knife or spatula, and after 1 or 2 minutes, turn to cook on the other side another 1 or 2 minutes. Remove to a plate. Add a little more butter to the pan, and repeat the above process.

In a medium bowl, mash the ricotta with a fork, add the egg yolk, the remaining salt, the *parmigiano,* and porcini and continue to mix. Add 3 tablespoons of tomato sauce and mix.

Drop 2 tablespoons of the filling in the middle of a *crespella* and spread it all over. Roll the *crespella* like a cigar. Repeat with the others. Put them in an ovenproof baking dish and top with ½ cup of the tomato sauce, a few more small pieces of butter, and a sprinkling of *parmigiano*. Bake for 25 minutes. Serve immediately.

POMMAROLA
Tomato Sauce

½ cup extra-virgin olive oil
1 small onion, minced
1 28-ounce can of whole tomatoes, or 6–8 firm fresh
    tomatoes, peeled
½ cup basil leaves, chopped
Salt and pepper

Heat oil and add onion. After 5 minutes over medium heat, add tomatoes and break them up with a spoon. Add basil and salt and pepper to taste. Cook for 10 minutes on high heat, uncovered, to reduce it. Makes 3 cups.

Bramasole

AT BRAMASOLE, I LEARNED TO IRON WITH MY hands. Fold and smooth, fold, then smooth, fold, smooth; the blue top sheet, lifted from the rack, smells of warm light. Flounces on the pillowcases yield to my flat hand; my yellow nightgown softens. The bottom sheet draped over two chairs tries to sail and would blow over the valley if I had not nipped the corners with clothespins. Ah, as my hand glides, I see that an iron has the shape of a hand. Red T-shirt, black pants, the waffle-weave hand towels—my hand slides over, just as the fish-shaped boat moves through water, the bird body of the plane parts the air, and a car mimics a horse's body with four feet—scratches off, the driver holding the steering wheel like reins. I like my dishcloths ironed and so I press hard; I stack them, red-checked, blue striped, sunflower print, toile of spring green, and the utilitarian white, worn to gauze, for drying glasses. Three silk shirts—fuchsia, white, a lavender print like Victorian wallpaper—twirl on hangers in the breeze, the wind urging them to give up their wrinkles. Folding laundry, sun in my hair, the basket stacked—the ritual of preparing the clothes seems like an offering to the household gods. Warm laundry, carried aloft, distributed among the rooms, brings a particular solace. All's right with fresh towels, snowy underwear, and a bed that welcomes the body.

At Bramasole, I learned to forage—pull on rubber boots, grab the clippers, and go. Even this cultivated landscape offers abundant *insalata di campo,* wild field greens; yellow plums like those I used to find along the honeysuckle-lined roads in Georgia—suck the juice and spit out pit and skin; the prized *amarini,* cherries the size of five-caret rubies, which are bottled with alcohol and brought out in winter to spoon over polenta cake. Volunteer pears, purslane, the low-growing wild mint called *mentuccia*, pine nuts, blackberries, wiry, bitter asparagus, fennel flowers, figs. My neighbor Placido would add *lumache,* snails, to my foraging list. He's first in line at the annual Sagra della Lumaca, where in a copper pot the size of a truck tire, a mountain of snails simmers in rich tomato and pancetta sauce. As the cook ladles, shells clatter into the bowl. I fail as a true gourmet; I pass up these creatures who make slime, though Ed relishes this dish once every year and insists that I don't know what I'm missing. If our huge vegetable garden had the boost of a cow and a henhouse, we could be almost complete locavores. (Attractive concept. Unattractive word.)

The land gives wildflowers eight months a year. Because on the first day I ever spent in rural Tuscany a neighbor came over with a sack of eggs and an armful of broom, vetch, poppies, lilies, and nameless yellow and purple wildflowers, that has been my best-loved bouquet. (Lilies—both orange and white—grow wild.) A foray through the fields, the bounty plopped into a pitcher, and *voilà*.

I love the setting forth, swinging my basket, roaming the olive grove and the terraces beyond. I know what I'm looking for (green almonds or tiny crab apples) but really I'm looking for surprise—coming upon a clutch of chanterelles or wild strawberries or blue-blossomed thyme or dark purple irises with intense grapy scent. If I return with only a dozen strawberries, they put a little magic in our habitual summer cocktail. A few figs, split, add an earthy touch to a platter of *salumi.* A handful of purple allium balls looks unexpected when poked into a bowl of roses. A branch of lemon balm I drop into my hot bath. Simplicity, an elusive goal, feels within reach as I arrange three pecorino cheeses on grape leaves I've cut from abandoned vines, as I roast a pan of knotty pears, or lay my three porcini on the hearth for grilling.

So many pleasures have come to me at Bramasole. Here, I learned to take cuttings of old roses and make healthy new plants. I learned to plant rosemary, santolina, and lavender in long curving waves, interrupted now and then by lion's tail. I learned to keep my knives sharp—a dull blade is more dangerous than a razor edge, and there's much to slice and chop. I learned to consider the scorpion, and the snake that lives in the dahlias. The scorpions love the shower and, I suppose, have their rights. Their beauty is particular, as is that of the amazing brown spider that looks like a bronze and topaz brooch. I've learned to care for my lemons just as they did in the Renaissance, bringing them out of their glass-fronted room, the *limonaia,* in late April, and lining the grand pots along the front of the house. For six months, they yield not only their fruit but also their narcotizing scent, which drifts into the downstairs rooms and sometimes even up to the third-floor window. In late October, as though they know this is a last chance, they give forth their most abundant bounty. This is the season to brew *limoncello* and to serve forth my grandmother Big Mama's tart, sweet lemon pie. I can see her white, white face, lips pursed and lacteal blind eyes staring just over my head as she rolled out the crust and whipped the whites.

The brilliant yellow lemons rival the beauty of the dangling orange persimmons, *kaki,* in many gardens. Before the first hard freeze of November, back the pots go into the *limonaia*. Each pot has been marked on one side and they're placed on risers so that the mark faces winter sun. Side windows open automatically if heat rises. They're watered only occasionally. Even in February, I can squeeze among them and find an emergency lemon.

I learned to mend my *vase*. People value their *fatta a mano,* handmade old terracotta pots. I thought it was the ultimate in thrift when I saw huge lemon trees in pots held together by wire. Even small geraniums on a step or wall often would be wired. This local habit developed long before superglue. Once when I returned, a *vaso* decorated with swags of fruit had completely split. I am fond of it because it holds a yellow tree rose in my herb garden. I got out the wire and the superglue. Now, several years later my pot endures. I've repaired several others, even cheap pots, and have come to like the look as well as the philosophy.

From Albano, who works up at Fonte, our farm in the mountains, we know that the *orto* fence must go underground about eight inches, otherwise little snuffling diggers root under. Albano takes no guff from night visitors. We learned that October strawberries are sweetest, juiciest, that chard reboots forever, asparagus plants last twenty years, raspberry canes must be pruned hard after the fruit is finished for the season. We learned to make tall bamboo teepees for beans and short ones for peppers. We shade the lettuce with a ring of sunflowers. And we never knew before to pick only the males (no zucchini developing at the end) for fried zucchini flowers. We learned to love the winter garden—black cabbage, cardoon, kale, rape, and the early spring fava. I save seeds from the best tomatoes. We have not discovered how to protect our small cherry orchard from the greedy birds, who leave us only half-pecked fruit. The trees are already too tall to drape, and tying old CDs to the branches seems only to attract more blackbirds to the silvery sparkles.

If I were a medieval woman weaving a family tapestry, the knowledge gleaned from living here would form my borders and backgrounds. Instead of a procession of men with falcons on decorated horses, or a lady mincing along on a unicorn, there would be the iconic long table, the gathered friends, the servers and diners, all loved faces, and richly colored threads for the rose, the lemon, the twining bean, sunflower, moon-flower vine, and all the creatures who also are as at home as we are where we live. Above the scene, I'd stitch the golden disk of the sun and jagged rays. Bramasole, from *bramare,* to yearn for, and *sole,* sun, means something that *yearns for the sun.*

The Romans respected their *lares* and *penantes,* household gods of the hearth, pantry, and food. The presence of ancient spirits appeals to one who chooses a house as a spiritual haven. Bramasole always has seemed to me, even when empty, more than a house. This is spooky; a house has an *anima,* a soul? When I am away, I miss it as I miss a person I love. I miss the house's colors, what the old painting manuals call *polvere di mattone,* brick dust, *rosso arancio,* blood orange, *terre bruciate,* burned dirt, *giallo caldo,* hot yellow. I miss the platters on my kitchen walls and the pear and almond tart cooling on the counter. I miss the fireflies, who make the best dinner guests. I miss the *girasole* terrace when the giant sunflowers face the au-dience, the whole dance corps gazing fondly down at our ad-miration. I miss the balcony when the jasmine, lemon, and *tigli,* linden, scents collide and seem to emanate from the moon. I miss the valley below, that pays homage to all greens, and the dark-hearted cypresses along the road, and my earnest coral geraniums escaping from their pots, joining with clematis and trailing down to meet the old roses below. I miss, in winter, the early dark, which comes suddenly, like a stage curtain let down with a velvet thump.

I don't need a celestial paradise; I'll take my immortality here.

∽

Today is Wednesday. Twelve-fifteen by my watch, whose face is obscured by moving stars and a crescent moon. I must shake my wrist to see the minute and hour hands. The pretty watch Ed gave me always reminds me of two kinds of time— this minute and the overriding mega-time of past and future. Maybe the designer intended such a connection. Time, the big breadbasket we fill, raid, fill, and empty.

In Tuscany, I learned to *take time*. Take time to have coffee with the one-armed man in my neighborhood, who tells me how he drives his stick-shift Panda with his dog in his lap, and how as a child he ate bread dipped in red wine for breakfast. Dividing the snarl of iris bulbs and replanting them around an olive tree takes time. I find that I have it. Time: reading until three, then sleeping until ten, if I choose; sharing a glass of sour wine with a farmer who walked back from Genoa after the Italian surrender in World War II; cooking with Gilda, who's incredibly efficient without ever using a processor or microwave. She came to work for us when her sister-in-law, Giusi, left to open her *agriturismo*. We learned from Giusi, a close friend, and we will be learning a long time from Gilda. We learn from Placido, who came over three afternoons straight to help us lay a stone path, who walks the horse so that my grandson can ride, who searches the woods all day for a basket of porcini mushrooms.

Time—that's what it takes for the slow tomato sauce, stirred until reduced to an essential taste of summer sun, for tying lavender in bunches and hanging them from beams to dry, for learning the imperfect tense, for checking the reddening pomegranates every day as they ripen, ripping open the leathery skin to reveal the juicy red hive within, sprinkling the fruit over a salad of field greens and toasted walnuts. Living well in time means *taking back* time from the slave-masters—obligations, appointments, the dreary round of details that attach like leeches in a stagnant pond. During intense periods of work, restoration projects, family crises, health scares, I want to wake up at first light, pull on hiking boots, and set off for an hour while the birds are still practicing their doxologies.

Wasted hours—they were mine; I meant to use them before they slipped through the hourglass.

AT BRAMASOLE, I often recall raising the big sail called "the genoa" on the boat my former husband and I owned. The genoa was suited to copious wind and when it reached the top of the rigging, suddenly billowed grandly and the boat seemed about to levitate into the sky. The memory parallels the rushes of happiness and the silent tilt toward peace that this *home* gives me. Sometimes houses embody not only memory but also a whole sense of the location itself. In the first months I spent here, I had the intuition that since the house was so at home in the landscape, I too would be at home. Living in these rooms, I linked myself to a force field—I am carried by something larger than myself that is at the same time very much myself. Seamlessly, in such a place, you create what in turn creates you.

Those early impressions about *place,* I later came to realize, all rested on *time*. On a metabolic level, don't you sense that the mystery of time is how it unfolds and folds simultaneously? Time, which devours, also stretches. Time is elastic and brutally rigid. Memory cuts and comes again. It does not know how to downsize, to render redundant, or to press a delete key. Old friends are not replaceable with new friends, early loves are still alive in bright rooms of the mind, and years and miles apart, what your Big Daddy told you is true, *blood is thicker than water.*

～

WHAT AN UNEXPECTED turn when strangers began to seek Bramasole, too. Occasionally, a personal book that goes forth modestly into the world takes on a life of its own and the author can only hang on and travel where she's carried. After my memoirs, Bramasole mysteriously transformed from the forlorn, abandoned villa, bought on an iron whim, into a symbol. Although it probably seems awful that one's house turns into a traveler's destination, that has not been the case. I think those who travel because of a book they've read are not ordinary travelers. Also, I think of my writing as letters to friends, so reciprocation seems natural. After the film of *Under the Tuscan Sun,* a new wave began. Still—romantics, all. With each publication in other countries, new visitors arrive. We're all amazed to find Estonians, Taiwanese, Tasmanians, Brazilians, et cetera, et cetera, in Cortona. Some officials are pleased that their promotional DVDs sent to tour leaders have been so effective in bringing the far-flung guests to town.

Other local people get it. They began to joke, somewhat ruefully, that Bramasole is more loved than the grand Medici villas, more visited than Santa Margherita, who lies in her glass coffin at the top of the hill.

Italians hate to be caught short, and who among them could have predicted that Bramasole ever would become a world magnet? "Imagine," the owner of the dry-cleaning shop said to Ed. "It took a foreigner—and a *woman*—to bring this place out." He handed over the shirts. *"Che vergogna!"* What an embarrassment.

After the man died who used to prop a fistful of flowers daily in our shrine, others began to leave sprigs of wildflowers, pinecones, coins, candles, notes, poems, and small gifts such as Christmas ornaments, books, saints' medallions, bottles of wine. Today I found a stuffed koala bear holding an Australian flag. Seven paintings of Bramasole line the top of my bookcase, all left by strangers. I love these secret links.

The children born into my family since I acquired Bramasole all inherited emotions similar to those Ed, my daughter, Ashley, and I feel. At two, Willie could say "Bramasole" when shown a picture of an Eden rose, an iron gate, a door knocker. We plant trees with Willie and tell him how high they will be when he's ten, twenty, forty. My great-niece hides notes under loose bricks, *Nancy McInerny was here,* just as Napoleon's soldiers wrote on the walls of San Francesco in Arezzo. In certain places, we long to leave a mark on the time continuum. Carlos, my editor's son, runs up the steps after a year away. "I remember this," he says, and his face shows that the memory is good. I wish I'd kept a guest book. Hundreds of friends, friends of friends, and family have stayed or lunched or dined here. "How's Bramasole?" they ask, as though the house were a loved person. On the annoying side, rumors constantly sizzle through town. *They've sold it.* We've heard that a hundred times. *It's going to become a restaurant. Russian millionaires have bought it.* And most recently, *It's going to be a museum!* A museum—of what?

This iconic position goes way beyond me. Are there, as the ancients thought, hot spots where raw energy or spirits reside?

Tourists who arrive with their cameras want to see the house more than they want to see me. Some stay for an hour, staring up. Friendships begin in the road, and one marriage resulted from two people meeting there. What these visitors don't know is how sound carries on the side of a hill. Up in my study with the windows open, I often hear blissful comments ("Isn't it dreamy, just dreamy," "Oh, my god, how spectacular—look at those roses"), speculation about my private life ("They got a divorce, you know" and, of course, the most frequent refrain—"She doesn't live here anymore"). Sometimes I hear, "This can't be Bramasole—that screen is wonky," "It's crumbling," and "My house is *much* bigger than this." Tour leaders, I've learned, can be quite inventive with facts about the history of the house and its inhabitants. At times, I've wanted to lean out the window and call down, "Don't believe a word he says!"

What I hope is that his captors may look at sun-saturated Bramasole and feel their own secret desires stirring.

⌒

LIKE A LIVING thing, a house evolves, changes, remains itself at core.

"In dreams begin responsibilities," W. B. Yeats wrote. Bramasole *is* my dream, Ed's too. After all the years here, systems in the house need responsible revision. The roof we never replaced must be fixed. After more than two hundred years, it deserves a little work. I remember that it was to cost $30,000 in those first rounds of estimates so long ago. I dread learning what that cost will be today. Regularly, an owl lifts tiles and squeezes itself into the attic, where he romps and tumbles. We wake up thinking a grown man is on the roof. Then, when it next rains, the corner of my study develops a plop, plop. Someone must tread across the dangerous roof and straighten the loose tiles until the owl's next attic visit.

Irrigating the lawn sucks dry our two water tanks and pulls air out of the house pipes, so that when I turn on the kitchen faucet, the water explodes with enough force to break a glass. The living room has a moisture problem. The house backs up into the hillside and whatever used to drain that area does so no longer. In spring a trickle of water makes its way across the living room floor. We stare at it, mesmerized. The wall develops lacy mildew patterns. *Muffa*—I'm fond of the fuzzy word and the white fluff is pretty but alarming. By summer, it's dry and I get out the whitewash so we can forget about it for another year. The terrace door is so weak that a stray dog could push it open. That's for starters. We're just used to the loose brick in the hall, the washing machine that can deliver a shock as you unload, the little bathroom window that closes with a wooden peg. Poetic? Yes, but . . .

Part of me wants Bramasole to remain quirky, but some of me wants grounded electricity that does not burn out the modem every time it storms, and yes, the tourist was right, screens that disappear when raised, not these wedged into the stone frames. When it's windy, they sometimes crash to the ground. The list is long and we are wary. A large construction project at Bramasole is daunting. I'm getting too old and impatient for projects that can run on for years. The dollar is weak, the euro mighty. We don't have normal jobs anymore. The United States slides irrevocably toward recession. Once I cooked pumpkin soup in a pumpkin. Just as I proudly reached the table, the bottom of the pumpkin gave way and the lovely soup flooded the table. Is my portfolio like that? Will I be left holding a hot sheaf of papers with the numbers falling off? If we live to a hundred, will we be reduced to a gas ring in a freeway motel?

Fonte delle Foglie, the mountain house, gave us the opportunity to work with one of Tuscany's best restorers, Fulvio Di Rosa, who is now thoroughly occupied with Borgo di Vagli, the medieval village he bought and revived. "Do the minimum," he advises. "Bramasole's charm is in how it is." I keep that advice in mind. Still, work *has* to be done. What will it take to incorporate a few graceful improvements as well?

❧

To INVESTIGATE, we turn to Walter Petrucci, a local architect with an impeccable reputation. Even when he has climbed around a ruin encased in blackberries, his shirt is never wrinkled. His shoes are unscathed. He's slender, slightly balding, and has a steady gaze with a practiced remoteness. Probably he's had to shield his true reactions many times to the outlandish ideas of foreigners. Last year, we worked with him and a master of restoration, Rosanno Checcarelli, on an addition to the mountain house. Quickly, we appreciated his genius for solutions. And if you don't like one, he finds another. I admire resourcefulness. *Get it done.* Like a good surgeon preparing the patient, he knows how to be involved and not involved at the same time. With all this sangfroid intelligence, I'm enchanted to learn the mad fact that he has been restoring his own villa for twenty-seven years.

He invites us there to dinner with his family and a few friends. A Medici would feel right at home. The Renaissance-influenced gardens with walks and geometric paths and pools are formal and perfect. Inside, local artist Eugenio Lucani has adorned walls and ceilings in the charming Pompeian style known as "grotesque." Walter points out arches and niches, leads us through bedroom suites, an impressive cantina, his library. Silvana, his vivacious wife, serves dinner from a kitchen that must have made a sizable dent in some marble quarry. In the dining room, our voices echo slightly.

Though the house has been ready for years, the family does not *actually* move in. They live, instead, in a comfortable, plain postwar house, nothing like this. "Maybe next year when our daughter graduates. We don't want to interrupt her studies," Walter explains. But friends have told us that every year there's a new reason. Has the villa become *Walter's Paradigm,* a book to be written and lavishly illustrated?

As we leave, Ed says, "Walter's dream house is like something in a Borges story. Or Calvino's invisible cities, if he'd written about houses instead of cities."

"Yes! Some abstract perfection hovering over Walter's mind."

"Maybe it will be reached, maybe never."

"That house *is* his mind—in 3-D."

Meanwhile, Walter finishes other projects on time and has designed the plans and overseen several friends' restorations. The work proceeds smoothly. We've admired his ingenuity, and now quickly learn to admire his droll wit and inventiveness.

As we walk around Bramasole together, he reveals to us possibilities we've not envisioned. We've been set on the practical. New laws allow us to expand *interrato,* into the hillside behind the house. He sketches a floor plan. We could double the size of the downstairs. The *limonaia* could become a phenomenal kitchen and the current small kitchen could be joined to the dining room, creating a place for large feasts. Further, we could request permission to consolidate the bathrooms stuck on the rear facade, and place them outside bedrooms, so that they become en suite. Guests would not have to navigate stairs to reach the bathroom. Removing the back bathrooms would allow the upstairs terrace to run across the entire back of the house.

This is heady. A laundry room here, he points out, and a wine cellar. Then he delivers the coup d'état. "This law allows you to build a garage into the hillside at the top of the driveway." He begins to sketch an extension of the stone wall, with an elegant iron and glass door into an underground room, which we see will be full of light because of the glass front. I don't see "garage" but, instead, a luminous writing studio lined with books.

Ed shocks me with an immediate enthusiastic response. I'm asking the architect how long it would take, would the work destroy my garden, how much would it cost. Ed's thinking of wine racks, creamy marble counters, and a grilling fireplace in the kitchen. I pore over the drawings Walter soon gives us. Yes, it would be astonishing to wrap the small upstairs terrace around the back. We could walk out into the olives and plum trees. I can't believe we're considering something so drastic. How do we bring forward all we've learned about Tuscan vernacular architecture without losing the individuality of the house? I have the irrational thought that the house will have an opinion.

After such remodeling, would it be the same house? Ed has a radical idea: "Maybe we should just sell instead. After Walter's revelations, can we really just patch up the roof, put in new windows, and go on? Or wouldn't it be easier to find another house already updated, made over, or 'tarted up.'" He quotes the writer Ann Cornelisen's expression, which she used so dismissively.

"Wait. Be serious. Could you ever leave Bramasole?"

He shrugs, making the Italian palms-up gesture, signaling "Who knows?" I smile and shake my head.

When I met Ed, I parted from my husband, Frank. He and I had a college-sweethearts connection, a child, graduate school, houses, moves back and forth across the country. We even loved Italy. I felt the Red Sea divide when our pact broke. Even now, after decades of happiness, I find that behind the intervening unpleasantness, I still feel an unbroken bond. The gold ring engraved *forever* lies among my earrings and bracelets. I think I once claimed to Frank that I'd thrown it off the Golden Gate Bridge, but I did not. Ties that bind. We can't invent them or dissolve them. Circumstances may be devastating, but love refuses to budge.

How could we ever leave? Three summers ago, I was ready. Hurt. Indignant. Mad. In profound disillusionment, I thought, *Time to move on to an alluring Greek island or a beach house on North Carolina's Outer Banks? A new place on the globe where we, blessedly, know no one.* Sartre is right, I thought: Hell is other people. Worse, I had to face that what I thought I knew, I did not know. Even now, I put off writing about that time.

I did not go, obviously.

Now a few more rolls of the scroll unfurl. New possibilities—Bramasole redux.

I'm tempted. This is scary. I'm not tempted. This is a relief.

⌇

BEFORE I GO to bed, I lean out my study window, a daily habit. I like to hear the night birds, but right now they are elsewhere. I lay my notebook on the stone sill and go back to my desk for a pen. When I return, a granddaddy of a black spider has settled in the crease between the pages. I blow on it until it rises on bent stilts and moonwalks into the folds of the white curtain. I write a few notes: *To taste the phases of the moon, to touch the aria floating down from a balcony, to smell the blond sunlight warming the child's hair and to hear the grand opening of the* favoloso *Eden rose that scrambles along a stone wall. What do you sense is coming toward you?*

⌇

THE NOTEBOOK LIES open. Still no owls, but the voices of two University of Georgia art students float up. "That fart-sack. He doesn't know shit about . . ." His voice is cut by a passing *motorino*.

Charming. As they pass, I hear, "Man, it was fuckin' Pompeii, not Herculaneum." The *motorino* is a wisp of white curling up the road.

Before I leave Italy this year, I decide, I will write about the tumultuous summer that had me looking at Portugal, at Sarasota, at Merida, at anywhere but here. Get it down. Get it out of the way. It's history. Not that important, is it? Then it truly will be over.

I write in the notebook: *The White Vespa*. There, wet black ink. The top of a blank page.

Torta di Suisine con Mandorle
Plum Tart

A dessert guaranteed to provoke extravagant praise, such as "This is the best tart I've ever tasted." It's equally as good with pears. This was inspired by a recipe in *Rogers Gray Italian Country Cook Book: The River Café* by Ruth Rogers and Rose Gray.

Makes 1 tart

PASTRY

½ pound very cold butter, cut into pieces
2½ cups sifted flour
⅛ teaspoon salt
1¼ cups powdered sugar
3 large yolks, beaten

FILLING

¾ pound butter
1½ cups fine sugar
1 teaspoon vanilla
2 cups almonds, pulverized to fine powder in food processor
3 whole eggs

7 ripe but firm plums, pitted and halved

First prepare the pastry: By hand or in a food processor, mix the butter, flour, and salt until crumbly; then mix in the powdered sugar, then the yolks. When well combined and adhering together, roll it into a ball and chill thoroughly, about half an hour.

Preheat the oven to 400 degrees F. Remove the dough from the refrigerator. Slice it into pieces and press it into a large glass pie plate or a 12- to 14-inch tart pan. Chill about 10 minutes, then prick the pastry dough all over and bake it in a hot oven until slightly toasty, about 10 minutes. Lower the oven to 350 degrees F.

For the filling, cream the butter and sugar until fluffy, add vanilla, mix with ground almonds, then add eggs one at a time, beating well.

Arrange the plums over the baked pastry shell, pour the filling over them, and bake until set, about 30 minutes.

The White Vespa

A PHOTO BOOK FROM SOUTH AFRICA, A POUCH
of paprika from Budapest, a ceramic angel from
Poland, Christmas ornaments from Germany,
wildflower seeds from Provence, landscape sketches
from everywhere, maple leaf tie tack from Canada,
honey from Estonia, wine, lots of wine, T-shirt from
Brazil, even hand towels monogrammed with a *B*
for the house: Many gifts are left at Bramasole. And
so I thought nothing of picking up the small parcel
wrapped in newspaper, left on the grass just inside
the gate.

I came down the steps first. We'd just finished
taking photos: Ashley, Ed, and I, dressed in summer
best—Ed in his white suit, Ashley in aqua chiffon,
and I am wearing a green and hot-pink silk shirt
and linen pants. We were going to a party for Ed—
a big surprise. Who took the picture? I don't know;
probably Willie's babysitter. Next, suddenly I am
walking down alone, trying not to catch my high
heels between the stones and crack my ankle. Maybe
Ashley went back inside to kiss Willie good night.
Maybe Ed went back to pick up his cell phone. I
start down to the road—wanting to hustle everyone

along because surely the guests had gathered. Just inside the gate, a "present" lies in the grass.

We were en route to Corys, just up the road, for the celebration. Because Ed gave pints of blood to the reconstruction of the fallen stone walls at Bramasole, with many mighty frustrations, and also to the restoration of Fonte, I had planned a party for him—twenty of our closest friends for a feast. He thought we were meeting four friends for a quiet dinner. Instead, Chiara and I had been to Arezzo and bought a retro-style white Vespa, straight out of Fellini. We hid it all week in the horse corral at her house. At dinner, we planned to hand Ed a tiny box holding a key. Chiara bought him a key ring. Resplendent with bows, the white Vespa would be moved out front by Simone just as Ed was led outside. He had *no* idea.

The narrative at this point always will replay as present tense.

⌒

I PICK UP the package wondering if I should wait to open it until we return. But there's no ribbon or string. A note flutters to the ground and I glimpse crude handwriting as it falls. I unfold the colored newspaper, the pink sports section.

I am holding a grenade in my hand.

I stare only for a moment before I lower it softly to the ground as if it were an abandoned kitten. I run fast, back to the house.

"Ed!" I call out. "There's a grenade in the driveway. It was wrapped . . . like a present. . . . I opened it."

"Holy shit, what are you talking about?" He grabs my arm and steadies me.

"It's real. Call Claudio." He's our friend who is the *maresciallo,* marshal of the *carabinieri.*

"Wait a minute. This must be some idiotic joke. Let's start over. What . . ." This is the first of many times that I will hear the word *joke*.

"Look, Eddie, I *know* what a grenade looks like. This is not plastic. It's real," I shout. "If I'd dropped it I might be up in the pine trees now."

"This is impossible."

"What's going on?" Ashley comes out of the house looking fresh and lovely. I don't want to say anything—also a reaction that reoccurs—but I tell her.

"Get inside," she commands us.

"Claudio's sending a car." Ed stares at his phone, as if there were someone else to call. He leans over the wall and looks down at the square of newspaper on the grass.

"This can't be happening." Who says this? We all say this.

Very soon, the *carabinieri* pull up in the driveway and Ed asks me, "I just told Claudio that we needed him. What's the Italian for *grenade*?" Neither of us knows, but we do know *bomba*. Ed calls down, *"Claudio, stai attento, c'è una bomba."* Be careful, there's a bomb. They pause in the act of closing the car doors.

"Che cosa, Edoardo?" What? Claudio then spots the crumbled newspaper and they stop. Claudio takes out his phone. The three men step inside and regard the grenade silently. We venture down the steps. I explain what happened. Visions shoot through my brain—the Red Brigade, the Mafia, the progressive mayor of Naples gunned down. My fear slides toward anger.

Claudio looks serious but says, "This must be a joke." The heavy gray ugly weapon in the grass does not look like a joke.

"Maybe it's not real," says the muscular one, who looks as if he could bite open a grenade.

"It's real," the third affirms. "But maybe it's stripped.

I think it's stripped?" His question-mark inflection defeats his opinion.

Even in this crisis, I can't help but notice how sharp they look in their summer blue shirts, black pants, with big guns strapped around their waists. Their presence comforts me. It seems that the grenade is not going to explode in our faces.

Even now, writing this, my heart starts to thud. I feel breathless. I keep writing "they" where I mean "we," still trying to distance myself.

Claudio picks up the note. He shows the others, then hands it to me.

Wait, wait, I think. *Fingerprints.*

"*Qualcuno che è maleducato,*" he says. "*Brutta figura.*" *Maleducato* doesn't just mean "badly educated." It means "crude," the opposite of *bella figura.*

"*Al meno,*" I reply. At least.

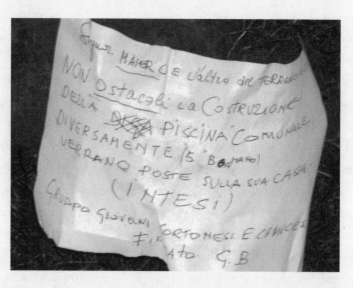

"See," the stocky one says, pointing to the signature. "*Ragazzi.*" Kids.

My Italian is not up to this discussion at this time. "*No. Non sono ragazzi,*" I insist. Not kids. Not.

Ed is shaking his head. "This is not the writing of a young person." He points to the penmanship.

"Look at the crossed-out word *diga*. *Diga* means dam; kids writing about a pool would not confuse pool and dam. Makes no sense." What seemed probable to me was that the hired thug who wrote the note was confused as to what his purpose was. He certainly did not know how to spell our name.

This is what the note says:

Signori Maier and the other neighbors
Don't block the construction of the ~~dam~~ *public swimming pool*
Otherwise 5 hand grenades
Will be placed in your house
UNDERSTOOD
Young people of Cortona and Camucia
Signed GB

A few months ago, we circulated a petition among our neighbors, a protest over the approval the town had given for a private recreational complex at the end of the Strada della Memoria, the road Bramasole overlooks. While we were in favor of a pool somewhere, the location made no sense at the dead end of this undeveloped, residential road where local people take their daily *passeggiata,* bike, and jog. It's narrow. We feared increased traffic in a *Zona del Silenzio,* totally unsuitable for the memorial road planted with cypresses, one for each local boy who died in World War I. This is a designated *belle arti* zone where nothing can be built. Nothing even can be altered without a full-court review. Woe unto you if you'd like to install a window in your dark bedroom. We'd offered to help raise money to replace the copper plaques with the name of the soldier under each tree.

When we'd circulated the petition, we were amazed that

only a few of the Italians would sign, even though they agreed with the petition and did not want "the wild side" of Cortona developed at all. I was stunned. In America, if you don't agree, you do something. You speak up. You organize. You make signs. You write to the paper. You band together and make common cause.

I learned new Italian words—*ritorsione, punizione, castigo, rappresaglia*. All of which, essentially, seemed to carry a heightened fear of reprisal. As Fulvio explained to me when I expressed amazement that the Italians wouldn't sign: "It's ancient history, *cara: You kill one of mine, I kill ten of yours.*"

"My taxes will go up."

"Signora, I'll get my new car damaged."

"They'll set my fields on fire."

"My business will be investigated."

And most primitive of all, "Signora, put a lock on your well," said Pietro, whose wife would not let him sign. My well!? What!?

Bizarre. You've got to be exaggerating, we thought. A simple petition is just a way of banding together to make a point. How strange—these boisterous, opinionated Tuscans. Cautious. Afraid!

The foreigners signed, a few younger Italians signed, and two business owners, too, which I by then recognized took guts.

We turned in the petition and I shortly got a big dose of what my neighbors knew. The editor of the little local news— he was also the person spearheading the development of the private pool complex—wrote an article about my interference. He said I had no right and that before Cortona gave me my books I was just an obscure poet. It went on and on, slamming me personally. Classic argument *ad hominem,* full of errors and brimming with vitriol. The upshot was that foreigners are guests and should be grateful for that privilege.

Since I'd lived there seventeen years at that point, I was short on sympathy for that position. I've loved the place and have made my contributions. Even if I had not, I believe that someone who lives in a town has every right to participate, even if the family has not been around since the fifteenth century.

I wrote back explaining my position, not to his paper, because I thought I might be edited, but a personal letter circulated around town. I was in California, so it all seemed quite distant at the time. I was incredulous, miffed, and, mostly, shocked.

When I returned in the spring, I was nonplussed to be greeted like the prodigal daughter. Though no one had written a public protest to the article, not even our closest friends, it seemed that I could not go twenty steps down the street without someone stepping out of the doorway, whispering to me, *"Che vergogna,"* what an embarrassment, *"Typical of someone from the south,"* shaking a finger, *"You know he is not Cortonese,"* even telling me how much everyone loved me. Other stories, *sotto voce.* I didn't want to hear them. I really was not interested in this bad actor in the piazza's latest play. I wanted to close it off, like white cells around an infection.

Everyone mentioned the editor's origins. *"He's Calabrese—they're like that. We are not."* Ironically, trying to comfort me, they reinforced the existence of xenophobia. *They are like that. We are not.* The editor had more in common with the foreigners than he dreamed.

We were trying to swallow the lesson. Not only had the residents in our area been afraid to sign, they didn't even stand up for us when we were unfairly attacked for a cause they believed in. They gave the situation the royal brush-off. *"No one reads that paper. No one believes anything in that paper."* And weirdest of all: *"This just shows how important you are."* Well, thanks, but I'd rather be less important if this is the benefit. To some, it was something to shrug off. Others became amnesiacs. Later, I understood. Not then.

All those fearful repetitions of *ritorsione, punizione, castigo, rappresaglia* I had heard when we passed around the petition—retribution. Oh, yes. Now I could see why everyone stayed shut up.

After the petition faded, and the brutal letter became almost a joke, the pool complex went forward. Construction was under way at the time the grenade landed in my garden. So, I'd already lost my case. Why terrorize me? Later we understood another layer of the petition issue. We learned that such an approach is simply ineffective. We learned that a letter back to the editor was similarly regarded as a waste of time. Resolution takes other paths.

"How could we not know these things?" I'd asked Ed over and over.

"Because we've never made waves. We've been happy as peas in a pod."

"You're mixing metaphors. And clichés. And you're absolutely right."

⁓

A CROWD GATHERS in the road. Our houseguests, who left before us, and several friends have walked down to Bramasole from Corys to see why we are late. They expected us a half hour after they arrived so they'd be ready for Ed's entrance. Passing cars stop to see what is going on. This feels disorienting. Everyone in summer party clothes, standing solemnly in the road. As I'm thinking the same thing, Ashley says, "Can't we rewind? Replay?" For once the Italians are speechless. Or they weigh in on the joke side—but no one touches the gravity of the grenade.

Ashley, with a small child in the house, insists that the *carabinieri* search the grounds. As a forensic psychologist, with a lot of experience with the criminal mind, she'd looked at the note and immediately said, "This is a hideous threat. And that it's amateur doesn't make it less serious." We take the baby and the sitter to the Cardinalis' house. Thinking back, I'm amazed that the babysitter didn't say, "I am definitely out of here. *Buona notte*."

The grenade, untouched, waits in the grass. Claudio calls the bomb squad in Florence. He promises that the men will stay overnight in the driveway and for as long as we want them. Doug, one of our guests, another forensic expert, calls a friend at the FBI and describes the event and note. The agent asks about anti-American sentiment in the area. She talks about tracing the handwriting; she reiterates that many terrorist acts are committed by the manipulated ignorant.

We telephone the consul in Florence, with whom we've shared a few dinners in castles and villa gardens. He says he's never heard of such an event and asks if we want intervention. We say we'll leave it with the local police for now, and that the bomb squad arrives tomorrow to determine if the grenade is live. We decide to send Ashley and Willie with our guests to the mountain house to sleep, if anyone can. Ed and I feel quite stalwart about staying in our house. Scared, yes, but someone out there in idyllic Cortona would be too pleased if we were driven out tonight.

There seems nothing more to do, surreal as it seems. We pick up our handbags and camera and go to the party.

On the way, I think, *I never ever will get beyond this*. I think, *Is it over for me here?* I struggle with the urge to *go, just go*. Right then. Night train to Rome, early flight to the United States.

But then we are pulling up our chairs at the long table

under the awning on a brilliant summer evening. Our friends applaud us, embrace us, speculate about the perpetrator. Giuseppe pours the prosecco liberally. I remember Lina in a bronze satin dress with spaghetti straps, Chiara with her hair up, and Renato going on about fascists and fools. I remember the word *joke* bouncing from chair to chair. I begin to understand that our friends are only trying to shield us. Still it annoys, as in saying "You're going to be fine in no time" to the ashen patient whose sands are free-falling through the hourglass.

~

ASHLEY REMEMBERS THAT the dinner was splendid. I, who remember divine meals as far back as third grade, recall nothing. I know everyone was very charged, many toasts were raised, and Ed truly did not know what the key in the little box was for. Chiara and I led him to the street where the Vespa was parked. She had tied red, green, and white bows to the handlebar, Italian flag colors. The metallic white paint shone incandescent under the streetlight, as though a lightbulb burned inside the trim form. Everyone cheered. Ed hopped on, fired up, and raced off, his white spiky hair, white suit, and white Vespa conspiring to look like an ad in the Italian *GQ*. He looked as carefree as he'd felt four hours ago. I felt a sudden sting of tears. He is the finest person; he does not deserve this. Then a surge of hot anger.

The Vespa—Fellini's Italy. Romance and freedom. If there's reincarnation, let me be sixteen, hair flying behind me, as I take off from the piazza. I loved giving one to Ed.

He made a U at the fork and returned, crossing an invisible border between *before* and *after*.

After

I WONDERED WHAT THE TWO *CARABINIERI* dreamed. From my study window at six, I saw them in the car below, still sleeping. Did last night really happen? The early sky, streaked with lilac light and pink-gold clouds, proclaimed its daily innocence. I spotted Ed on an upper terrace clipping something that probably did not need clipping. He was awake when it was still dark, having kicked off the sheet and several times performed a kind of turning over that seems acrobatic—levitate and flip. I probably thrashed too, flashing a thousand times on the threatened other bombs mentioned in the note.

As the *carabinieri* backed out of the drive—surely seeking espresso and a bathroom—I felt an irrational conviction: They're gone; it's over; erase; delete. I considered the colors of the sky, now brightening to a blue like the veins inside my grandmother's wrist. Violet. Violence. I curled my hand into a fist, still feeling the weight of the grenade. Some things are heavier than their size suggests. I imagined heaving the grenade myself, but at what? Violence begets. *You kill one of mine, I kill ten of yours.*

By ten, the parade began at Bramasole. Everyone casually passing by stopped to chat with the *carabinieri* posted below. The chief arrived with Claudio and another handsome, fearsome specimen whose adze jaw contrasted with pouty lips. This time they'd changed from the informal summer uniform to the red-trimmed black one, signifying the formality of the visit. The chief described how the fingerprinting and handwriting analysis would be sent to Rome. "How long will it take to get the results?" Ed asked.

"Maybe two months," the chief admitted. We nodded, dumbfounded. We didn't say, "Christ Almighty, man, two months! Why not two days?"

"Meanwhile?"

"We will be investigating and interviewing."

"Is there any way we can keep this out of the papers, out of the news? With all the people stopping in the road, I doubt that. But my wife would hate the publicity . . ." Ed stood behind my chair, his hands on my shoulders.

"We'll do what we can."

"Do you have any idea who did this?" I already knew he wouldn't say, if he did know, but I wanted to see his face as he answered.

"Mmmnn. No." He maintained eye to eye. The furrow of his frown merged his eyebrows. He didn't even twirl the hat he held on his lap. They stood, again expressing their regret. Cortona has little crime and certainly nothing remotely like this, ever. I knew they were mortified and I was sorry to be the troublesome foreigner who attracted such an event.

Next came the young mayor, Andrea, smoking furiously, and his assistant, also Andrea. Somehow, we always laugh together. He gestures wildly, paces, acts out whatever he's saying, and when he leaves, I'm never quite sure what actually has happened. The mayor was concerned, rightly, about negative publicity for the town. We all had visions of articles: "American Writer and Family Evacuated by CIA." What a disaster for the hotels, the restaurants, the merchants. "Goof-ball Terrorist Lobs Grenade at Americans." Tour buses gunning out of Piazza Garibaldi. Camera crews rolling in. He hoped the incident was a joke, although when he looked at the note, he dropped that line of thinking. No *ragazzo,* young man, in the fine Cortona schools wrote that badly. Simply impossible. But. No. Need. To worry. Everything is under control.

After friends stopped by with melons and beans, after the cicadas provided their screeching background music, after everyone stepped around the grenade in the grass and paused at the top of the driveway to admire the white Vespa, after a call to Ashley urging them to take a day trip, after expat friends asked if one of the five thousand Muslims in the province were involved in an anti-American gesture, after I stood with my back against a tree and stared into the valley below, after a morning that lasted a week, the Florence squadron arrived.

Five men in high black boots, black shirts, tight gabardine pants, and shoulder holsters stepped out of a menacing black sedan. They'd closed the road at Corys and asked us to stay inside. Good. They meant business.

After about fifteen minutes, one came to the door and told us the grenade was not live. We took some bottles of water down where they were gathering their evidence. Soon they were joking, asking about the olive trees, asking about the movie of my book. Under their fierce demeanor and serious outfits, they're like most Italian men—gregarious, ribald, warm. I wish they would stay in the driveway all summer.

That the grenade was stripped made us feel slightly better. Gilda had her theories. Giorgio, too, but never mind. Gilda made a soup. Giorgio, who helps us here, walked the land.

Usually we have fun together; I felt sorry that they had to be concerned. Ed took a rag and wiped a film of dust off his sweet Vespa until it glowed white as the moon and immaculate.

I went into town once that week and faced a repeat of the famous petition aftermath. Quite a few people, though, seemed not to have heard—or perhaps preferred to pretend. The guesses about the perpetrator, the repetition of *"fascisti,"* the arousal of old left-right political feuds going back a century (memory is long in Italy), the cynical shrugs, the certainty that someone had been hired—it was all interesting. Secret. Nothing in the open. No one spoke to us in the piazza about the grenade. We were called into tiny shops, spoken to in doorways, smiles on the faces seemingly speaking everyday greetings but really recounting an uncle's dealings with a certain unsavory person, World War II grudges from when someone turned in a partisan, dreams of revenge over a broken rental agreement. Bewildering. "Ed, maybe it's the architecture of the town—all the steep, dark *vicoli* [tiny streets] leading off the main street, winding into nether Cortona."

"Really. The city as a metaphor for the collective brain." We were in a trance all week.

The algebra we were learning: Equations that balanced to our American ways of thinking were all x's equaling other x's here. A small notice appeared in the Arezzo paper. Astonishing, astonishing. It said:

BOMB THREATS AT A BUILDING SITE

It didn't explode and wasn't able to explode: It was an old reminder of the war, an empty casing found frequently in the stalls at flea markets. Moreover, it was also without powder. That does not mean that the message wasn't still disturbing: a hand grenade, "pineapple-type," placed in the construction site for the building of a new sports center of the Parterre, already the focus of a thousand arguments. This particular rift has divided Cortona. The construction of the pool seems to be connected to the discovery on Saturday. It was the *carabinieri* who discovered the bomb, which was lying next to a threatening handwritten sign.

The surveys conducted by the *carabinieri* have just started and may continue: The fact is that someone made a serious gesture, someone who has decided to continue the battle against sports center by other means, other than mere words, from mountains of paper that have been filled in recent months, the mountains of speeches, pros and cons, which characterize since the beginning of the year the controversy in the city.

We couldn't help but laugh. Our very own grenade transferred to the *pool site*. Discovered not by me in my summer party clothes but by the *carabinieri*. Not against us but against them. Oh, *mamma mia!*

Who managed this and why?

⁓

THE SUMMER RESUMED. I reclaimed the *centro* of my heart for my own.

What became clear over the ensuing months was that our relationship to the town changed. From the day we arrived, we were overwhelmed by friendliness and hospitality. We'd always felt totally welcome. But while we'd felt a belonging before, we got the sense that the people just now knew we really belonged, that we were here to stay, and that since we knew the worst, we could become not just *residenti elettivi,* elective residents, but familial. *"Cari, siete cortonesi."* My dears, you're of Cortona. Two people gave me a *corno,* the coral horn-shaped ornament that even tiny babies wear to protect them from the evil eye. One *barista* said, "I thought you only had good luck."

Previously, I'd often been pulled aside and told a personal story. "You can write about that," the teller would say proudly. Always there was plenty of news of liver problems, adultery, the secret nicknames that bounce around town, occult tumors, family histories, proud moments, and jokes. *After*—the level of confidences didn't double, it cubed. I didn't even know I was on the outside looking in until I was suddenly on the inside looking out.

⟡

WILLIE HAD A fine summer. Ashley was wary of every car that passed. Me, too. Ed was reluctant to leave us alone, even to go out with Placido and the falcon. We spent more and more time at the mountain house. I began my wanderings on paths in the chestnut forest, emulating the followers of St. Francis. I often thought of Neruda's lines:

> *I have to go much farther*
> *and I have to go much closer . . .*

Ed devoted himself to cooking. He bought me a dark red helmet and we explored back roads, bumping along on the Vespa.

Someone handed me another minute newspaper article. A large stone was heaved at night onto the vinyl bottom of the new pool, ripping it. Later, there was a false rumor that a girl was raped there. The drama continued without us. I found the clandestine workings-out of the situation very disturbing. Miss Insomnia was my permanent houseguest.

~

LONG AFTER—THE pool was a flop. Too small. Too chilly under the majestic cypresses. I liked to think that the memorialized World War I soldiers cast a cold spell on the whole project. Mainly, too out of town, too *scomodo,* inconvenient. Ah, Sherlock Holmes, what a discovery. Ditto the pool restaurant and plans for theatrical events. The damage was done to the dreamy hillside. What everyone must live with: horrid lights like an airport (and electricity is exorbitant in Italy) and an ugly gash of turquoise on the hill that formerly resembled the landscape behind a Signorelli Crucifixion. We can't see the site from Bramasole, but many can.

As the failure grew more apparent two summers ago, the desperate management resorted to disco evenings with a sweeping light like those on suburban used car lots. We heard the monotonous lyrics of "I Wanna Be Your Girl," blaring at three A.M. Condoms littered the Strada della Memoria on Sunday mornings. Italian discos usually stop around six A.M.

The absurd moment was when the pool owners suggested that those who did not want noise should *pay* for the shortfalls the management was experiencing. If each resident coughed up a couple of thousand euros a year, then they'd turn off the music. Everyone on the hillside laughed maybe louder than the disco.

Taking our previous miscue, another petition was circulated by an Italian friend who has lived his adult life in America. This time—no repercussions. Maybe we started an idea that you can speak up. This disco idiocy roused everyone on our side of the hill, and Ed and I did not have to be the ones who protested. We simply spoke to a few influential people around town. Privately. No one was put on the spot. See how we learn! The following summer permission for the disco was denied by the comune.

At the pool now, children can take swimming lessons. A few Dutch tourists stop by for a dip. All is calm. *Per ora,* for now . . .

The *carabinieri* never found the person who left the grenade. I often wonder if he drives by, if he regrets what he did.

All the evidence sent to Rome for analysis had revealed nothing.

But secrets will out. The gold necklace hidden in the toe of a shoe will be found by the small child. The forbidden email tends toward the forward click, not the delete. The deepest confidence awaits transformation into orange-bannered truth waving in the wind. There exists someone who protects someone else and at the same time longs to open his hands and hold out that forbidden knowledge like a ripe apple. Already, someone is rehearsing. Someday, I'll hear a voice just behind me as I look in the bookstore window or select the local cream meringues for Sunday *pranzo.*

Signora, I just want you to know . . .

⁓

THE EDITOR NEVER apologized for the libelous article. He exited from the pool management. I ignore him when we pass on the Rugapiana, which is often. A close Italian friend says, "Maintain Olympian disdain." Actually I don't hold on to animosity. A few have suggested that we should forgive each other. I replied that I would accept flowers from him in the middle of the piazza at noon. No roses have been forthcoming.

Bring Me the Sunflower Crazed with Light

If a story begins with finding, it must end with searching.
—PENELOPE FITZGERALD

ROSES, CUTTING ROSES AND PLACING THEM IN a pewter pitcher, satisfies my solitary instinct. All the colors complement one another, even red Abe Lincoln, not my favorite. He's the dark splash of venous blood among the silky apricots, yellows, and pinks. Pronouncing the name in Italian, Ah-bay Link-o-nay, tweaks the dour president into someone who might samba instead of play "Jimmy Crack Corn" on the harmonica.

C'era una volta, so tales begin, once upon a time. I like the archaic "upon" in English, as though the story sits atop time and therefore is outside time. Assaults refuse to fall into mere time, mere story. It seems wrong that happy times often blend into time, blur into a smear of well-being, while vicious events remain vividly themselves. How to make one's own life the polar opposite? After the platelet shift settled down again, this question preoccupied me. That's the question I want to answer.

～

Nothing really happened, I tell myself. I go about my day. Oddly, I do think of when a man crazed with drugs broke into my house in San Francisco. We were at dinner when he burst through the window and landed in the middle of the living room. He staggered toward us screaming, "I want to kill," and as he lunged near, I threw my wine in his face and we fled. He shouted after us, "Give me a knife." I ran to the left, to our new neighbors; Ed ran across the street, where lights were on. He called 911 as he ran. Our visitor followed and tried to break through the door as our startled neighbor raised a golf club over his head. The intruder was caught that night. Two weeks later he was on the street again. In my mind he broke through over and over, a sunburst of glass shattering around his goofy, druggy face.

～

Days of solitude; ah, this is *my* life. *Don't mistake the wound of the world for the world,* a wise friend told me years ago. So I cast about in art books, write thirty sentences that could open a novel, try to find the exact word for the green aqueous light falling through my studio window, look up words in the dictionary and list good new ones in my notebook. I'm asking: What informs, what inspires, what feeds, what amuses? Such days deeply refresh.

Maybe close skirmishes with violence, like small earthquakes, release pressure, warding off those doozies that seize the Richter and shake the fillings out of your teeth. Those shakes I've lived through in California, the glasses tinkling against each other, were nothing like the earthquake of 1989, when I was tossed from side to side as I ran down the stairs and out of the house. Life's little wake-up calls. (Do they have to be so numerous?) Scroll down the list and start to wail—or shout out *Carpe diem.*

~

AND ED, MUGGED while walking home from Fillmore Street, a few blocks away from home. When he fought back and was slugged and pinned down, he suddenly realized he could be killed and stopped struggling. His assailant climbed off him and said "Sorry, man." When Ed went in the house, our cat Sister smelled the stink of the fight and ran crying all through the rooms. I was in Spain; he was leaving the next day and had converted his dollars. There was some satisfaction that the robber opened his wallet to find pesos and lire. We later moved to a more remote San Francisco neighborhood of Spanish-style houses and shady streets. St. Francis Woods was known to be the safest area in the city. That's where the drugged guy leaped into our lives. The next year we moved north to Marin, to a secluded cul-de-sac with a locked gate at the top of the road and a serene view of the bay.

I begin to realize: Time to seize the day, ruthlessly, as my aunt Hazel seized my grandmother's fur coats and jewelry during the funeral she was "too upset" to attend. By the time we trailed in, her Lincoln was packed.

~

ROBERT RAUSCHENBERG wrote this about his painting process:

I had been working purely abstractly for so long it was important for me to see whether I was working abstractly because I couldn't work another way, or whether I was doing it out of choice.

Why not take this time of solitary self-exile to unlearn, shake up the compass and veer off into other territory, shake off "the lethargy of custom," as Coleridge called it. Maybe then come back with new insight? At my last crux, I jumped ship, quit my university job to travel and write *A Year in the World.* Since I'm reviewing past choices, I might as well start with revitalizing my own most private and creative life.

∽

I REMEMBER WHEN a student was murdered in an elevator at the university where I taught. Another was raped in the women's bathroom. We couldn't go into the bathrooms without a partner for months. We couldn't open our mail either, unless it had been screened, because the Unabomber was suspected to be nearby and, who knows, might have secreted a bomb within the pages of *The Gettysburg Review.*

∽

CERTAIN PRACTICES CAST a benevolent, protective spell over the hours. One habit: choosing a book of poems, or a book on fresco cycles, or any artist, or meditations, and starting each day with a dedicated time of reading and gazing, becoming an apprentice to a mind I admire. I select my friend C. D. Wright's poems. I miss her. She's southern to the core, and all her poems have a handful of ferrous red dirt in them. In person or on the page, she challenges the language, turns subjects inside out, plus she owns a fine and rough sensibility that is often funny, antisentimental, and embodies the word *fierce.*

> *I have been to Pilates   I found my old coat*
> *I took my will to the notary   I found my good glasses*

I have filled my tank   I am going to the market
Then I think I'll cut my hair off with a broken bottle

The reader embarks. The writer heads out to the open waters. Carolyn's work offers revelation, the hand of a true original, and the pleasure of synesthesis: "the slur of cars," "The petal of one eye shutting," "Aloe vera and bromeliad felted with dust," "a curtain of bougainvillea." *Dear Carolyn, can we take a road trip in the South together?*

～

I THINK OF two neighbors in Pacific Heights, one carjacked, one robbed and beaten severely with a crowbar. Our garage was jimmied open and the bicycles stolen. Those were San Francisco's hard crack cocaine years and our gentle Victorian neighborhood a bull's-eye target. I slept with an electronic panic button beside the bed.

～

WHY NOT PLACE large *X*'s in those white squares on the calendar? Cordon off time—well in advance—and be accommodating to my desires? What do I want on those magic blank days? Not lunch with Julia, not a walk with Michaela, not a yoga class or a movie. I want the mental equivalent of a bottomless black pond surrounded by long grasses and a willow tree. Sitting just *there*. Luxurious are the protected hours to read poetry, to draw, to listen to Ravel, all of Ravel, and read everything I can about my time-warp *fratello,* Luca Signorelli. Self-excused from daily life, I want to practice the art of catering to my own interests. My own steely whims. May I now reclaim my childhood right to explore for myself? To indulge in exploration for its own sake, which is the way I advance my cause. My cause, of course, is wisdom, which comes to some at birth and to some by contemplation.

⁓

FARTHER BACK, A peeping Tom raised the white curtain with a coat hanger on an August night when I was newly married. My husband slept. I dropped off the side of the bed and crawled silently into the hall and called the police. They caught him a block away. I learned later it was a boy in my summer school class who'd called me on my wedding day asking me not to marry. *Mea culpa,* I admit I'd flirted even though I was engaged.

Oh, but, as Eduardo Galeano wrote, *Let's save pessimism for better times.* From my collection of pristine blank books—I have so many I could never fill them in three lifetimes—I open a yellow and white marbled one and write the last line of a Montale poem:

Bring me the sunflower crazed with light.

I resolve to observe something of the natural world every day, an image or paragraph, and write it here. I know all the boar paths, fire lines, and cart tracks on my side of Monte Sant'Egidio, where like St. Francis's followers, I roam and observe, practice sitting still and observing dragonflies and butterflies in the wild heather. I'm fortunate when I see a falcon in the *"Spirito Santo"* position. The bird finds equilibrium between his wing motion and a breeze so that like the Holy Spirit in paintings, he stays poised, hovering over his miserable prey below until the moment he strikes. Although I'm wearing jeans and a T-shirt, I may be like the medieval hermits, living my own idiorhythmic day.

Rereading my notes later, will they quickly reconnect me to fresh, startling nature?

- *Green lizard flying from the rim of one geranium pot to the next*
- *To see the perfume of a handful of wild strawberries*
- *To feel the greeny translucence of a thin slice of fennel*
- *Golden October leaves sticking to a marble statue in the park*
- *Three ancient ladies in dark print dresses, their backs to the view of Santa Maria Nuova, visiting in the winter sun. Immortal.*
- *Rolling fields of late June with clumps of late red poppies amid tawny wheat. I noted the purple-black Maltese cross printed inside only a few of the thousands of red poppies volunteering for service. Years of seeing poppies and now I discover the magical hidden cross in the center of the blood-red petals. How life continues to open and amaze.*

In my early Italian years, the natural renewal I experienced came largely from being at home in nature again, playfully as in childhood. As we began hacking brambles from the land and planting gardens—a rose garden, an herb garden, a vegetable garden, a shade garden—I realized that the blistering work, the aches and sweat and scratches of restoration were, like writing, where work and play became the same. As an adult, my feet were accustomed to concrete. Sleeping with the door open, waking with the splendiferous Tuscan dawns, listening to the bees mining the linden, lying in the grass at night watching the falling stars, walking to town instead of driving—all realigned me with my love of the natural world. Circadian rhythms usurped the clock.

For my nature notebook, Thoreau is my inspiration because he looked intimately at the small plot of the world he lived on. Wisdom is packed into his sentence "I have traveled much in Concord."

- *Three tabby cats curled under a lavender plant*
- *Coral geraniums spilling from a baroque balcony*
- *Stonemason soaking his work-sore feet in hot spring water*
- *Cornucopia-shaped eel nets drying on the golden stone street*
- *By a canal in Venice—huge pink panties flapping in the breeze*
- *A ziggurat of ripe peaches at the market*
- *Black morning glory seeds soaking in a glass before I nick off a sliver of each so it germinates*

What you see, you know. In my notebook (handmade paper, thank you Alberto, and real ink) I arrange these tactile pieces of time, as I might three russet pears on an ochre napkin for a photograph.

⁓

CLOSE CALLS WITH violence—they're microcosms. We're well into the twenty-first century and still resort to barbarian wars. It's profoundly distressing to realize how we do not go forward but always pick up the stick.

When someone picks up the stick, someone else has less control over life. Post-traumatic stress must be the most underestimated affliction on earth. How people go miraculously on after the Warsaw ghetto, the streets of Baghdad, and other horrors, defies psychology.

But one can't live by comparing personal experience to historical extremes. If you were spun in the dryer by your brother when you were two, if your home were bombed, if your sister cut off your long braid while you slept, if your parents were blown to smithereens . . . Against what rod do you measure? Moving along toward a civilized world, isn't it best to compare experience to a paradigm good instead of a worst scenario?

~

FIRST IN MY personal war-torn series—an ordinary day in May when I was five. A cotton mill employee pushed into my grandfather's office and shot my father in the side. He'd stepped in front of Daddy Jack, my grandfather, and taken the bullet. I remember hearing later that the man, Willis Barnes, was "disgruntled." I thought that meant that his stomach was growling too much. Willis Barnes had killed another man inside the mill before he crossed the road to the office. He killed another man after he shot my father.

I was at home with my mother when our friend Royce Williams came to tell her what had happened. She ran to the bedroom, crying, and I followed, jumping up on the canopied bed. I began bouncing, grabbing onto the tester and pulling at the organdy flounces. "Get down," she shouted, swiping at me and searching her drawers for a handkerchief. "They think he's going to live," Royce said, as the mattress dislodged and the bed collapsed.

At the trial, I sat in back of the courtroom in the colored section with our cook, Willie Bell. My father was brought in on a stretcher and was asked to identify the murderer. He rose on his side to point at Willis Barnes. He was never completely well after that and died nine years later. The daughter of Willis Barnes was in my class all through school and spit on me several times. Willis Barnes was electrocuted. I remember hearing people say, "He's gonna fry," and he did. Did a party from our town, Fitzgerald, go over to Reidsville to watch the execution? This is part of my memory but I'm not sure it's true. Still I see them at the glass partition and, how strange, my memory takes Barnes's point of view, not the perspective of a child standing among grown-ups but how he'd see them if he looked up from the medieval-looking electric chair.

Home from the hospital, my father lifted his pajama top when I asked to see where he was shot. My eyes squeezed closed as I saw the red gash sewn shut with thick black thread. On his back was the puckered hole where the bullet exited.

~

I DON'T STEP on ants. Ed takes scorpions outside under a glass. Spiders in the tub get a chance to crawl up the towel and be taken to the windowsill. I live with a gentle man who always will turn the other cheek, unless brutally attacked on the sidewalk. I walked toward him in the Madrid airport, almost not recognizing his cement-scraped face, bruised cheeks, and split lips. "Don't worry," he said right off. "It could have been worse. Much. I am so glad to be here."

It could have been worse. I am so glad to be here.

Yeah. And it could have been better.

~

SINCE A LARGE percentage of control over fate doesn't exist, how to go forward?

Cultivate interior life as though it were a garden sanctuary.

Give away what you can.

Squander your love.

~

As A YOUNG woman—actually beginning at age fourteen—I was always falling in love, deeply in love. I loved, still do, romance. Growing up, I was steeped in Deep South mythos. Reading kindled a kind of manic belief in the flames of ecstasy. I actually wanted to be swept up onto a horse and carried by a man in a cape to a castle in Ireland. My college studies were barely tolerated. When I transferred junior year from the strict women's college to a big university, I went out every single night of the year. So many cute boys, so little time.

A revelation about love came to me in my mid-twenties. An older friend came home from a week in New York. She was ecstatic over Picasso and Miró. She'd seen an exhibit, brought back a stack of books she pored over. What she said struck me. "It's as if I'm in love." The look on her face—just as if she'd met her prince.

From inside a marriage by then, I adored my husband, but there was no tango at midnight, no roses on the sheets, no love letters with the edges of the paper burned. The friend's remark stuck, and it was several years more until I, too, understood that all the play and energy—laser focus, really—that I'd put into the quest for the ultimate soul mate could redirect. Passions and interests could reinvent my everlasting desire to fall in love.

⁓

TRAVEL WRITER JAN MORRIS writes about her take-it-or-leave-it attitude toward art before she encountered a painting by Giorgione. She'd looked up at one of his luminous, mysterious paintings in a church in Venice and lightning seemed to strike. Obviously she fell in love. Since, she's seen every remaining Giorgione in the world and can tell, with a lover's instinct, if the authorship is doubtful.

I had a similar experience with music in Granada when I heard Manuel de Falla's *Nights in the Gardens of Spain*. We were staying in a hotel just under the Alhambra and a stone's throw from the blue front door of de Falla's house, where he once wrote his music and entertained García Lorca. Then I heard Angel Barrios, another composer of the period. I already loved Lorca. The music and poetry and the stunning experience of seeing the Alhambra—well, yes, I was in love. And still am.

- *Cypress shadows striping the road black/gray/black/gray.*
- *Circle of flames inside the bread oven. A little hell.*
- *Oak tree reflected in water. A creepy, bony hand outspread.*
- *Chickpea bushes drying in crotches of olive trees.*

How to go forward? Pick up the pebbles already dropped in the big woods. Are some of the ways forward also the ways back? Then gather the crumbs.

La mia cucina, my kitchen life, makes a difference in how time adheres to my skin. The kitchen stays serene with music wafting in from the living room. But now I turn up the sound. Up, up until the house pulses with vibrato. Tune out. Tune in. Lang Lang, Hélène Grimaud on the piano or Joshua Bell on the violin, Jovanotti, Buddha Bar, Barry White, Giorgia.

The voices seep into the pan heating on the stove, the arias of Jussi Björling cause my apron to swirl, Bobby McFerrin's verbal play with Yo-Yo Ma brings back the prelinguistic jubilation we all were born with. Chopin, Villa-Lobos, Penguin Café, and all our friends who grace the Tuscan Sun Festival. Music lifts the air as I snap the beans in rhythm with "The Great Pretender," whisk the whites in the swirls of Shostakovich, letting the music in, raising my natural exhilaration and zest, washing the blood stream free from lead.

Delight. Joy. Excitement. Surprise. And then, flip side: Wisdom. Tolerance. Knowledge. Worldview. *Occhi spalancati sul mondo*—eyes wide open on the world. My thoughts magnetize around these words.

2

Summer into Fall

Orto and Oven

GARLIC BURNS EASILY. EVEN THOUGH I START with a splash of cool olive oil, the slivers begin to brown by the time I swab off the cutting board. From the braid hanging by the fireplace, I snap off a bulb and start over. How tightly the papery crescent moons fit together to form a neat miniature mosque dome. When I return to Tuscany, my senses feel hyperactive for the first few days; even simple things appear super-real. The volatile oil in the just-planted basil, tiny pointillist olive flowers, my neighbor Chiara's magnificent smile, the jaunty outline of my yellow Fiat, dark cypress trees brushing against the night sky—I experience everything as if for the first time.

My Italian friends always squash the clove with the side of a knife, then give a quick chop. That way the garlic melts into whatever you're cooking. I'm slicing today, just prolonging opening day in my kitchen. The farro has soaked; I put it on the stove to simmer until barely done. Our garden's tomatoes won't be ripe for another month, but Annunziatina at the *frutta e verdura* recommended oval ones called *dateri* from Sicily. They're ripe, taut, and, other than their oblong shape, bear no resemblance to dates.[1] Chopped tomatoes, parsley, onion, celery, carrot—all these tastes and textures will seep into the farro all afternoon. By dinner, the salad will be irresistible.

Before you use an outdoor bread oven for the first time, you must season it every day for a week by lighting a small fire and letting the warmth temper the inside dome and base. If you just fire up the *forno* for a pizza party, high heat might split the brick and stone. Where is that written? If Albano, who works as our *uomo fisso,* "fixed man," at the mountain house, had not told me, I would have a damaged oven. When I mention this to Italian friends, they are surprised that I was not aware of this universally known procedure. So many years in Tuscany, and still the learning curve continues to rise. Will I never lose my ingénue status?

Domenica, true woman of the mountains, patiently has educated me out here in the wilds. In fall she showed me which are ordinary chestnuts and which are the more prized *marroni.* "The *marroni* are bigger," she explained, "and they look like *marroni.*" Helpful, but finally I began to see the plumpness of the delectable nuts, which can evolve into *marrons glacés,* and that towering Tuscan dessert, Monte Bianco, a sweet peak of *marrone* purée mounded with whipped cream. I've disguised my squeamishness as she's demonstrated the best way to hack a rabbit into pieces or stalk a duck and twist off the head. All the while she's kindly insisted that I'm *"bravissima"* in the kitchen; she's quietly made sure I put a pinch of baking soda into the chard to keep it green, has kept my fridge stocked with her fresh eggs so I won't use ones from the grocery store, which are bound to be a week old. She's made sure I push down the tomatoes, releasing all the air in the jar, before we seal it. If she were in my American kitchen, would I have as much subtle instruction for her? I somehow doubt it.

Today she will help me make big batches of pizza dough and teach us how to gauge the temperature of the bread oven.

I'm overprepared. To initiate the new oven, I've been gathering ingredients for many different pizzas and reviewing several recipes for dough. I have my cakes of yeast, a vat of tomato sauce, and slabs of mozzarella. Ed wants anchovy and capers. I like gorgonzola and walnut. Locally, the classic, plain margherita is favored, possibly because Margherita is the favorite saint of Cortona. I like the margherita with *rucola* and *parmigiano* on top. Our neighbors, the Cardinali family, always crumble raw sausage on theirs. Visiting American friends have suggested shrimp and fennel. My absolute first-choice pizza is the thin-crusted margherita topped with caramelized onions.

The sweetly crafted bread oven is my shrine to the household gods. In fact, it looks like a miniature stone chapel. On either side of the opening there are niches where I can stash olive oil and herbs, but these small indentations could as well hold religious icons. Not only that, the chimney resembles a bell tower.

When we bought the ruin Fonte delle Foglie (Font of Leaves), by the front door we found a large *forno,* collapsed and strangled with blackberries and nettles. I could still see a portion of the curved brick dome, so much like an apse on a Romanesque church. Had the friars who followed St. Francis of Assisi baked their rude *pane* here when they built this stone house? And did it serve the potato farmer and woodcutter families who later lived here for centuries?

A house this old profoundly reassures me. Even during the snowed-in months of restoration, the stalwart position of the enduring stone house on the hillside folded me into a continuum of time. I could turn my back on the frozen mud of the construction site and look out at the two eternal volcanoes on the horizon and the distant spur where the ancient outline of Cortona steps down the hill. Even when I wanted to bang the one-handed (other hand held a cigarette) workers with a cement bucket, I could feel the strength of the house planted in the landscape and the generations of *contadini,* tenant farmers, lifting their own water buckets and walking downhill to the spring surrounded with Etruscan stones. I was eager to step into that stately dance.

Standing among the pulsating cicadas and the weeds, I tried to conjure a whiff of ashy, crusty bread, abundant loaves of it piled in a basket and taken inside—by someone very much like Domenica—for the week's meals.

The structural engineer immediately pronounced the old oven too crumbled to rebuild, but because it once existed, the strict town board allowed us to construct another. I've never been a bread baker—my loaves are good only for propping truck tires to stop them from sliding downhill—but I immediately envisioned myself unfurling a round of dough onto a metal peel and sliding it into the contained inferno inside the oven. In a flash, I saw Ed and me shoving the peel under a toasty crust, removing one after another, lining up an array of proper pizzas on a wooden board for guests to sample, a rising fragrance of smoky chestnut and oak wood lingering in the air. Now that is about to happen.

On another side of the new oven we built in a large grill, so that while the pizzas bake, and everyone eats, we could fire up for another course—skewers of lamb and vegetables, robust Tuscan sausages, or the giant Val di Chiana steaks. As the bread oven heat turns moderate we can slip in a pasta to bake, or chicken under a brick. We've learned from Placido to grill on a wood fire, which he makes quick work of building. He forages for ten minutes, comes back with an armful of sticks. Soon the fire lowers and he hoists the great steaks on the grill for a quick sear. Ed says no, Placido really just waves the steak over the coals to warm it. *Al sangue,* bloody, is the preferred degree of non-doneness, a moment on the heat, a quick dip into a platter of olive oil and rosemary, then onto the plate.

Fourteen adults, six children arriving in two hours.

Ed hauls every lawn chair he can find. I set a table for the children under the oak. They can roll down the grassy hill, jump in the pool, throw the Frisbee, and play hide-and-seek into the twilight while the grown-ups linger at the long table under the pergola. Before we eat, Albano has promised to give everyone a lesson in how to play *bocce*. I already know that he will play like a champ. He does everything well. The skill and movement of his compact body always make me wonder why Americans value big, tall men. We have over-heard Italian men discussing tall Germans and English tour-ists. *"Brutto. Troppo alto,"* ugly, too tall, they said. Albano could only be Italian. His profile looks like a Roman senator on a medallion.

I wonder if anyone ever studied what part immigrants play in maintaining the customs of their new country. You hear about what food and expressions remain from their old country's ways but never about how they adopt the new folkways, even as the natives abandon them. I remember the Vietnamese manicurist in San Francisco telling me about her Thanksgiving dinner—much more traditional than mine.

When we first came to Cortona, there were several *bocce* courts and the game seemed integral to the groups of guys who, then and now, gather and play cards at bars. Out back, bare bulbs strung overhead, the muffled clunk of balls strik-ing each other, and the easy fun, the shouts of "you cuckold," and *"porca miseria"* and *"porca madosca,"* a mild slang expression that uses a nonsense word instead of saying the more serious "Madonna," the usual curse. I teased Ed, "Maybe someday you'll be invited to play." Now, only one court in town remains, a roofed one in nearby Tavernelle. We missed this lively piece of local life. When Ed asked Albano if the terrace above the fruit orchard would be wide enough for a court, Albano's face brightened and he immediately measured. Soon he and Fabio and Bruno, other friends from the mountain, were leveling the land and clearing rocks away. Their enthusiasm for the project showed poignantly that they missed *bocce* too. A friend of theirs brought in a *scavatore* and dislodged a stone the size of a woolly mammoth jutting out from the hillside. Ed suggested that the thick, flat stone would make a perfect table beside the court. The men quickly built a stone-faced cement base and in a few days we watched them guide the stone as their friend's mini-crane lowered it into place. The miracle of Italia—some things are accomplished at the speed of light. Unlikely as it is, I am good at *bocce.* My secret is eye contact with the target ball, letting my throwing hand just follow my eye. It feels something like walking with a full cup of coffee—if you look ahead, you don't spill.

⌇

"SIGNORA FRANCES!" DOMENICA—whose booming voice raises birds from the trees—announces her presence with a shout at the kitchen door. She strides in, and, oh, wonderful, her son Ivan is with her! They've brought two blackberry jam *crostate* made in their own bread oven. Kisses all around. She's told us that Ivan is a pizza *maestro.* The two of them move like dervishes in the kitchen as we look over all the bowls and jars of ingredients I've lined up on the counter.

Easy to tell that they've worked together thousands of times. Ivan's characteristic posture—arms flung open, kind eyes smiling. He looks like one of the saints in Luca's paintings, only he's constantly in motion. Domenica gives the counter a quick scrub and dry just as he's brought out the flour. She exudes confidence. I suspect she thinks we don't know the kitchen from *borscht* but is going with the flow. Ed is strong. Domenica may be stronger.

"Quante pizze?" Ivan asks.

"Oh, maybe thirty. Will that be enough? We'll be around twenty." I say "around" because Italians often show up with an extra guest or two. I hand them aprons.

He's rummaging in the cabinets and sideboard, rejecting one bowl after another. Finally I drag out a gigantic salad bowl and he nods. Flour, yeast, water—he starts the dough by making a huge mound of flour. Soon he's up to his elbows. He's as nimble as his mother is solid. She watches with hands on hips. *"Lui—bravo,"* Yes, he's good. When the yeast is ready, he quickly forms more than thirty puffy moons on the floury, cool travertine counter, then covers them with dish towels to rest and rise. Like all experts, he makes the work seem effortless.

"You are *so* fast—why did you quit being a chef?" I ask.

"Frances, the hours. Now when I finish my work at the Co-op, I clean the pool at home, take care of the garden, I see my friends, I can cook for you!" Ed comes in from the garden with baskets of salad greens, which we take outside to rinse several times in a huge bucket, then soak in the sink. I finish my farro salad and a platter of roasted vegetables—simplest of dinners: pizza, three salads, cheeses, their toasty *crostate,* and my standby lemon hazelnut ice cream that I hope is hardening in the freezer right now. It seemed determined to remain soft and creamy this morning. I've always hated it when you get to "freeze according to manufacturer's directions" in a recipe. I haven't seen those said directions in many years.

⁓

THE CHOREOGRAPHY OF the kitchen—I peel, you scrape, wine spills, bag splits, beans simmer, sink slurps, petals fall, flour drifts, crust splits, aromas spread, lights flicker, chocolate melts, glass shatters, sauce thickens, finger bleeds, cheese ripens, crumbs fall, sweat drips, spoon bangs, meat glistens, oil spatters, wine breathes, garlic smashes, lettuces float, silver shines, apron snags, you sneeze, I sing *oh, my love, my darling,* and dough rises in soft moons the size of my cupped hand as planet earth tilts us toward dinner.

⁓

DOMENICA, WHOSE NAME, Sunday, I love, lives in a mountain house called Il Poggio del Sole, Hill of Sun, with her husband, two grown sons, and her mother-in-law, Annetta, who is a bright-faced woman the size of an eight-year-old girl. She sits by the woodstove in the kitchen in her apron, with a scarf around her head, as she has for all her eighty-six years. She says little but her eyes are so friendly that I always feel that I've had a conversation with her. She watches Domenica roll out the pasta and begin cutting it into strips. She rises to stir the pot on the stove and yanks open the oven to check on the hare she's axed and skinned this morning. I've never seen her in town and suspect that long years when getting into town was difficult disincline her now that it's easy. *La vecchia stampa*—a person of the old stamp. They're disappearing fast from Cortona now, those self-sufficient old-timers who used to sit inside the huge fireplaces trading stories and passing around the *vin santo.* When I see women near town with bundles of sticks on their backs or with their armfuls of greens for their rabbits,

I say to myself, *We won't see her kind for long.* Simultaneously, my own life is running quickly through the same hourglass. The changes coming fast now to Italy are sometimes painful. Out in the mountains, though, time is not so relentlessly transformative.

Since restoring Fonte delle Foglie, I've had the good luck to meet many fiercely independent mountain people of *la vecchia stampa.* I sense more than know that Signorelli lived nearby. His original name was Luca d'Egidio di Ventura, suggesting that his family was of the mountain Sant'Egidio. In his self-portrait, his face looks determined. He looks like a man who knows exactly who he is, a kind of face I've seen on many mountain dwellers. Their isolation promotes independence. Curiously, I've found an intense friendliness and a warmth people give forth generously when not bombarded daily with dozens of social encounters. They've revealed a wilder side of Tuscany to me.

The first neighbor I met was Angelo, who stepped from behind the house when it was still a ruin and fixed me with a silent stare, which I took for a greeting. His tail-thumping mongrel stood almost eye to eye with Angelo. They were out gathering *vinco,* a type of willow. A sprite of a person, Angelo carried a carved stick and wore thick brown wool clothes that must have fit when he was more robust. The pants, secured by a rough belt, gathered in folds around his middle. From a strap slung over his shoulder dangled a bottle covered in woven *vinca.* "We're buying this place; I know we're crazy." I held out my hand, which he regarded as though it were a dead bird before he stuck out his own small hard hand and cracked my metacarpals. He took a swig of whatever was in his distinctive flask. He cocked his head, and lifted his face of a thousand wrinkles to the sun. I realized he was nearly deaf. He seemed otherworldly to me and probably I seemed to have landed on his wild mountainside from another galaxy.

I soon met his wife, Irene, she of the single yellow tooth and big smile, and visited their house, which looked barely changed for hundreds of years, except for the blaring television that dominated the dark cavernous kitchen. Angelo beckoned for me to follow him into an even darker room where, among hanging salamis, rows of cheeses, and the prosciutto secured on a carving stand, I saw the cunning, artistic willow baskets he wove all winter by the fire. I put his egg and vegetable baskets on top of the cabinets in my kitchen where we can admire them every day.

Angelo roams the woods all year, and they also invite us to roam. I love stepping over our low electric fence and onto the rutted road leading absolutely nowhere after passing a rustic cottage, a ruin of three attached collapsed houses, and an architecturally pure small stone chestnut-drying barn.

I'm out in the territory of wild cherries, apples, heather fields, and wildflowers. Succulent strawberries the size of a pea especially prefer the edges of the road. Occasionally I startle a mother boar herding her young along the mud holes and torrents. When I meet one of the beady-eyed, nut-seeking maniacs, I adopt the old southern advice about snakes. Don't bother them; they won't bother you. No eye contact. Exit in the opposite direction. I back up and she runs. This works so far.

At night we hear the *cinghiale* snorting in the dark. Their attachment to the acorns that fall near the house prompted the electric fence. They'd rooted up the irrigation system and the stone patio in their zeal for the crunchy nuts. Ed was looking out every morning to see if we'd find one in the pool floating feet up. British friends, who returned after a long absence, immediately noticed a putrid smell in their tap water. A two-hundred-pound boar had somehow shifted the stone off the well and fallen in.

Since our fence began delivering a zing to their hairy snouts, they have stayed out, ripping up the hillside above us and delivering frequent avalanches onto the road. We're fond of them—so brutal and wild—and when they run we laugh at their cartoonish, rocking-horse gallop, those absurd tusks, and tapering legs attached to pointy hooves.

The mountain people regard them differently. Their corporeal form simply embodies the first phase of *cinghiale in umido,* a long-marinated (to get the raunchy taste out) stew that falls apart on the fork and reminds you of a smoldering fire on the morning of the first *brina,* frost. During hunting season, our friend Giorgio always has brought us bags of bloody boar. Now Domenica's other son, Mirko, sometimes drops off a hunk. I hate the way they're hunted. A squadron of men, who look dressed for combat in the latest American war, spread out across a wide flank of hill and flush them out. Given that they are hunted, the best fate for the meat is pasta sauce. Every trattoria in Cortona serves long-simmered *pappardelle al cinghiale,* wide pasta with rich boar sauce.

❧

To WALK, GOING nowhere. The sensation deeply relaxes me and leads me to walk for miles through the woods on old logging paths and Roman roads. Following the ancient stones through the pine and chestnut forest, picking the sweetest blackberries, finding patches of pink cyclamen, yellow and purple crocuses, and seeing the neat falcons called *pellegrini,* little pilgrims, peering down from a branch—*che gioia,* what joy. I sing. Loudly. Loudly because when I took voice lessons at fifteen, the teacher, reaching for a compliment, said I had a "soft, sweet voice." San Francesco's followers sang as they wandered the mountains, but not my "Nessun Dorma" or "American Pie." I wish Robert Frost had never written that always-anthologized poem about two roads diverging in a yellow wood, because at every separation of path I recall that he took "the one less traveled by," a choice that influenced his whole life. Here *all* of the branching Roman trails are less traveled by, and the snags in my sweaters and scratches on my arms prove that.

To be where there's *no one*. Solitude, the real luxury item. Clearings show me views of Lake Trasimeno that look like backdrop painted scenery, the distant Val di Chiana, forever the fruit basket of Tuscany, with apartments and shops now creeping out from its edges, and always Cortona below, which I see like an eagle from one vantage, and then in a fanned-out position, a fine little city spread like a bolt of green-gold embroidered silk over the hill.

The Etruscan spring still runs, even in drought. The spring house that once protected the bubbling source lies in heaps, with water finding its way among the stones. Ed wants to rebuild it—but what did it look like originally? Or maybe not originally, but even recently, say 1600. Wild as our mountainside seems to us, many traces indicate that it was not always so. Our house and the two nearby are called *"Cassacie,"* the bad houses, on the old maps, although one has spider-leg script labeling ours Fonte della Foglia, Font of the Leaf. We changed it to Fonte delle Foglie. Plural leaves made more sense. A section of a Roman bridge and medieval monastery ruins remind me of other travelers, other lives. During our reconstruction, we found two sections of Roman aqueduct. Coming upon these things makes me question what *else* is just under the surface of where I roam.

Emphatically, what is *not* underfoot or in the air is the Tuscany of the Renaissance. Here we feel the more primitive biotic pull of Tuscany before it was Tuscany. At this time in my life, I'm loving the raucous waterfalls, stone pushing up from deep tertiary levels, grandfather chestnuts, some with hollow trunks you could camp in, freshets that open after downpours, big prelapsarian silences I don't even want to interrupt with a single word. This is where I came for comfort when we experienced at Bramasole our own private terrorist incident. This is where I come now for the pure joy of loving a place so purely itself.

Who would not be happy, this far in the country? Happiness, what an elusive elf, how to hold happiness, how to find it, how to live inside a great happiness of your own making? *The Sustainability of Happiness*—some philosopher should write a treatise. Maybe it would be very long, or perhaps it would be only a few sentences.

⁓

DOMENICA DOES NOT toss a pinch of flour onto the oven floor and count the seconds until it browns, as I'd been told to do. She sticks her face close to the open door and the reflective coals burnish her tanned skin to copper. *"Pronto,"* she shouts, and we begin rolling the pizza. Our American guests toast Domenica and gather around to watch. The Italians stand back, bemused, having seen this process since birth.

Forno, I must remember to ask Ed, has an etymological relationship to "fornicate."

Almost as soon as the pizza glides in, out it comes, the yeast blistering the dough and the crust toasty in the intense heat. Ed quickly cuts and our friends devour them as quickly as we can get slices on plates. The children dispense with plates and eat on the fly. Everyone has brought wine and the new stone table already shows a few red circles and splats. No matter. Let the entire stone absorb the runoff from these magical summer evenings. In the mountains, people really eat. After a day outside, Ed has the appetite of a marathon runner. Domenica and Ivan brush the flour from their hands and speed off like the genies from a bottle that they are.

Every crumb, every grain of farro has been consumed. Franco practices his English. *Where is it that you come from?* Becky practices Italian. *Quanto tempo ci vuole per adare ad Arezzo?*

Ah, *brava,* that *ci vuole* jumps away from the phrase book into the vernacular. How much time do you need to go to Arezzo?

We hear "Marco" and "Polo" from the pool, then the children are running by, wrapped in their towels, hiding behind the oven and oaks, chasing fireflies. The Italians gather at one end of the table, not being able to bear any longer our guests who don't speak Italian—they need to *talk*—though they pour them grappa and pass it down to the other end, where plans are laid for day trips to Siena and Montalcino. Edo and Placido light their cigar stubs, to the amazement of the Californians. Fiorella and Chiara help me serve the gelato and the *crostate,* all praise to Domenica, then a few Beatles songs unite all of us. "Yellow Submarine," it seems, is a universal language.

May all the guests make it up the rough road. *Buona notte. A domani . . .* Until tomorrow. The fire falls to ashy embers now. We face the kitchen littered with plates and glasses— how can we have used every glass in the house? With my thumb, I rub the soapy water around the lipstick prints. "Ed, what was it with *forno* and *fornicate?*"

"Oh, the Roman whores used to hang out at the public ovens to keep warm. They'd go after a night's work and wait for the warm bread."

"But which came first, *forno* or *fornicate?*"

"Both are old as time. But *forno* originally meant *arch* so I guess that's the dome of the oven." Ed and I start the dishwasher, sweep the kitchen, and turn out the light. We step outside for the deep night sounds of owls calling to each other. A little chill has arrived and we lean against the still-warm oven and listen.

May the scurrying animals who are owl prey hear those haunting oboe notes and find a burrow. The far lights of Cortona string down the hill. I know the piazza is still hopping. A line runs out of the gelato shop. The *trattorie* are resetting the tables for tomorrow and a cat sleeps outside Isa's antiques store. We are near and far. I have come to love the chestnut forest and this stone house, already old when Signorelli did or did not walk along the path to the spring. Tomorrow I will be up early to sow arugula seeds. Summer begins.

PASTA AL FORNO CON SALSICCE E QUATTRO FORMAGGI
Baked Pasta with Sausage and Four Cheeses

With the bread oven hot, we can slide many different dishes across the brick floor—bread, of course, roast chickens, three at a time, and baked pastas. Ed adapted this recipe for home use. We've served this a hundred times at casual suppers.

Serves 6

Olive oil
1 onion, minced
1 carrot, minced
2 ribs celery, minced
3 garlic cloves, minced
Salt for seasoning
½ pound sweet Italian sausage, casings removed, meat cut into small pieces
½ pound spicy Italian sausage, casings removed, meat cut into small pieces
½ cup red wine
4 or 5 sprigs of oregano, leaves torn
1 28-ounce can of whole tomatoes, chopped
1 pound dried rigatoni
1 cup ricotta
½ pound Fontina or Taleggio, cubed
½ pound mozzarella, cubed
½ cup parmigiano
½ cup bread crumbs

Preheat the oven to 375 degrees F.

Bring a stockpot of water to the boil.

In a large pan, heat 2 tablespoons of oil. Sauté the onion, carrot, celery, and garlic on low heat for 5 minutes. Season with salt. Add the sausage to the pan, cooking until browned, about 10 minutes. Add the red wine, turn the heat up to boil, and cook until most of the liquid has evaporated. Add the oregano and the tomatoes along with their juices and continue cooking for at least 10 minutes.

When the water in the stockpot has come to a boil, salt it, and add the rigatoni. Cook a minute or two less than the time required on the package (since it will continue cooking in the oven), then drain, reserving a bit of pasta water.

In a large bowl, mix the ricotta with the Fontina and a splash of the pasta water, then add the drained rigatoni, and continue mixing. Add the sausage mixture. Add the mozzarella to the bowl and mix well, then pour into an oiled 8- by 13-inch baking dish, sprinkling grated *parmigiano* and bread crumbs on top.

Bake uncovered for 20 to 25 minutes, and serve hot.

VARIATION: *For the ingredients listed before the cheeses, you can substitute 2 cups of homemade ragù.*

❧

INSALATA DI FARRO
Farro Salad

Farro is sometimes translated as spelt but is actually its own distinctive grain. Tuscans love it with chickpeas in a rousing winter soup. In summer, farro salad is an inspired choice for lunches because it is easy, abundant, and tasty. Leftover farro salad keeps in the fridge for 3 or 4 days and is handy for wraps or to serve in radicchio leaves on an antipasto platter.

Serves 10

2 cups farro
4 tomatoes, chopped, or ½ cup sun-dried tomatoes, diced
2 or 3 ribs celery, chopped
½ cup green olives, cut in half if they're large
2 shallots, minced
3 garlic cloves, minced
¼ to ½ cup extra-virgin olive oil
1 cup basil leaves, torn
1 cup parsley, chopped
Salt and pepper

Follow the directions on the package of farro. Usually it cooks in less than 2 hours. While the farro is cooking, mix the other ingredients together. Drain the farro and add it to the vegetable mixture, correct the seasonings, and serve at room temperature.

Verdure Arrosto
Roasted Vegetables

When you cook out of your garden, invention becomes a necessity. What to do with an abundance of onions, eggplants, and pears, not to mention a side of pancetta or speck a friend brought over? Roasting is quick and easy. Try Brussels sprouts, shallots, garlic, and lemon peel together.

Serves 4

> *1 eggplant, cut into 1-inch pieces*
> *8 garlic cloves, peeled*
> *Salt and pepper*
> *2 onions, cut into 1-inch pieces*
> *Extra-virgin olive oil*
> *2 pears, peeled, cored, and cut into wedges*
> *6 slices of pancetta, speck, or bacon, cut into 1-inch pieces*

Preheat oven to 400 degrees F.

Toss the eggplant, garlic, seasonings, and onions with some oil and put in an ovenproof dish. Cover with foil and bake. After 20 minutes, remove the foil, add the pears and pancetta, and return to the oven for another 20 minutes, tossing once.

⌒∽⌒

CROSTATA DI MORE DI IVAN
Ivan's Blackberry Crostata

We once wondered why you see so many jars of fruit preserves in Italy, a country, unlike England, that doesn't have a toast-and-jam breakfast culture. We soon found out. The contents of the jars—apricot, blackberry, raspberry, quince, fig, and plum—are for the famous and ubiquitous *crostata.*

Ivan—pronounced E-vahn—and his mother, Domenica, make the most wonderful *crostate,* the default dessert of Tuscany. They gather wild blackberries in early September and Domenica makes the jam. We serve their fig jams with cheeses and their quince with roasts. Like the jars of tomatoes lining their pantry, the jams seem to contain summer. Grab a jar and roll out the pastry—there's Sunday dessert.

Serves 8

1½ cups flour
3 eggs (2 egg yolks and 1 whole)
10 tablespoons sugar
10 tablespoons butter, at room temperature
Grated zest of 1 lemon
½ glass red wine
¼ teaspoon salt
2 cups blackberry jam

Mound the flour on a *spianatoia,* a pastry board. Make a well, and put the eggs in the center, along with the sugar. Start to work the mixture with your fingers or a fork, then add the small pieces of soft butter, the lemon zest, the wine, and salt, blending everything. Roll the pastry in a ball and allow to rest, covered with a cloth, for about an hour.

While the pastry is resting, butter and flour a baking dish and preheat the oven to 350 degrees F.

Roll out ¾ of the pastry and fit it into the dish. Spread the blackberry jam on the pastry, then roll out the rest of the pastry, cut it into ½-inch strips, and make a lattice over the jam. Bake for 30 minutes. The pastry will look toasty.

Vine Yard

IN PIAZZA SIGNORELLI, ED PAUSES ONLY LONG enough to signal Marco that we've arrived. Melva and I are in the backseat like good wives, but really it's because Jim and Ed both get carsick unless they're in the front seat. Marco and two ex-pats lead the way out of town and onto Marco's secret back road to the Brunello countryside.

A benefit of being friends *and* good wine customers of Marco is that he invites us to vineyards for lunch and tastings with winemakers. Today, we are going to Fonterutoli in Montalcino with a few other Americans and the Pantes, good San Francisco friends who have a home here and entertain magnificently with the best of Tuscan wines. I'm always telling Melva that she should write a table-top book. Her flowers and china perfectly set the mood for dinners overlooking olive groves and the silhouette of Cortona. I would just as soon admire her arrangements of white hydrangeas, roses, and lilies, as devour whatever delectable dinner she has prepared.

As we wind downhill and across the valley, I remember another friend's wine-tasting trip with

Marco. Secondo, a Tampa friend who has an apartment in Cortona, was with a larger group, going to two vineyards in a small bus. After the first stop, five wines, and a long boozy buffet of Tuscan specialties, the eight or so imbibers boarded the bus again, heading for the next stop. An Italian man sitting behind a proper English woman became ill and had a spasm of projectile vomiting that quite covered the blond chignon in front of him. Bus stopped, bottled water was thrown over all, Kleenex appeared from handbags, windows were opened. An American, also vomit-spattered on his polo shirt, stepped out of the bus, facing traffic, and moaned, "Kill me now."

As the bus pulled off, the mortified Italian man fell asleep, but he roused at the next stop and proceeded with the tasting, while the English woman retired to the bathroom to sop her blouse and hair. The vineyard owner graciously served an elaborate lunch.

Secondo, telling this story, kept bending over with laughter as it got worse. Reboarding the bus, the Italian man in his stylish Armani sport coat and pressed pants, along with his wife, sat in back. Everyone was stunned with the heat, the lunch, and the curvy road. Not far into the trip home, Secondo and the others heard a tremendous barf, and the bus filled with the sour smell. When Secondo saw a stream of vomit running down the aisle, he lifted his feet. Everyone on the bus was groaning, leaning out the windows, shouting "For Christ's sake," or laughing. Secondo shouted out, "I'm so glad that at least he's not an American!" Back at the parking lot, the Italian man looked at no one from behind his sunglasses as he stepped down, balled up his Armani jacket, and threw it in a ditch. Secondo said at that moment he never wanted another glass of wine in his life.

And these trips are usually so sedate.

We will try to be sedate.

⌒

FONTERUTOLI PRODUCES A million bottles of wine a year. "That's gigunta," I remark, but Ed shrugs. We usually seek the smaller vineyards for the sense of discovery that comes from a *vellutato,* velvety, Nero d'Avola syrah from Sicily, or even the homemade wine from the shepherd down the road.

"It's only one bottle a year for a million people. One bottle," he says. "That doesn't seem like so much."

Fonterutoli turns out to be not just a vineyard but a pale stone *borgo,* completely owned by the Mazzei family and inhabited by employees. We meet the Marchesi Mazzei, a slim man in a mustard-colored suit who welcomes us, then turns us over to Silvio Ariani, who looks as though he could be mounting a horse or pulling the crossbow in a Piero della Francesca painting. He takes us on a tour of the *borgo,* into the courtyard of the family villa (I would love to see the inside), into old cellars and into the family wine library, where all the vintages are stored for their own celebrations. We meander downhill to the shockingly modern facility where the wine is now made. En route, Silvio shows us how the vines are planted close together. I love it that he pronounces *vineyard* "vine yard." "If they are close, the plants sense each other," he tells us. "They go deeper instead of spreading out close to the surface. That's better—in drought they reach water; in time of much rain, they are not soaked." As metaphor and philosophy, this sets me reeling. They let the weeds and wildflowers flourish in the aisles, which helps force the vines downward for their nutrients.

In an association test, in response to the word *landscape,* this quintessential Tuscan vineyard would always come to mind for me—undulating hills, the cross-hatched patterns of planting juxtaposed from one field to another, a distant hill fringed with cypress trees, and a clean sky skittered with clouds. The day is unsurpassable, especially after weeks of continuous rain.

Seen one, seen them all, or so I thought, of damp stone cellars full of oak barrels. But this super-techno facility fascinates everyone. What I took for lights in the vast courtyard actually are openings for crushed grapes to fall through big tubes into stainless steel vats on the subterranean floor below. This immediate transfer keeps the just-crushed grapes from getting "stressed."

Silvio explains that the skins are used to make grappa. "What's left," he says, "goes off to pharmaceutical companies to make alcohol." Ah, so that's why Italian rubbing alcohol is pink. The flat cone-shaped vats look like gigantic medical equipment or, as Melva says, "That thing that left Apollo when they walked on the moon." In the warehouse-sized room of small barrels where "we sleep the wine," I feel as though I'm inside an immense tomb where strange burial rites were practiced. The floor frequently is doused with water to keep the humidity at around 70 percent. One wall of exposed rock weeps water constantly. In three years, little calcium stalactites have formed, prompting Silvio to remark, "See, wine is better for you to drink than water."

❧

THE COOLLY MINIMALIST tasting room allows all our attention to go to the wine and to the view of the distant Chianti hills. It's noon. Silvio pours first their Serrata, a light-hearted rosé that catapults me to a long-ago picnic in the South of France. Sometimes as my lips are just wet with wine, a flood of images overtakes my mind just as the taste of the wine overtakes my mouth. So that now as I'm given the lissome, faintly flowery wine and the expansive view of distant Siena, I simultaneously receive a rough, shell-crusted Bandol beach, sausages and baguette, salt wind and the Englishman's sweater with his aroma of sandalwood around my shoulders. Rosé in a paper cup. A memory more distant than Siena. Then Silvio tells us that the rosé is made in their Maremma vineyards near the Tuscan coast. Running through the wine must be refractions of Mediterranean light, mysteriously acting on memory.

The blond Englishman with the mesmerizing lips disappears as we try the big-mouthed, juicy Tenuta Belguardo, the Zisola made from mostly Nero d'Avola in Sicily, and the Castello di Fonterutoli, made from Sangiovese grapes with a hit of cabernet. Here's the *vino dei sassi,* rock wine of the local hills, fruit-basket rich with a potent balance of mineral.

Downhill in the *enoteca,* the chef serves ten or so antipasti—not the usual prosciutto and *crostini,* but instead, chickpeas with lemon peel, chopped radicchio with cubes of pecorino, bruschetta with arugula pesto, rice salad with chopped vegetables, a platter of fennel topped with local salami with fennel seeds echoing the taste. No pasta, which would cause imminent collapse.

As the Siepe wine is poured, platters of chicken and rabbit with roasted potatoes circulate around the table. Fonterutoli's top wine, Siepe, comes from their lower hills, a Sangiovese with a judicious dollop of merlot. Best for last—but, really, others to me were just as fine. Or maybe after so much sun, food, and wine, we've all just mellowed into total enthusiasm.

～

FORTUNATELY, ON THE road back to Cortona, we all feel terrific. Sedate, we were, but a thousand images and tastes whirl through my brain all the way home. We've arranged to meet Silvio in Florence at a restaurant we both admire. A new friend, new tastes, a memory of toast-colored stone houses where people have poured out a daily wine for five hundred years. Secondo should have been with us rather than on the bus.

Antipasto Platter

For a crowd or for an outdoor lunch, I rely on antipasto platters and often follow them with a pasta and dessert. The first list comes from Chef Nicola Borbui, who served these alluring antipasti to our wine-tasting party at Fonterutoli vineyards. After that, some of our additions. Both informal and lavish, the platter starts off a dinner with a festive note.

Ceci con Olio e Buccia di Limone
Chickpeas with Olive Oil and Lemon Peel

Raddicchio con Pecorino a Cubetti
Chopped Radicchio with Cubed Pecorino

Insalatina di Baccelli e Marzolino
Fava Bean Salad with Fresh Pecorino Cheese

Frittata di Asparagi
Slices of Fresh Asparagus Omelette

Bruschetta con Pesto di Rucola e Pomodorini
Bruschetta with Rucola Pesto and Cherry Tomatoes

Sformato di Parmigiano con Crema di Asparagi
Parmesan Flan with Cream of Fresh Asparagus

Tagliata di Morellini con Mozzarella di Bufala Olive e Pinoli
Sliced Artichoke with Mozzarella, Olives, and Pine Nuts

Insalata di Finocchi con Sbriciolona
Tuscan Salami with Fennel Julienne

Tortino di Carciofi
Artichoke Frittata

Other favorite additions to the platter:

roasted peppers
olives baked with lemon peel and herbs
artichoke hearts with vinaigrette
fennel slices sprinkled with fennel seeds
prosciutto and melon cubes on toothpicks
halved figs
radicchio leaves filled with farro salad
small chunks of hard cheeses
grissini (breadsticks) wrapped in prosciutto

Gite al Mare— Little Trips to the Sea

PORTOFINO, LIGURIA

THE WORD SPOKEN MOST OFTEN IN CORTONA these summer days is *mare*. Everyone is going to, or is just back from, the sea. Popular *trattorie* close at the height of tourist season. Why? Gone swimming. So what if tourists are looking longingly at the posted menu in the window? Sea air lures us.

Kids go to Rimini on their motorcycles, drawn by cheap package deals, all-night discos, and a beach jammed with the youth of Italy. The fortunate go to Sardegna. Many hop over to Viareggio and Forte dei Marmi for a few days, or to the beaches around Grosseto. Since Cortona is two hours from the Adriatic and two from the Tyrrhenian, we go in both directions. Although we're seduced by the Adriatic towns, especially Senegallia, for their wide, long beaches, we often choose to spend a couple of days on the other shore. Elba is especially fun and a quick ferry ride from Livorno. A stroll around the deck, a gelato, deep draughts of sea air, and suddenly you're driving out the ramp into Napoleon's territory. Relaxation starts immediately—maybe it's the

Mediterranean air, the easy driving along the sea, the blooming little towns where not much is going on, the friendly people. Renting a boat lets you explore the coast and find tiny
beaches where you can swim and sun alone. We stayed a week
on Elba and want to go back.

On the Tyrrhenian mainland, we have spent days over the
years in Capalbio, San Vincenzo, the protected Riva degli
Etruschi, Talamone, dramatic Cinque Terre, and Punta Ala—
all good seaside destinations. I'm a fool for beauty, however,
and nothing compares with Portofino, where we are heading
for a short idyll.

"We are going sailing to Corsica," Fulvio said at dinner last
Sunday. "Why don't you take our place at Portofino for a
week?" Then he and Aurora provide us with a key and a list
of their favorite things to do. Fulvio's father bought this piece
of dreamy real estate many years ago, and he grew up spending summers there. He keeps a sloop in the harbor. It's hard to
budge his family, Aurora, and their son Edoardo, from there
all summer. But boats are second nature to Edoardo, as they
are to his father, and they like sailing to Corsica because
Mediterranean winds, which seem balmy on shore, slap a boat
around pretty fiercely, providing sufficient adventure for these
two. Aurora sometimes visits family during these excursions.

We accept, but only for three days. We have guests arriving
Thursday. On Monday morning early, we drive over, parking
our car once and for all in the town garage. It's nice to walk
away from a car, knowing you won't start it for days.

The delicious earth colors of the houses—terracotta, ochre,
sand, and gold—line the harbor; crisp boats with their blue
stripes and flying flags repeat in their reflections, and concentric ripples of light on water play and change at all hours of the
day. I say colors and light, but underlying this inviting surface,
architects Alberto and Fulvio might agree, let's acknowledge

the gift of geography—the U shape of the harbor, whose open-arms provide a delicious intimacy. When you're strolling there, you've been gathered into the heart of the place.

Portofino, unlike the secretive, layered hill towns of Tuscany, gives you everything at once, one beauteous splashing wave of Mediterranean perfection.

I'm sure the Di Rosas know every soul in town and every cornice, stone, and house name. Their apartment, up three floors, occupies a small corner of a building on the harbor with windows facing two directions. "If you've ever seen a postcard of Portofino, you've seen Fulvio's place," Ed notices.

"We're on a yacht. Look at these narrow teak floors. They're like a deck. And the kitchen—so very shipshape." The furniture is super-modern and sleek. From the bed we can hear the clangs of rigging in sailboats and watch boats nosing in for the day. One is megabucks-huge and even has a helicopter and a Smart Car on board.

If I should ever win the lottery, I'd love a grand swoop around the Mediterranean. Not on that floating mansion but in a great old wooden sloop that could tuck into tiny ports. In my first husband's sailboat, the *Primavera,* I learned to cook in a gimbaled kitchen. The San Francisco Bay was not conducive to complicated recipes. We were constantly tacking and tossed and sometimes we ran aground. Surprisingly, the bay is not very deep, in places, and somehow our sonar was often kaput. On one New Year's Eve sail, with several surly teenagers, we ran aground and had to wait until the tide lifted us off the mud. They were envisioning themselves at discos with dates, not out with friends of parents, high and dry with the alluring skyline of San Francisco in the distance.

In the Mediterranean, who would not fancy leaping off the boat early in the morning, gathering produce and fresh fish at a market, and producing simple, elegant dinners on deck, with guttering candles, white linen, a bowl of figs, and libations of Ligurian white wines?

⌒

WE LEARN RIGHT away to jump on and off buses. Driving can be tedious because of slow traffic snaking into the peninsula of Portofino. On the harbor, we talk to a boat captain who embodies the expression "old salt": frizzy white beard, pink cheeks, and navy beret. His small launch looks basic but seaworthy, so we hire him to take us over to Camogli, a port town around the promontory. He seats us in front and begins to talk nonstop about the history of the area. With the outboard noise and the wind against him, we can't understand anything. Now and then Ed calls out *"Si!"* or *"Buono!"* He slows at a cove and offers a swim, but it's windy. "Fulvio and Edoardo would have been in the water in an instant," Ed says.

Camogli! Heart-stopping! Approaching by water, we see the whole sweep of the vibrantly colored town, anchored by a castle and harbor full of small fishing boats. The town curves along the shore, with buildings rising five or six stories high. Doubtless, many women have looked out to sea from the windows, waiting for their husbands to come in with the catch. The name may mean *ca' moglie,* house of wives.

We say good-bye to our captain and take off to explore. Built on narrow terraces, the town backs right up to a mountain. Many steep staircases lead from one level to the next. Toni and Shotsy, our friends from California, love Camogli. Why are they not up there on a third-floor balcony, writing in their notebooks and pouring glasses of fresh orange juice? If only they'd spot us and wave, call us to come right up—but instead, a woman brushes a little dog and smokes.

We visit the Maritime Museum, poring over all the ship

models, and drop into a couple of churches. Mainly, we just
stroll, photographing the bougainvillea and doorways and vis-
tas. After lunch—big platter of fried fish and squid—we hop
on the train and make our way back to Portofino, via a bus
connection. A plus of Italian travel is the chance to jump spon-
taneously on trains. We're back in time for a rest, me with Fulvio's art books, Ed with a Pavese poem he's translating, and the
peaceful sound of voices and boats below.

The next day we take the bus to lively Santa Margherita,
wander the town, almost buy an antique fragment of a marble
hand for my collection, think better, and settle for lunch in a
small restaurant. Since we're late and the only customers, the
owner lingers by the table. She perks up when we say where
we live. "Better, Tuscany," she exclaims, when Ed says how
fabulous Santa Margherita is.

"We love it here," I say. "Maybe we should move here."

"The Ligurians," she assures us, "have no manners. I'm
from Tuscany and there they have manners." A life story en-
sues and lunch lasts longer than we planned. You really can't
be in a hurry in Italy.

Santa Margherita has an old-movie glamour. Mellow
painted facades with tromp l'oeil windows and fanciful deco-
rations, the grand harbor lined with palms, the transparent
light—will Marcello Mastroianni pull up in an Alfa convert-
ible and offer us a lift back to Portofino?

⌒

DESPITE THE GLITZY reputations of both, Portofino, like
Capri, is for hikers. Old donkey paths wind around the hillsides. If you take the footpath to San Fruttuoso, as we did on a
trip years ago, you're rewarded with eye-popping views and a
swim in a blue, blue cove.

Although the restaurants of Portofino do not achieve high marks in the best guidebooks, we find the seafood utterly scrumptious. Aurora told us that some of Liguria's best *focaccia* comes out of the town bakery. We buy slabs for breakfast. Every restaurant serves the pungent Genovese pesto with a twist—diced potatoes cook along with the pasta. If there is a celestial paradise, I expect to be served the baked shrimp from Portofino at every meal.

Dining harborside with lights shimmering in the water and boats rising and falling on their kaleidoscopic reflections—a moment of perfection. Not even marred by the burly man who leans over to Ed and says in a heavily accented English, "You Americans make ugly wars." His eyes are black as fishing holes in ice. I look at his wife, who resembles a wasp. She lowers her eyes. She must know she lives with someone crude. Although we could mention a war his country visited on the world, although we want to tump his chair backward into the harbor and see his dome head sink, we say nothing. This enrages Mr. Burly Man and he speaks loudly to his wife in German.

The waiter overhears his snarly voice and as the lumpy couple leaves—weaving a bit—he brings over several glasses of prosecco and sits down to discuss with us some of his prime prejudices. When we tell him that we are friends of the Di Rosas, he brings out his brother and we stay until no one is left. From a window above, piano music wafts down and the notes seem timed to the lifting, falling motion of the water.

On our last morning, we climb up to Castello Brown, a stunning garden and castle/house where *Enchanted April* was filmed. And enchant, it does. Bees are mining the orange trees and everywhere I look the view is blue, blue, blue. The position defies description: The house is a pivot around which the sea turns. It's empty this morning and wandering the rooms, I easily can construct a fantasy life.

⁓

DRIVING HOME, I want to turn down many tempting roads. Italy is an immortal playground. Does any country come close to its sustained, heady concoction of joys—serene landscape *and* magnificent art *and* layered history *and* savory cuisine *and* glorious music *and* welcoming people? So many *ands*. All in an elongated peninsula slashed down the middle with mountains, packed and stacked with dialects, great cooks, the Renaissance, hill towns, evocative cinema, ruins, castles, mosaics, villas, church bells, beaches, on and on. Just as we think we won't find anywhere to eat on this back road, a small osteria appears.

This is Italy—such an out-of-the-way, inconspicuous hole-in-the-wall—and the meal leaves us wide-eyed. The waitress just brings out what they're serving, a penne with tomato sauce and basil, veal roast and potatoes, sautéed spinach, terrific bread, and panna cotta. Simple, very simple, and perfect.

We feast, then drive on, making it back to Bramasole in time to shop for the weekend. Cortona is abuzz with tourists—fewer this year and the merchants are dismayed—but still the piazza throbs with talk and laughter. Ah, Marco's has a wine tasting in progress. We join friends and strangers there and meet the makers of the local and impressive Gemelli wines.

Evening falls softly and the intense sky fades to thin turquoise streaked with gauzy clouds. Everyone looks wonderful glazed with this radiant light.

"This is the happening place," Jim says, handing us glasses of dark red wine.

"Yeah, rockin'." Ed clanks glasses with us.

Yes, Luca, so nice to be back. Are you joining us in the piazza?

No wonder swarms of travelers converge on Italia, expecting to be dazzled. Washed and unwashed masses hoping for, yes, plain fun, hoping for enlightenment, for relaxation, transformation. Perhaps that bolt of life force that shoved the Middle Ages into the Renaissance also sparked the idea that Italy is *the* place. Humanism's blaze of glory still draws us. Witness this piazza on a summer evening. Perhaps the big old Mediterranean sun, throwing its golden arrows across the piazza, continues to pull us, too.

"Did I ever tell you," I say to Valentina, "that once I got on an empty bus. Then a woman got on and of all the empty seats, she chose to sit beside me."

She looks at me blankly. *"Perché no, cara?"* Why not, darling?

SENIGALLIA IN THE MARCHE

We've been wanting to explore the Adriatic coast, so when Riccardo and Silvia, just returned from Senigallia, recommended a hotel, we looked it up on the Internet and found the description on the website irresistible:

> To the natural offer of a still fierce landscape of the own authenticity, the Marine Terrazza Marconi Hotel and SPA spouse the own ability to receive and to satisfy the requirements of the present. Is the meeting of the precious and atavistic equilibrium between desires, habits and resources, it rocks of a harmonious daily ritual to measure of every host. It is also a fascinating dialogue between architecture and landscape, an invite towards one pause of well-being in a generous and cordial context; it is the source of found again union between space and the time.

I book a room immediately. We see right away that Senigallia not only lies on the opposite coast from Portofino, but the town is opposite as well. Portofino is one of the most exclusive spots on the entire Mediterranean; Senigallia, instead, is a relaxed beach resort, ancient in origin, and welcomes everyone to its broad strand, known as Velvet Beach: African men selling scarves; sun-seekers actually lying on towels and folding chairs as well as lining up at the concessions of umbrellas and chairs; children building sand castles; and boys playing volley ball. Senigallia is one of the EU Blue Banner beaches; the golden sand has been drawing sun-seekers since the Romans.[1]

Getting a bit lost gives us a look at the gritty, colorful port area. The Misa River runs through town and such advantageous access must have been what originally attracted settlers in the fourth century B.C. This was the first Roman colony on the Adriatic.

We meet several blocked streets teeming with people. During the Middle Ages Senigallia held a gigantic market fair. The tradition continues, with stands set up to sell clothing, household items, and beach toys instead of oxen and farm supplies, although the fish, herb, and vegetable market in Foro Annonario probably doesn't veer much from its earlier model.

We've come to Senigallia for walking on the beach and because of two culinary meccas—Uliassi, a short walk from the hotel, and, a little out of town, La Madonnina del Pescatore. I couldn't say which I prefer. They're diverse but similar. For both innovative chefs, local ingredients star. "Write what you don't know about what you know," a colleague of mine used to tell her fiction students. That's the mode in Senigallia. The chefs seek what's new in what's familiar, especially seafood. A few days of sampling both kitchens, walking the beach at dawn, taking a massage, reading a book on the terrace—here's a recipe for an instant sensation of liberation.

The hotel keeps bicycles parked out front, with wicker baskets and no gears. Pedaling up and down the promenade, stopping for lunch at a simple fish restaurant on the beach (where moisture always clogs the salt shaker) would feel like an old-Florida beach experience if it were not so quintessentially Italian.

An art nouveau pavilion suspended over the water prods the memories of every Italian over forty. They all know the words to the seventies song "Una Rotonda sul Mare"—"A Rotunda on the Sea." All the friends are dancing at the sea but where are you—that kind of song. For Italian friends, it carries the kind of nostalgia that "California Dreamin'" does for me.

While leaning on the rotunda railing, I'm catapulted back to the beach casino on St. Simons Island, where my family spent vacations when I was a child. My older sisters in their summer sundresses went off with their boyfriends to dance to *Somewhere there's music, how high the moon* . . . In memory the casino is round, columned, open to the night sky, smooth terrazzo floor, a jukebox glowing gold, red, and green. Did the casino actually look like a Greek temple? I can see the tanned lifeguards my sisters dated and the secret anticipation I felt that someday I would flounce off on the back of a scooter, my hair a mass of damp curls, my toenails painted hot pink, and my arms encircling the waist of someone semidivine.

If we'd been Italian, would I have gone to the *rotonda sul mare*? The high moon shines the same silver on the water, dancing in an open pavilion at the sea is the same, my sisters nowhere in sight. The local boys of summer are dark, with black eyes, and as a teenager I would have loved to dance with them.

We take several drives down the coast, where we find a splendid stretch of the Adriatic, the natural park of Conero, and the tiny towns of Sirolo, Portonovo, and Numana. Who would not love a home along this coast? We make a plan to visit Portonovo with our grandson next summer. The hotel there is an authentic walled Napoleonic fort from 1810, perched over the sea.

Before we check out, we take a soak in the hamam downstairs. We lounge in the tile chairs and let the warm waters swirl around us. The hotel description is right. It does rock of a harmonious daily ritual.

Circles on My Map— Umbria and Beyond

ASSISI, HOME OF SAN FRANCESCO

IN UMBRIA, ASSISI HAS A PROFOUND ATTRACTION no number of tourists can dissipate. Ed and I often return for the immense pleasure of seeing this pale stone town dramatically positioned against its hillside. We come here to venerate San Francesco and Santa Chiara, immortalized in their own churches, to see the Romanesque facade of Duomo di San Rufino, and to gaze at the Tempio di Minerva, whose severe columns stand strongly for the ancient world. We're only an hour away, so this is a gift we often exchange. "Why don't we drive over to Assisi," Ed will say on an idle day.

The main parking lot heaves with buses unloading religious tour groups and art lovers who throng the lower church of Basilica San Francesco for the Giotto frescoes. We all file onto the outdoor escalator that raises us (assumes us?) into town. The great pilgrimage sites always have been crowded with seekers and sellers. Seeing nuns from all over the world in their various habits, watching pilgrims buying wooden San Francesco crosses, hearing bearded young men singing and strumming in the piazza is part of the experience. If you haven't heard "Kum Bay Ya" since Methodist Youth Fellowship, this is the place.

As we enter the main gate of town, the July sun seems to pour down from a great chalice onto our baking heads. Today the crush of other tourists is daunting. I try to follow my photographer friend Steven's advice: See as through a lens. Look up, or down, or around at the carved stone and magical street shrines and green courtyards and doors that open into palaces.

An African group in colorful garb sits down in the first piazza and starts up a lugubrious hymn. "Do you think there's such a thing as a global soul?" Ed asks out of nowhere.

A global soul. I have to think. "Well, I suppose so. Isn't the mineral content of the human body compositionally the same as the mineral content of the earth—I mean, in the same proportions?" He seems okay with the response, but I don't know how the Africans singing a Catholic hymn provoked him. Probably just the United Nations component of Assisi.

❧

DURING A SIESTA stroll through this ancient town, where well-fed alley cats curl under a lavender plant, I suddenly experience a joyous release from the present tense. I madly wish I could photograph all the fantastic iron door knockers, or paint the coral geraniums tumbling from a balcony. The aroma of roast chicken drifting from a window makes me want to tap on the door and introduce myself to the man in the wife-beater undershirt reading the paper at the window. He's privileged to glance up at any time of day and look at the rose window of San Rufino, as we do now.

"That rose window looks like a doily that Domenica crochets on her winter nights," I notice. This is a church Ed particularly likes for its solid bell tower from 1028, the oldest part of the church, and the stone zodiac signs around the main door. The construction lagged so long that you can trace the change from Romanesque toward Gothic as your eye and time move up the facade. The inside has been remodeled and no longer speaks the stark primitive language of the outside, but you can run your finger around the rim of the marble font where both Francesco and Chiara were baptized.

~

I MUST VISIT the flying buttresses of Santa Chiara's church of striped pink and white stone, and go inside to say *ciao* to her mortal body lying on view, her face a waxy brown, like beef jerky.

"That's a poem," Ed says, pointing toward Chiara's rose window.

"Do you think the form simply evolved from the older oculus windows of the ancient buildings?"

"Maybe, seems logical. What makes them so pure? I guess it's the contrast of the hard stone carved into a lacy design."

"Yes, stone so heavy and the design absolutely airy."

"I like the name as much as the windows. Rose windows. These are so much simpler than Notre Dame and Chartres."

"A whole different gesture."

The upper church of the Basilica has an important rose window, too. Not that these windows are the prime attractions of Assisi. We'll leave that to Giotto's frescoes, and to those of Cimabue, Simone Martini, and Lorenzetti. But the perk of return visits is that you get to ferret out nuances of a place, and often those connect to you personally more than the five-star attractions.

Wandering neighborhoods, arm in arm, we glance in open windows. The laughter and shouting inside, dishes rattling, cage with a finch, the crocheted curtains, climbing roses, and pots of hydrangeas all speak clearly about life in Assisi. Ed stops to inspect a pot of basil on a stoop. I just stare, imprinting a faded blue door into my brain.

San Francesco in his rough brown robe lies inside, sleeping off the heat and dreaming of holding out his hand to a wolf.

⁓

ITALY IS ENDLESS. My favorite short trips are to places that remain uniquely themselves. Small towns especially yield an intimate experience—and you find an immediate sense of the place's essence. You may also have closer encounters with people, always a bonus in Italy.

Last week, en route to Venice, where we met friends, we hopped off the train for a night in Ferrara in Emilia Romagna. Ferrara deserves a long chapter and I can't wait to go back. If "Best Places to Live in Italy" lists are compiled, surely Ferrara makes the top echelon. The town is flat and open, with handsome buildings, numerous palaces, bell towers, arcaded walks, and a populace on bicycles. Bicycles everywhere, with clusters of people who've stopped to talk while balancing their bikes. From just a whirl in this marvelous city, I absorbed its strength and dignity. What other city has such extensive Renaissance town walls, open splendid piazzas, and tree-lined streets full of birdsong?

The forceful Palazzo dei Diamanti, Diamond Palazzo, takes its name from the faceted stone facade. Inside, we had the Ferrara School of painters to ourselves. The security guards were all reading books. The Este family powerbrokers, who held court here, left their indelible stamp of culture and history. More recently, the Bassani novel and De Sica film, *The Garden of the Finzi-Continis,* leaves a scrim of sadness over the place for the Fascist-era fate of Jews, who'd previously, from the seventeenth century until the mid-nineteenth century, been shuffled into a ghetto area. Under the plaque listing names and commemorating lost Jews, café tables host throngs of cheerful people partaking of a late-afternoon *aperitivo*.

We happened into a small restaurant that I like to think represents the town well, Quel Fantastico Giovedi (That Fantastic Thursday), the name taken from the translated title of John Steinbeck's novel *Sweet Thursday*. Memorable, the *budino* of peas with gorgonzola fondant, the scallops with fennel, spinach ravioli stuffed with quail, then the ambrosial peach sorbet.

Lacking bicycles, we walked for hours in Ferrara.

~

CLOSER TO HOME, we often drive guests over to Bagno Vignoni, where a thermal spring with curative properties runs downhill through a travertine ditch. Often our guests have pulled a muscle hoisting suitcases or twisted an ankle walking on stony streets in high heels. We take them to the waters. Early morning is the time to go and soak your feet, even if they don't hurt. By noon, many Italians have arrived, ready for the mineral properties of the hot water to infuse their work-sore feet. They hike their skirts and trousers, lower their feet, and heal. In town, a thermal pool takes the place of the usual piazza and you can imagine Lorenzo Il Magnifico floating like a water lily.

~

ON ISOLA MAGGIORE, an island in Umbria's Lago Trasimeno, a walk at midnight returns you to a lost time when the village was home to fishermen and the castle-monastery brooding on the end of the island hosted St. Francis for a visit. Cornucopia-shaped nets still dry on the main street. Through a window, you see a woman making lace by lamplight. In a place with no cars, a human proportion asserts itself. You can walk in silence, watching the dimpling light of stars on the water.

⌒

IN RECENT YEARS, we've been attracted to the south. Matera, way down in Basilicata, is a strange town where people once— not long ago—lived in a vast hive of caves, most now eerily empty, some restored to use. The rest of the town seems to thrive, but at its heart lies this primitive maze, a place to wander and contemplate life as you don't know it.

Then on to Alberobello in Apulia, with white conical houses called *trulli,* which look both ancient and at the same time like something from another planet. You half-expect space cadets to emerge.

You could happily spend a month exploring the castles and hunting lodges of Frederick II, the unique Baroque town of Lecce, and the charming port town of Gallipoli. Despite growing tourism, this whole region is still fresh with the possibility of discovery. I especially like the duomo towns of Trani, Bitonto, and Otranto. It's worth the trip just for the bread, gargantuan loaves that could feed a tribe of forty, and for the hearty pasta dishes created by those who worked hard on the land.

Amalfi, Capri, Vicenza, Cormons, Verona, Torino, Trieste. Italy *is* endless.

Signorelli's Bones

Vade Mecum—Come with me.

— ROMAN TOMBSTONE INSCRIPTION

IF YOU ARE DEAD IN ITALY, YOU ARE NOT AS dead as you could be. Looking out from the Piazza del Duomo, I see the walled cemetery just below town, on the same slope. From here it seems to mirror the town, only the paths among the graves are more ordered than the snaky streets of Cortona. I can't see the flowers that I know are there—fresh, too, not just dusty plastic. The comune recently constructed a sidewalk down to the cemetery for all those who walk that way on Saturday afternoon with their armfuls of glads or jars of yard roses. They're on their way to the weekly care and feeding of the dead. Funerals, too, go on foot from the churches in town. Mourners, sleet or sun, follow the hearse for the second part of the service.

I am walking down myself, though it is Monday. I am going to lay a spray of lavender on the grave of our friend Alain, who died last week. Lavender because he was French and I associate lavender always with Provence. I must meander, because I don't know where he lies.

In the past few years, we'd unaccountably lost touch with Alain and I didn't even know he had died until three days after. In our early years here, we were tangentially part of a tight circle of older writers who'd been expats together in Rome. All of them permanently migrated up to Cortona, where several had bought houses earlier, during the Red Brigade years. Alain was the wittiest of the group and entertained often. They were, one and all, imbued with the fatalism, ribald humor, and cynicism that overcomes expats.

Even in the country, he maintained a formality. I'm sure he wore a nifty sport coat and tie even sitting at his bedroom desk. He held forth, a one-man show, and never repeated an anecdote. He loved to talk books and politics. Muriel Spark often was at his table when we dined. At least once a week for years, we met at each other's houses, often for feasts under the olive trees or at Il Vallone, a pizzeria where the sun-loving owner wore bronze makeup in winter. With her also bronze ringlets piled above her head, she looked like a misplaced opera singer, except that she wore slip-on scuffs that reminded me of an exhausted housewife. It was at Alain and his partner Ben's house that we met Ann Cornelisen, that strong prose stylist, who became our closest friend in Italy. Now, it seems impossible, almost all of these forces lie under the earth.

At the cemetery entrance, two large bins mounded with empty soda bottles attest to the number of people who come to water plants on graves. Through the dark of an arched corridor, I emerge into the harsh light of the bone yard. As they lived in town, so they lie—the stone dwellings with hardly a handspan between them. The first name I notice—the painter Gino Severini. His is a plain box above ground, rather like an Etruscan sarcophagus. Here he is, dead as anyone. But his epitaph proclaims otherwise: *Non omnis moriar.* Not all of me shall die. I wonder if Signorelli lies anywhere near, though no grave seems to be older than 1850.

The walls hold chest-of-drawer graves, each with a heart-rending photo of the inhabitant, caught at a moment of full life. There are the motorcycle graves. At least every year we lose a young man to the adrenaline rush of passing on a curve. Many photos show the gnarly faces of the old *contadini* generations that are now quickly passing. Others proclaim Conte and Contessa, superior even in death. I run my finger along the worn carved letters: Artemisia, Laudomia, Sparteo. Lovely old names—Girolamo, Oreste, Assuntina, Felicino, Salvatore, Conforta, Oliviero, Guglielmina, Ersilia, Zeffiro, Quintilio, Italo, Candida. Will anyone ever again choose to name a boy Giovanni Battista, John the Baptist?

So many Umbertos from the late nineteenth century when Umberto I reigned, so many Elenas a little later, namesakes of Elena of Montenegro, mother of Italy's last king. I stop before Orte Baracci, whose stone simply says, *Fronte Russo, 1943.* His rough wool uniform probably did not protect him from Russia's frozen steppes, but he's smiling under his regimental hat with an outrageous feather plume drooping to his shoulder. And near him a man born in 1918, end of another war, with the strong name of Libero, Free.

I do not find a fresh mound heaped with decaying flowers. Perhaps he is outside the walls. I navigate through internal hallways lined with the floor-to-ceiling dead, pass a dank crypt, and step out into the open field. Ah, better to rest out in the *campo* with the infidels and paupers, amid the blooming lacy white flowers and the weedy grasses. The rose-topped recent grave is not Alain's. A ladybug tests a rose leaf and promptly flies off.

Most of these lack stones, which will hold down the bones

on Judgment Day. Out here the skeletons can just claw through the dirt, stand erect, and assume their bodies again. Signorelli's great fresco cycle in the duomo at Orvieto depicts souls emerging from under the crust of the earth. In the painting, as in a dream, you can feel a literal rush of ecstasy and astonishment as the beautiful flesh returns. This must be our most profound hope: *Say it isn't so.* I wish I could summon a particle of belief that a Judgment Day will restore me, along with billions of others. I would again be twenty in a yellow bathing suit, sitting on the side of a pool with three gorgeous boys in the water around my feet. If I were truly religious, I think life would cling to me less. After all, it's only a proving ground for eternity where I will greet my parents and we'll dress in snowy cotton and attend a long choir practice. Heaven is a fantastic idea. I'm afraid, though, that death is an absolute. For me, a walk in a cemetery makes me want to throw myself over an Alpha and Omega and weep.

I remember Alain's upstairs study with all his books in French, English, and Italian. I remember Sunday lunches in winter with the lemon soufflé made on top of the stove and a fire in the grate warming my back. I remember the glint in his eyes before the punch line and the affable laugh afterward. His little salon with draped couches and cushions, deep reds and blues, seemed exotically foreign and I remember the charge of the new I felt encountering the old world. I remember his French cuffs and his big dog, the stepped garden and the grape pergola where he served Campari and soda. I don't find his grave.

◦～◦

IN HIS *Lives of the Most Excellent Painters, Sculptors, and Architects,* Vasari tells a revealing and moving story. When a plague swept through Cortona in 1502, Signorelli's son, already training to be a painter, died. Signorelli undressed him and drew his naked body "so that, by the work of his own hand, he would always be able to have before his eyes that which nature had given him and which adverse destiny had snatched away." Signorelli is said to have made anatomical studies in the local cemetery. Did he have a body exhumed, or did he appear with his sharpened *lapis* before burial? Of all the Renaissance painters, Luca's forms are the most alive. He loved distracting you from the main subject with a well-placed male buttock, tightly clad, a servant's copious thighs through her skirt, or the quite buff chest of a minor figure off to the side of a martyrdom in progress. Weird to think his dynamic bodies originated here among the dead. I always look at his paintings and recognize people I see in the piazza. I trace the cast-down eyes of the pizza server to an exalted Annunciation Mary, and the rippled curls and short legs of a local antiques dealer to the flagellated Christ. He must have crouched there, against the wall, with his pens. I like Vasari's story of his dual life as an artist and as a family man, active in government as a Cortona magistrate. His death at eighty-two catapulted him into a new and eternal relationship with his chosen place. *Where do your bones lie, Luca?*

〜

BY NOW WE have attended many funerals. Although I've stood by while graves were filled with dirt, I can't locate any of them. I was sure Lorenzo's brother Umberto was *there,* but no. And Francesco Zappini. I thought he was in the right wall. When Francesco died, we visited him at home, where he rested on the matrimonial bed with the family's cat asleep at his feet, as on a medieval marble sarcophagus.

The baker has died, the tailor, Anselmo, and Placido's brother Bruno, whose liver transplant finally failed him. At the end of the olive harvest season last fall, our dear Primo Bianchi, restorer of Bramasole, fell from a ladder in his grove. In our winter absences, we lost the wandering artist who hitchhiked all over the area with canvases under his arm, and the hunchbacked man who delivered groceries. At Ernesto's wake, he lay under a veil over the open coffin, surrounded by Anna and his daughters. Margherita would not let go of his cold hand, which seemed to have reached out from under the veil. Then, last winter when we were here, Amalia. On a freezing March day, we sat around the open coffin in the cold church with the family. From my vantage, only her gray nose was visible above the side of the coffin, a little sail setting out for the afterlife.

The church is always jammed. The priest always weeps, which engenders waves of weeping all the way to the back of the church. I find it offensive that volunteers pass baskets for collection. Once I saw that someone had dropped in a breath mint. Hardly anyone sings the hymns, but everyone knows the words to the funeral mass. Even I have picked up phrases. The crowd takes the long walk together to the cemetery, where the gaping grave is not disguised by Astroturf. The coffin goes down and two grave diggers set to. Then final handfuls of dirt are thrown while the priest prays. The grave diggers pound down the dirt into a smooth hump, the headstone is placed, flowers arranged, and that's that. Everyone knows with total finality that the person is dead.

⌒

Only one other person is here. On Mondays the dead are left to their own devices. A woman in a printed housedress is mopping out one of the mausoleums. The family members' slabs line the side walls. Fresh linen and flowers adorn the altar. One prayer chair furnishes this home away from home.

I peer inside several others. Some are neglected, the trinity of plants dead, the altar cloth dusty.

Out the back gate of the cemetery, I find discarded tomb-stones and iron crosses. Did their families die out, leaving no one to pay their rent? I could take them to my house, prop them up among the olive trees. Would anyone mind?

The most affecting part of the cemetery is a wall lined with the oldest stones. These send back messages. One commemo-rates two small *sorelle,* sisters, taken by *la cruda difterite,* the harsh diphtheria, in 1874. Another marks other sisters, victims of *malevoli insinuazioni.* What? Malevolent insinuations? Am I beginning a heat stroke, here at noon in the July sun? What could that mean? Another mourns *"La cruda difterite tolse la vita a me."* The same diphtheria "took my life." The sun beats a slow rhythm on my head. This is a long audit of the past. Since the mid-twentieth century, with the sperm count spiral-ing down, ten, twenty percent, approaching forty percent, the future should be my worry. If I want to worry, the low Italian *birth* rate should be my focus. We're on a course so that long before five thousand million years, when the sun evolves into a red giant, ready to collapse, no one will be around to care. This place will have joined the jillions of specks in the universe along with Alain's lemon soufflé, his crisp blue shirts, Francesco's memory of the long walk back from Russia with no shoes, the flour on the baker's hands, the stunned faces of Bruno's young daughters, the cold wake in the octagonal church, the veil over Ernesto, the amused twinkle in Primo's blue, blue eyes, the priest who cried.

But Zelinda Dragoni's 127-year-old passion, for now, en-dures. She must have had time to compose her epitaph in 1881. She addresses Luigi, "My first and only love on earth. I will always speak with God of the great affection and of the com-passionate care, that you vested in me and to Him I will recommend our Ida. *Addio, Addio.*" Ida must have been a daughter, who seems here to be something of an afterthought. Another stone (1852) implores the reader: "Scatter tears and flowers on this field of death." Okay, no problem.

My phone rings, shattering this communion. "Where are you?" Ed asks. "Do you want me to reheat the chicken for lunch? It's after one." I glance up at the town above, where I see a woman as I was earlier, leaning on the duomo wall, looking down at the small city of the dead. Briefly I wonder what she is thinking.

And so I leave my bundle of lavender propped against a lichen-etched stone cross with no name.

Addio, Addio.

Amici—
Friends

"WHEN IS THE CUBAN INVASION?" MASSIMO ASKS.

"Have you heard from them?" Lorenzo calls from his doorway.

"What's the news of the *Cubani*?" Edo gets out his phone. "Let's call them."

"*Ciao*—you know Luca was looking for Alberto?" someone I don't even know asks me.

As the nearest neighbors and good friends of the Alfonso clan, we're constant conduits of information about their papal-level entrances and exits from town. Their annual arrival signals *vacation* as clearly as if the word appeared over the town in skywriting. They bring their Cuban laid-back charm and contagious *gusto di vivere*. Everyone has fallen in love with this family, seventeen strong, who bought Casa Caravita, an ancient house just above Bramasole. They can't all stay in the house, so a couple of apartments are rented for various configurations of the three brothers, their wives and total of eight children, plus mama Rose, Uncle Enrique, and sometimes an aunt from Spain. Though the father died several years ago, I often sense he's come along for the prolonged party and just happens to be invisible.

I will not forget the summer night I met Alberto at the Cardinalis' pergola table. Placido had sold him a piece of land adjacent to his house and invited us over to meet *"questo Cubano molto simpatico."* We had heard in the piazza that a mysterious Cuban-American had bought the house above us. Because trees hide it, I'd never even seen this oldest farm on the hillside. The chief of the *polizia* used to live there. We heard him every day summoning his dog. *Vieni qui,* he called, come here. We always referred to the hidden house as Casa Vieni Qui. Alberto's restoration had been accomplished in record time. Miracle. I was curious.

We were a little late, and Placido invariably calls out *"A tavola,"* to the table, on the stroke of eight. We squeezed in, shoulder to shoulder, as Fiorella was bringing out the platter of prosciutto and melon. I had the luck to sit across from Alberto. He was there with two colleagues from his architectural firm, Elizabeth and Secondo, both of whom had bought apartments in Cortona and were in stages of restoration. From down the table there were lamentations over what was or was not hooked up and excitement at progress. Ah, hot water. Windows that open and close. Italians like roof and drainage discussions, too; they're dealing with their own stone nightmare dream houses.

Normally the subject enthralls me, but I was riveted by Alberto. He has a full-out laugh and looks like someone Caravaggio would have liked to paint: black dense hair like Bacchus, tropical skin, and a look in his eyes—the shining brown of chestnuts—that's quick, direct, and keeps something hidden. I could see that he was ready to be amused. Later, I'd learn of his empathetic nature, his god-given talent as a painter, his ambitious architectural projects, and his knowledge of Italian architectural history.

"Well, what are you working on?" Alberto asked me. I explained that I was in the middle of a book of travel narratives and Ed and I were on the road a lot. "What do you want to do next?" he persisted.

"I've been looking for a house in the South—in North Carolina—and I would love to build a little town there, based on things I like about Tuscan houses." This popped out, not premeditated.

Ed and I recently had decided to leave California and move back to my southern roots. He went to grad school in Virginia and always had an attraction to the South. We had not then found a house with an intact soul. We had been talking a lot as we filed in and out of houses about what we, right now, value in four sheltering walls. I mentioned a term paper I wrote in college on "The Ideal Place of Learning." *Come down out of the clouds,* my professor had written across the top in a crabbed scrawl. B plus. We were looking for a little farm and hoping for a creek, but had found only perfect new houses or cramped cottages.

Alberto laughed. "Really! A *town?* That sounds so *interesting.*" "Interesting," I found, is one of his words, pronounced with a drawn-out first syllable and used either sincerely or ironically or to mean *not* interesting. This time he obviously was intrigued by the wild idea.

We fell into conversation about the mutually favorite subject, architecture. We talked stone, we talked water, we talked land. The dinner swarmed around us but we had found shared obsessions and it's hard to stop that, even for Fiorella's apricot *crostata.* I learned a little about his practice, the airport, museums, and houses he'd designed, then the *sotto voce* admission: "What I really want to do is paint; I bought my house here so that it would bring me closer to painting."

And I confessed, "I wanted to be an architect. Back then, I just did not have the vision."

We've been talking ever since: emailing, meeting at his office in Tampa, meeting in Rome, sending books, calling from airports, meeting in North Carolina, and best of all, meeting in the piazza or my herb garden or on a trail at Fonte.

Our families just give us space. After all, who wants to listen for hours to talk about the layout of a William Werther farmhouse built in Santa Cruz in 1926? Or to discuss how a church near the Florence airport looks like Corbusier's chapel at Ronchamp? Who will tramp through Rome in the rain to verify whether Bramante's Tempietto actually measures the same as the oculus in the Pantheon?[1]

I have had the gift of several such friendships in my life, just enough to know how rare they are. When you meet a true friend, I find, you recognize each other immediately. "Do you remember the first time we met?" I asked him recently.

He answered, "First in the bottega in Firenze the summer of 1492, just after Il Magnifico's death, where we learned to crush pigments."

Yes, exactly then.

~

A COUPLE OF days after that dinner, Alberto called. "Are you serious about your Utopian town? Because I'd like to work on something like that."

~

WE CALL OUR town Montelauro, mountain of laurels. We see it near a river. We run all over Tuscany photographing houses and details and entrances to towns and piazzas and bridges and pergolas and arches. We each buy a better camera. We love the golden mean. We measure felicitous buildings, getting to the square root of ideal human scale. Ed loves the idea. He wants Italian chefs coming in to Montelauro on a rotating basis. Alberto's brother Carlos, an architect with business sense, becomes enthusiastic, as does brother Tony, who starts scouting land on Internet sites. Alberto buys black sketchbooks for each of us and we make notes of street names, lenders, and trees to plant. I feel that I'm again inside a club-house made of packing crates. Password: Montelauro.

⌒

As it happens this morning, when I'm asked all the questions about the Cubani, I do have an answer. "They're arriving on Tuesday. All of them."

⌒

On Tuesday morning I cut a big armful of blue hydrangeas and Ed prepares a basket of olive oil, jars of our tomatoes—enough for their month-long visit—and fruit, bread, and cheese. Even though their house is close enough that we can shout to each other—sound carries on a hillside—the climb is steep. We load the Fiat and drive around Torreone, then along their goat-track road. I see wild white lilies on the hillside and the ginger-speckled orange ones below the Etruscan wall that borders their land. What an extravagant wildflower—spontaneous lilies. I take it as omen. In the Renaissance someone would have built a chapel there. A housekeeper is airing sheets on the line.

Just as we're unloading, the first wave of Alfonsos arrive: Tony, the middle brother; his wife, Joy; their three children; Uncle Enrique (called Nico); and Mama Rose. First item out of the van: Tony's guitar. We flash on great evenings to come. They're wild to see the rose pergola, the new pool, and the lavender planted last year, now waving wands of scent.

Later, we hear Carlos and Dorothy arrive with their three, then we get a call from Alberto—late plane—driving madly with Susan and their two children from Rome.

We expect they're tired and will throw together a pasta and turn in, but around ten, as we exit from the pizzeria, there's commotion in the piazza and we know the Alfonso clan has taken up residence again. Luca, their architect, Massimo, Edo, and Maria have found them, and the Cynar and Averno and grappa are pouring. The children are coming and going from the gelateria and kicking a soccer ball. There is always laughter in the piazza, but with them around, the stones reverberate.

We're all back again the next morning. The women shop to stock the kitchen, the men arrange tennis matches and wine delivery, the children explore. Our table in the piazza fills and shifts—Placido, Chiara, Simone, Claudio, Melva and Jim, Sheryl and Rob, Marco, Cecelia with her new baby, and her English husband, Lee, who is obviously smitten with little Tommaso. Some leave and come back. Ed goes off to the bookstore in search of a dialect dictionary. Fulvio pauses only a second; he's always in a hurry. I am not in a hurry this morning. Alberto and I stay because there's much to say. Davide waves from the door of his hair salon. He's ready for Ed's appointment. When we asked him how he achieves Ed's finger-in-the-electrical-socket haircut, Davide said, "First I make a thousand errors, then I connect the errors." Ed thought it sounded like a life philosophy. Massimo brings out another tray of water and coffee. We plan a trip to Orvieto to look at Signorelli's frescoes and have lunch at a place he and Susan read about. Marco announces a dinner on the porch of the Teatro after a late-afternoon wine tasting at his *enoteca*.

᭐

ABOUT FIFTY GATHER for the buffet. We sit with Dorothy and Carlos and catch up on news. "Sharon Stone, welcome back," several call to Dorothy. There's a resemblance, but Dorothy is really prettier. Marco proposes a toast to the Alfonsos' return, then we have another toast to Marco's birthday. His mother, Eta, is an estimable person. Her lavish buffet draws us all back to the table. She presides, insisting that no one is eating. I've seen pictures of her as a young beauty in white holding an armful of flowers in some long-ago parade. Now she's a matriarch, pale and tall for an Italian woman, with three grandchildren. With Marco and his brother Paolo, she and husband, gentle Giuliano, run the efficient market on the piazza, as well as the *enoteca*. They *work*. Their store is smaller than the chips-and-dips aisle at an American supermarket and yet everything you need is right at hand. Somehow Eta has time to pause for a chat, to offer a recipe, and to tell me to buy one brand over another. You can see her striding through the parterre park early in the morning and heading home at one, no doubt about to prepare a hefty *pranzo*.

We tease Marco that he should become mayor but he prefers ever increasing his knowledge about Italian wines. Paolo prefers soccer. Enza, Marco's smart wife, works with the University of Georgia art program, while Paolo's wife owns a baby clothing shop—so the entire family mingles and chats in the piazza all day. Nothing passes their notice and all of them have a bright *ciao,* a hug, or a joke for everyone passing through. Even Marco and Enza's boy is falling into stride. At nine, he's having fun restocking shelves and running errands.

Marco makes many rounds with his wines. Each one has its own story. Just over the town hall, I catch a glimpse of a high full moon, coming out just in time to light the piazza like a lamp in one's own living room.

I think one reason Cortona fell hard for the Alfonso clan is that they remind everyone of something Italians miss—the big, close family. With the lowest birth rate in Europe, Italians have lost an integral part of their culture in one generation. The norm is one child, or none. Couples often wait to marry until their mid-thirties. Unmarried grown children usually stay at home. It's still common for the elderly to live with their middle-aged children, but no longer are there several small ones running around to care for.

The Alfonsos radiate family. They also have many friends who visit and they obviously love their friends, another quality Italians cherish.

The "herd," as Alberto calls his group, will be invited to share many dinners during their time here. A stereotype persists about how expats live in Tuscany. It goes like this: Every day the rich property owner goes out to lunch, drinks several glasses of wine, and retires to the villa until time to go out to dinner. Locals are seen as curious fauna placed strategically for said foreigner's amusement. Expat speaks no Italian and relies on speaking English loud enough that *surely* the locals will understand. Expat will be tolerated because of spending power, but will not be invited to private homes.

Maybe this curious specimen exists somewhere, but I do not see him or her around these parts. I'd guess that foreigners own fifty houses. Many who've bought here have stretched to do so. Or they've moved savings out of traditional investments and put it into a place they can enjoy. Smart move. Some few are really rich but not in any ostentatious way. The Americans I know are genuinely involved in the community, have many friends, and work on their own land and projects. They do everything from contributing to charities to singing in choirs. They travel with a sharp sense of cultural interest and an adventurous spirit. The houses they've restored were, generally, not snatched out of the hands of Italian buyers but were, like ours, abandoned or falling into ruin. The foreigners

have—whether they thought about it that way or not—
rescued important parts of the patrimony.

The local people like the energy of the Georgia students
and the expat residents. An English woman told me that a
merchant called her a "filthy foreign bitch" when she put in a
small window—with permission—facing his house. I had my
xenophobic incident, too. But this behavior remains rare.
There are nuts anywhere! More typical is Placido, who invites
total strangers he meets in town to come to dinner, or Lapo,
who lives down the road. He often stops by and drops off a
round of fresh pecorino. Sometimes we go to his place and
help make the cheese. When he invites us this time, I say that
we have guests, my nephew and his family, and that the
Cubans are coming over, too.

"Bring them all, *tutti, nessun problema.*" He throws open
his arms, which is part of his invitation. And so we arrive, our
own little tour group. Lapo is a shepherd but also a canny busi-
nessman. He and his wife, Paola, with their daughters, Laura
and Ilaria, turned two stone farm buildings into guesthouses.
They built a pool and, lo, they had an *agriturismo*. They are
happy to meet their guests, and those who stay there couldn't
have landed in a more hospitable setting. Lapo and Paola grill
almost every night and the outdoor tables seldom have empty
seats.

Now he starts cooking the fresh sheep milk and then adds
the rennet. After a few minutes for cooling, he rolls up his
sleeves and starts to raise and dip the curds that are quickly
bonding. When the mixture forms an oozy, primitive clump,
he sets us to work pressing milky glops into molds, easing out
the water, compacting the mass.

This feels like the work of the world, something so fundamental that it seems we already should know the whole

process. The children are engrossed. We each make our own satisfying, truly artisan cheese. Paola sets out platters of their cheeses at various stages of aging, their own salamis, and wine. Lapo puts an LP on the turntable. The youngest child has never seen such a relic before, which makes me recall the wind-up Victrola in the back hall of my grandmother's house.

"This is the music of my father from before the war." Lapo turns up the volume and pulls me to the middle of the cheese-shed floor. The music takes us back a lifetime or more, half polka, half torch song. He twirls me around—oh, he's good; these Tuscans always know how to dance. He's my height, five foot four, but in the confidence of his muscular body, he feels tall and lithe.

He gives everyone hunks of pecorino to take home and a week later drops off the rounds we've made, along with some of his own ricotta, honey, and olive oil. The Alfonsos take an album of photos and my nephew's children send text messages to friends in Atlanta, a world away from the dusty donkey they rode in the afternoon.

⁓

WILL THIS MONTELAURO, place of beauty and harmony, ever rise off the North Carolina dirt? Will we ever give classes in stone-wall building or import *cotto* for floors? As many before me have said, *the journey, not the arrival, matters.* The project becomes an *aide-mémoire,* and keeps us aware *of why* Tuscany is the way it is. *How* it works. We talk to Italian architects. Alberto draws floor plans on napkins in the café. We build a scale model of our village. What fun to use equipment architects take for granted. You can press a few keys and "see" the building from various elevations and perspectives. Alberto paints watercolors of our ideal buildings and I plan landscaping and write descriptions of fields of goldenrod, wild plum, and lupine. I can see a riverine walk through lush grasses spiked with blue chicory. We talk about a medieval garden of simples. With words and paints we create an ideal town. I can almost walk the streets, see inside a window a stone hearth with a little fire of twigs, the benison of Carolina afternoon light striking a pewter bowl of pomegranates on the table.

In Book Ten of his *Confessions,* St. Augustine wrote of memory as a "great field or a spacious palace, a storehouse for countless images of all kinds." Montelauro is our memory palace.

Playdates for grown-ups—the pleasures are immense. Plus, even better, we laugh in the same places.

⌒

IN OUR EARLY years here, we used to avoid other Americans, which was easy because there were not many. We had our tight group of writer friends, but otherwise, we came to be with Italians, we told one another. Gradually we realized that we came to be with people we loved, no matter where they hailed from. Being friends with Americans and English and French residents also increased our numbers of Italian friends because we met friends of friends. Also, I got lonesome for American women friends. Now, especially with three couples, we keep a book exchange going, help each other haul plants from the nursery, and trade info about construction, changing immigrant laws, and news from home. We go on hikes and little trips, entertain each other at long dinners, and, of course, run into each other in the piazza. Lavishing attention on proper stonework and authentic colors, our friends have made spectacular gardens and homes, one small jewel, one farmhouse, and one villa.

Through chance meetings in the piazza and at Marco and Arnaldo's wine dinners and tastings, we've met other expats like us, though generally they are new and we've been around so long by now that we feel that metaphorical taproot probing down among the Etruscan middens. My former attitude—we're here to be only among Europeans—was provincial. Our connection with other settlers complements the primary experience. I am yet to meet someone who is here by lucky choice who does not *get it*.

There is a group of other Americans, mostly painters and photographers, who don't live here but out of love for the place return every year. They, too, have their circles of friends and habits of work. One woman, Anna, a great reader, lives for a couple of months a year in one of the convents where the nuns dote on her. Another, Robin, who has a beauty like a thirties film star, comes in for a few weeks, dazzles us with her photographs, and suddenly is gone. I watch for the artists painting watercolor landscapes in the hills around town and sympathetically inhabit their perches overlooking cypress lanes with columns of light and half-melon domes punctuating a vista of olive groves.

Is it too late to take painting classes? Candace, teach me how to daub that lavender light behind your three white jars. No, not white—I see subtle cream streaks and gray undertones (so pure with the lavender). How? By staring long at Morandi's pure forms? *Do these artists feel themselves under your protective cloak, Luca?*

Up at the Alfonsos' house, every day after lunch, Alberto, Carlos, and several of the children retire to private outdoor spots and sketch or paint. Carlos sometimes gets up at dawn and goes out photographing that delicious silvery light on the olives and architectural fragments. Albert Joseph, Alberto and Susan's son, at age eleven tries out the geometric style of Gino Severini, the Futurist painter who was born in Cortona. Olivia, their fourteen-year-old, brings me a sunflower she has painted. The face almost fills the paper and, yes, it feels *crazed with light*. I prop it over my desk for inspiration. If I knew where Luca is buried, I would leave it on his stone. *See, Luca, your legacy.*

∾

WE SET THE table inside because the forecast says rain. Once when I heard the report, the meteorologist apologized at the end and said he was sorry but he'd read last week's weather. So, we'll see. No clouds all afternoon when the Alfonsos come up for a swim. Gilda is coming to help us and she will bring several dishes. I know because when she starts up her bread oven, she just won't quit.

I could dine on the flowers alone—face-sized white hydrangeas in a white pottery bowl. We often have casual dinners but tonight—glasses for each wine, place cards, two *secondi* (Italians often serve two entrées but I usually serve one), candles in hurricane lamps, and the napkins Melva gave me. They're the size of head scarves and monogrammed with the initials of someone long gone. We leave a small flashlight beside Placido's place, as we always do to tease him because he complains that he cannot see what he's eating in dim candlelight.

Alberto takes the children home, settles them in for the evening, and returns with the other adults. They arrive just as Melva and Jim and Placido and Fiorella are turning in the gate. How joyous to see this phalanx of friends, faces brushed with late sunlight, crossing the grass in their summery colors of pink hibiscus, saffron, aqua, and lemon.

No rain at all. Gilda brings out an *aperitivo* she's invented with grapefruit juice and Campari, so pretty in the glass pitcher with floating tiny berries and mint leaves. We serve the *crostini* and slowly move to the table.

～

THE MENU

Fiori di zucchini fritti
Fried zucchini flowers

Crostini:
Aglio arrosto con noce
Roasted garlic with walnuts

Tre pomodori (arrosti, secchi, e freschi)
Three tomatoes: roasted, sun-dried, fresh

Gorgonzola e salvia
Gorgonzola and sage

PRIMO
Lasagne con tartufo e besciamella
Truffle and béchamel lasagna

SECONDO
Anatra con miele e arancio
Duck with honey and orange

Faraona arrosto con pancetta
Guinea hen with pancetta

CONTORNI
Patate arrosto al forno
Potatoes roasted in the oven

Bietole con aglio e pignole
Chard with garlic and pine nuts

Insalata del orto
Salad from the garden

DOLCE
Pesche ripiene con mandorle e mascarpone
Peaches stuffed with almonds and mascarpone

Torta di susine
Plum tart

⌒‿‿◦

After dessert, Tony takes up his guitar and we all sing "Guantanamera," "Ivory Tower," "Blue Moon," and several Beatles songs, Tony's specialty. He and Alberto harmonize. I love it when Tony shifts to falsetto. Clearly, they've done this before. Uncle Nico tells stories of Rome when he lived there in the seventies. Placido and Carlos talk hunting. We plan an excursion to the Etruscan tombs. Talk, talk, talk. On into the night.

In summer, every day turns into an adventure. Just a morning in the piazza is adventure enough, but the trips and cooking marathons and *bocce* matches draw all of us into closer and closer circles of friendship.

Riccardo and Silvia celebrate their anniversary with a party at their cooking school. They've recently converted an outbuilding at Il Falconiere into a large kitchen with a long table for prep work and, later, dining. Like everything else they've accomplished at their sybaritic inn, the teaching kitchen has a welcoming atmosphere and particular character. Riccardo and Silvia embody not only the Italian concept of *la bella figura* but also the more subtle *sprezzatura,* the art of making something difficult look easy. Their sense of décor never falls to standard-issue thinking. Silvia could be a flip-this-house maven, if she were not busy realizing her own projects. Whatever she touches turns to *Silvia,* and that's a fine thing.

Riccardo meets everyone under the wisteria pergola. *"Sempre bella,"* he welcomes each woman. Always beautiful. And, "How is it that you are returning more beautiful than before?" To the men, *"Grande!"* and a hug, which is short for *"Grande amico,"* great friend, the affectionate way local men greet each other.

We've arrived at six, plenty of time to prepare a goose sauce for pasta, lamb *en croute,* and a scrumptious chocolate dessert. Richard Titi, the chef at Il Falconiere, spends the first hour with us before he has to go down to the main kitchen. We are given aprons, a glass of wine, and a few tips about kneading, whisking, carving the lamb. Silvia keeps everyone on task but the noise level of fifteen cooks starts to rise. As the lamb slides into the oven, some drift to admire the dusky light on Riccardo's vines and the view of Cortona. Finally, a few other guests arrive and we migrate to the oval table in the garden, ready for several hours of toasts to the day twenty-five years ago when this amazing couple stepped into marriage.

ALBERTO AND HIS family take off for the Dolomites, Carlos goes fishing, Tony and crew pack the van and go sightseeing. I get down to work on ideas for my furniture collection. Ed works with Giorgio, pruning the olive grove. We scatter and come together and scatter. But on the night of the World Cup, we all gather, with every other live soul in town, in Piazza Signorelli, where a large screen has been mounted in front of the bank. Everyone is there except the Cardinalis, who stayed home to watch. Placido maintained that it would be a madhouse in town.

Italy plays France. This is big. Culmination of sixty-four matches. All around the piazza, people are leaning out their windows, shouting at every kick. Somehow Carlos has found plastic chairs inside the museum courtyard and set up our cheering section right out front. Most people are too excited to sit. The crowd breaks into a soccer chant everyone but us seems to know. The Alfonso kids, wearing bright blue team shirts with players' names on the back, bounce around. They've painted Italian flags on their faces. At each good move by Totti, Del Piero, Grosso, or Zambrotta, the child with that name emblazoned on his back takes it personally.

The sportscasters seem about to pop. They shout *"Incredibile! Incredibile!"* and *"Bello,"* and at each triumph the players tumble with one another like a pile of puppies. *"Forza Azzurri!"* "Go, Blue!" The tension mounts. Everyone stands now. They could hear our cheers and moans down in Camucia, if anyone were listening to anything other than the match. Banners sway to the rhythm of spontaneous songs and the theatrics on the field are matched in the piazza. When the ball bongs on a player's chest or head, hundreds repeat the action with their fists.

The explosive moment comes when Zidane, star French player, literally head-butts an Italian. This loss of cool probably cost the French the Cup, because Italy gets a penalty shootout and as the ball hits the net at 5 to 3 Italia, the entire piazza erupts as though a world war has ended: spraying water bottles, screams, hugs, dancing. This joyous moment echoes in every single piazza in Italy. The players on the screen kiss the trophy. They embrace one another, their faces pure bliss. We're in a bacchic rite, an ecstatic mob pulsing through town. Victory! Motorcycles appear with four or five riders precariously weaving through the hundreds of us. Several girls are draped in the Italian red-white-green flag. Marco appears with a jeroboam of Chianti Classico and paper cups. Suddenly we spot the red hat of Placido. Fiorella waves and grins. We weave through—how many times have we each been kissed?—and greet each other as if we've made it off the *Titanic*. Of course they *had* to come to the piazza to rejoice. Three boys attempt to kick a soccer ball. Kids in jeeps and convertibles cruise through the closed-to-traffic street. Who cares tonight? The *carabinieri* and *vigili* twist and shout, too. Firecrackers startle us—violence? Then we laugh. We've—none of us—ever experienced such a night. Some stay until sunrise. *Forza Azzurri!*

~

ON THEIR LAST evening, the Alfonsos throw a big party for all their friends. Paolo, who owns Trattoria Dardano, offers to help man the pizza oven. Their house is an eagle nest with a stupendous view over terraced hillsides as dreamy as a page out of a medieval book of hours. Below lies the lake where Hannibal defeated the Romans in 217 B.C., Bramasole's roof (oh, needs work), and the sweet valley dotted with ancient houses. People arrive and keep arriving. Joy, Susan, and Dorothy, three graces, serve *salumi* and several salads. They've placed bouquets of sunflowers on every table and stone wall.

Soon Mama Rose calls for music. Cuban music. She has the chairs pushed back and summons all of us to the samba. ONE, two, three, ONE, two three. She's incredulous that many of us have lived so long without learning the samba. Well, we'll change that tonight. Tonight's the night. UNOS, dos, tres, she's right, what was wrong with our lives that we did not samba? ONE, two, three . . .

Late, late, everyone drives out the impossibly narrow lane without incident. Must be the protective aura of wild white lilies, spot of miracles. As we climb the steps to our house, we hear voices and banging noises above us. "Isabella, bring in the candles." "Carlos, find the girls' bags." "The fire is still going." Then, faintly, we hear the five syllables of "Guantanamera," the family singing as they clear up the party.

❧

WHEN WE WAKE up tomorrow, they will be gone, gypsies stealing away in the dawn, leaving a large silence in Casa Caravita and a piazza strangely empty.

I came to Italy for the art, the cuisine, landscapes, history, architecture, wine, and the ineffable beauty. I stayed for the people. Cortona has a grand congregation of hearty, hospitable, generous souls. And not all of them are Italian.

IL FALCONIERE TORTINO SOFFICE DI CIOCCOLATO E PERE CON SALSA DI VANIGLIA
Il Falconiere Steamed Chocolate Cake with Vanilla Sauce

When we cook with friends at Silvia Baracchi's school, Cooking Under the Tuscan Sun, we often whip up this very simple dessert. I never thought of chocolate as seasonal, but in Tuscany, it's considered more appropriate for fall and winter. Seldom do you find it on a summer menu, perhaps because we have a plethora of plums, melons, and white peaches for hot-weather *dolce*.

With this, Silvia suggests a full-bodied sweet red wine with enough alcohol to "clean your mouth." Her choices are a passito from Pantelleria or an aged Recioto. I'm partial to the passito from Arnaldo Capraia.

Serves 10

> 8 ounces (1 stick) butter, plus more for the ramekins
> ¾ cup flour, plus more for the ramekins
> 1 cup fine sugar
> 4 eggs
> 3 tablespoons rum (or Tia Maria)
> 2 tablespoons strong coffee
> 1 tablespoon plus 1 teaspoon baking powder
> ½ cup ground cacao (high-quality cocoa)
> 4 pears, peeled and diced (optional)
> Vanilla Sauce (recipe follows)
> Chocolate bar or chocolate-covered coffee beans

Preheat the oven to 250 degrees F. Butter and flour 10 ramekins and set aside.

Beat butter and sugar to a soft cream. Add eggs, beating them in one at a time. Add rum and coffee. Sift flour, baking powder, and cacao into a bowl, then incorporate this into the butter mixture. Gently fold in the pears, if using. Pour into the prepared ramekins, filling halfway. Bake in a bain-marie by placing ramekins in a baking dish and filling it halfway with boiling water. Bake for 10 minutes, then increase temperature to 350 degrees F and continue baking until set, about 15 minutes.

Unmold onto individual plates or simply serve in the ramekins. Spoon vanilla sauce over the cakes, and garnish with curls of chocolate (use a vegetable peeler) or chocolate-covered coffee beans.

Vanilla Sauce

1 quart heavy cream
½ vanilla pod
8 egg yolks
4 tablespoons fine sugar

Heat the cream and vanilla pod to boiling, then quickly reduce heat. In a separate bowl, thoroughly beat together the yolks and sugar. Using a wooden spoon, stir the eggs into the cream and continue cooking on low, stirring constantly, for 5 minutes, until mixture slightly thickens and coats the spoon.

The Signorelli Trail

One's destination is never a place but a new way of looking at things.

— HENRY MILLER

ART LOVERS COMB TUSCANY FOR CHANCES TO see the work of one of Italy's greatest painters; from Florence to Arezzo to Monterchi to Sansepolcro, then over to Urbino, we travel the Piero della Francesca trail. We linger longest in Arezzo, where his only major fresco cycle remains in the church of San Francesco. Finally released from scaffolding after a fifteen-year restoration, the *Legend of the True Cross* is not his only work in Arezzo. Even some guidebooks miss the painting of Mary Magdalene in red on an inconspicuous wall in the Duomo. She's a force to encounter as she stands regarding you with her hair wet from drying the washed feet of Jesus.

Her even more powerful counterpart, *La Madonna del Parto*, *The Madonna of Childbirth*, reigns over its own museum in nearby Monterchi. Also a full-length portrait, this incomparable painting shows the Virgin Mary, standing with her hand slightly parting the blue dress covering her ninth-month pregnancy. The gesture—one never seen before—suggests that she is about to open her dress and give birth before our eyes. Despite calm colors and her cooler-than-thou expression, she's dynamite, the fuse lit.

Mothers-to-be visit her in supplication for safe birth, as they have for centuries. When she was removed from the Romanesque cemetery chapel to her new domicile, local women protested. I always wish, when I stand before this painting, that she could go back home. Too many people breathing on her, damp stone walls, humidity, and security drove her caretakers to secure the fresco. But surely the original setting could be made safe. To those who knew her in the chapel, where Piero intended for this homage to his own mother to live, the new one-painting museum seems stripped and soulless. Although the climate and air quality control protect the fresco, seeing her out of the rightful context seems like seeing an ethereal wedding dress in a thrift shop. Luckily, the sheer power radiating from the Madonna on the brink of changing the world manages to triumph over poor circumstance.

Sansepolcro, birthplace and home of Piero, is a top Tuscan town. I like the provincial market atmosphere, small shops, flat streets, and a trattoria with a mixed grill and antipasto selection so delicious that we always leave in a state of euphoria. I'm sure other notable dishes exit from the kitchen, but we always order the same thing. About once a week all year, Ed mentions Da Ventura's succulent *stinco di vitello al forno,* oven-roasted veal shank, and their *maialino in porchetta,* crusty young pig spit-roasted with herbs. To step out of Da Ventura, after a *pranzo splendido,* and walk down the narrow street anticipating Piero's paintings—there's the essence of Tuscan travel. Such a lunch suffuses you with well-being. Then all

you have to contemplate is whether or not *The Resurrection* is
the greatest painting in the world.

La Pinacoteca Comunale, the Civic Museum, smells like
chalky erasers in an old elementary school. The wan light inside falls benignly on Piero's four (three? *San Ludovico*'s cre-
ator is disputed) paintings. The memorable face of *San
Giuliano* looks vulnerable, shocked by whatever he's looking
out toward. Perhaps this is the captured moment when he re-
alizes that an old spell has caught up with him. Like Oedipus,
he fled his home because of an evil prophecy concerning his
parents. He made a marriage and life far away. While he was
on a voyage, his unsuspecting parents found his new home and
hospitable wife. They were sleeping when he returned.
Thinking his wife had taken a lover into their bed, he murdered his parents, thus fulfilling the prophecy.

The majestic *Resurrection* dominates. Christ emerges from
the tomb, his eyes already *al di là,* beyond the beyond. You
can't help but recall the same otherworldly look in the eyes of
the *Madonna del Parto,* as she fingers the opening to her dress
at an equally defining moment. His left foot steps up onto the
edge of the tomb, the right still inside. Spring has arrived in
the background behind his emerging foot, while winter remains behind the foot inside the tomb. He's dressed in lilac-
rose dawn colors as he prepares to step into the new day. Four
guards sleep below him, oblivious to the miracle. Legend says
that the second one from the left is Piero—is that a goiter on
his neck?—depicted as completely conked out.

The Resurrection is particularly precious to Sansepolcro,
which means Holy Sepulcher. At the time of the painting's
conception, viewers also saw a local symbolism. Piero's town
was experiencing a growth spurt and revival (resurrection)
after freeing itself from Florence's clutches. The artistic patrimony of Tuscan small towns continues to stagger me. What if

my hometown, Fitzgerald, Georgia, owned such master-pieces?

In an everlasting tribute to liberal arts education, a World War II American pilot on a bombing mission in the area vaguely remembered a professor speaking of the small village of Sansepolcro as the home of great Renaissance paintings. He spared the city.

Seeing Luca Signorelli's *Crucifixion with Saints* in Sansepol-cro makes me think *he* needs a trail to follow. For me, he is *the* Renaissance painter who seems to step ahead of his time. His revelry in depicting the male body, the life-force he infuses into form, and, most of all, his passion for individual faces give him a visceral energy. He loved muscles, movement, tension, feel-ings, force. Gertrude Stein said of her obsession with her char-acters, "I wanted to see what made each one that one." Luca would concur. Faces! Each so revealed. In his work a recurrent blond woman obviously obsessed him. So close an observer was he that you see his locals in the piazza today. Another quality catapults him toward the contemporary sensibility. He often strikes the viewer with the impression of more action continu-ing outside the painting's borders. He cuts off the drama at the edge of the frame at the last minute, instead of keeping action framed with space around. He seems precocious. In *Italian Painters of the Renaissance,* Bernard Berenson agrees: "His vi-sion of the world may seem austere, but it already is ours. His sense of form is our sense of form; his images are our images. Hence he was the first to illustrate our own house of life."

I had sensed the vivacity imparted by his dynamic compo-sition but had not articulated the effect I felt until I read and pored over the prints in *Luca Signorelli* by Tom Henry and Laurence Kanter. From them, too, I found *what* Signorelli is *where,* and which ones (especially in Città di Castello) are not totally by Luca's hands. The authors are rigorous art historians but also top detectives. They've traced several panels and pre-della sections to the paintings they once joined. I was jolted to learn that two panels of Luca's *Lamentation* in Cortona's San Niccolò now live in my home state at the High Museum in Atlanta. Please, give them back.

Besides dissecting what's authentic, what's not (and what might be both), the authors catalog and comment on all of Signorelli's work.

They opened my eyes to Signorelli's very smart use of architecture in his paintings. How brilliant to observe that the left-side light source in the *Annunciation* in Volterra came from Signorelli's conceit of using the three actual windows to the left of the oratory altar where the painting hung. So it appeared as though natural light bathed the angel. And Signorelli also repeated the oratory's vaulted ceiling on the Virgin's side of the painting. This blending of the place itself with the painting subtly created a feeling of intimacy for the viewer. (Since the *Annunciation* was removed to the Pinacoteca Civica, these connections are lost.)

In frescoes, sometimes a figure actually is stepping or leaning outside the painted frame. So much to admire. I love the details Luca often places in his foregrounds: a dropped red hat, a glass of wildflowers, hammer and skull, a lizard, an open book—each a tiny still life to savor and contemplate.

⟋⟍

WHILE ED DRIVES home from Sansepolcro, I jot down a basic three-day Signorelli route. Luca's trail leads to the wilder side of Tuscany, with a dip into Umbria. For anyone not passionate about art, this *gita* delivers anyway, for each town has righteous piazzas, good coffee, and people always worth watching.

Museum hours are usually dependable, but churches open

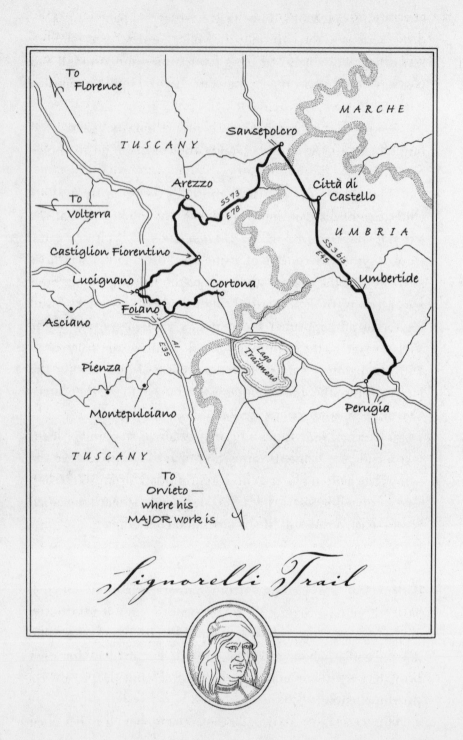

To Florence

MARCHE

TUSCANY

Sansepolcro

Arezzo

Città di Castello

SS73
E78

To Volterra

UMBRIA

Castiglion Fiorentino

SS 3 bis
E45

Lucignano

Cortona

Umbertide

Foiano

Asciano

Lago Trasimeno

E35
A1

Pienza

Montepulciano

Perugia

TUSCANY

To Orvieto — where his MAJOR work is

Signorelli Trail

at erratic hours. Sometimes you can ring for a custodian, some-times the side doors are open, and often the local tourist office will be able to help. When I want to be sure a church is open, I check for the hours of mass and visit just as the service ends.

Start in his native Cortona, which is graced with a trove of Signorellis. Most remain in great condition since they never had to travel. A tour of his paintings in the Museo Diocesano, San Niccolò, San Domenico, Santa Maria del Calcinaio, and Museo dell'Accademia Etrusca e della Città di Cortona (MAEC, also known as the Etruscan Academy) almost com-prises a tour of the town.

The best place to start is the Museo Diocesano before Luca's magnificent *Lamentation at the Foot of the Cross*. By my lights, this intricate work ranks as one of the high moments of the Renaissance. I isolate every face, every detail, and see a rare perfection, then regard the whole breathtaking composition. In the left distance, crucifixion takes place and on the right, resurrection, with Christ triumphant within a gold almond-shaped light. The cross, with dripping blood, bisects the painting—but, typical of Luca, the measurement is slightly off center. In the foreground, the deposed Christ lies with his head in the lap of Mary, his lower legs sprawled across the legs of Mary Magdalene, seated on the ground. A crouching woman holds his arm tenderly and leans to kiss his palm. One reason this painting is so moving is that three women are in physical contact with the magnificent body just removed from the cross. Other sorrowing holy women and men look on, and each face reflects a very particular emotion. Their sumptuous clothing gave Luca a chance to paint the folds and drape and grace of fabric. The gold leaf, dusty greens, tarnished copper browns, burnished coral, and ashy blues of the entire painting present a palette of complete harmony. An idealized village on a lake centers the background and reminds us subtly that somewhere, life goes on unperturbed by the momentous scene before us.

Another great Luca in this museum shows Christ giving communion bread to his apostles. If you focus on each face, the intensely individual portraits show a gamut of emotions. You see Signorelli's passion for human grace—and the opposite: Judas, closest to the viewer, furtively slips the Host into his satchel. Fox face, sly eyes, he's the only one disengaged in the scene.

Not all of Luca enchants. In front of the *Virgin and Child with Saints Louis of Toulouse, Bonaventure, and Anthony of Padua,* I feel unmoved. The figures are static. I'm puzzled how my rock-and-roll Luca painted such a dull group. The saints around the Virgin seem to have stepped forward for their photo ops.

Also in the Museo Diocesano, you'll see *Presentation in the Temple,* which I like to imagine in its original (vanished) oratory right on Piazza Repubblica, and the poetic *Immaculate Conception with Six Prophets.* Two angels shower the Virgin with flowers while God looks on. Frida Kahlo would have liked this impregnating floral cascade. Executed mostly by Luca's nephew Francesco Signorelli from his uncle's design,[1] this painting probably was done when Luca was eighty-one. Increasingly in his late years, he let his workshop assistants carry out his designs. The museum is so rich; you'll find Luca's *Adoration of the Shepherds, Scenes from the Life of Saint Benedict* (much more on Benedetto later at Abbadia Monte Oliveto Maggiore), *Nativity,* and *Assumption of the Virgin.*

A joy forever is Fra Angelico's *Annunciation.* The angel's hair glows popsicle-orange; the Virgin looks very *uh oh, not me.* The divine painting remains from Fra Angelico's thirteen years of work in Cortona. He left another painting behind in this museum, a polyptych, *Virgin with Child and Four Saints,* and a dim, almost unknown demi-lune over the main doors of Chiesa di San Domenico.

Before leaving the museum, don't forget to go downstairs to the weirdly placed Chiesa del Buon Gesù, Church of the Good Jesus, below the museum. Access is down a steep stone staircase. Once upon a time you entered from the lower street but now the secret church seems as though it's in the basement. Way below, you enter a mysterious and intimate holy space.

⤙

I'VE LOOKED THROUGH reproductions of all of Luca's paintings hoping to find an image of his hometown or local landscape. Here it is in the Etruscan Museum on Piazza Signorelli. Because Luca's *tondo,* round painting, *Virgin and Child with Saints Michael, Vincent of Saragozza, Margaret of Cortona, and Mark,* arises directly from Cortona, it seems precious to us who live here. There's the venerated local Santa Margherita in gray habit, and St. Mark, our patron saint, holding a still-recognizable model of the city. The *tondo*'s bottom third shows Mary's feet resting on heads of putti and below them a scramble of snakes, devil, and lizard. Mary, quite objectively, looks down at the balance scale held by St. Michael, from which one tiny man tumbles toward the devil's creatures. The other homunculus turns toward her. Judgment Day in Cortona!

Since wise people began collecting for this museum in 1727, quite a stash has accumulated. The Etruscan artifacts should be lingered over down in the old prison basement. Having benefited from a major intervention, the astonishing collection shines in the new cases and displays. In upper galleries, our Luca has several moments. His *Adoration of the Shepherds* is a disquieting painting. In the upper left, the Annunciation angel is on final approach. Baby Jesus lies in the foreground behind some peculiar silhouetted black plants. If you wander enough, you'll come across wooden panels of putti with coat of arms and inscriptions. There must have been lots of such work around town when Luca was called on for every little *festa* and every rich man's need to immortalize himself.

⌒

I LOVE UPPER Cortona's secret terraces overlooking the broad Val di Chiana, the neighborhood shrines with faded paintings, fortress-like convents, and the old joined houses facing a neglected park. I often stop at San Niccolò, set back among cypresses. I ring for the caretaker, then feel privileged to enter this mysterious and private sanctuary. Front and center, Signorelli's *Lamentation of Saints Nicholas, Francis, Dominic, Michele, and Jerome over the Dead Christ* lends a somber air to the charmed space. Christ, propped on top of his tomb, slumps to the side. An angel, who appears to support his weight, holds him up. He is truly dead at this moment. The resurrection, which they may believe will happen, has not yet happened. The stone tomb juts into the sight line of the viewer. In a conventional composition, it would be placed horizontally or vertically, but Signorelli's decision to cant the stone gives the painting a jolt of tension.

To see the flip side of the Signorelli standard, the caretaker must press the button that reverses the painting. This is done with a great deal of seriousness. The reward, a sweetly colored *Madonna and Child with Saints Peter and Paul.* She looks melancholy; the Child is more adorable than Luca's usual babes.

There's also a fresco in San Niccolò that may or may not be Luca's. My book says no. The man who opened the doors says yes, and he seems old enough to have known Signorelli. I vote yes, at least for partial authorship. Maybe it's the lavender and saffron robes. Or the Baby Jesus leaning away from St. Christopher and holding the world in the shape of an orange. And the strong and delicate Sebastian. These just look like Luca's hand.

Because it's on my daily route, San Domenico is the church I visit most often. I light my votives at a side altar when I am worried for someone. The lofty ceiling and austere atmosphere calm me. I visit with Luca, too, his *Virgin and Child with Saints Dominic and Blaise, Two Angels and Giovanni Sernini.* The latter commissioned the painting and thereby earned his own spot. I always pause to look closely at the unidentified fragments of frescoes near the entrance, which could be in Fra Angelico's hand, since he lived at the San Domenico monastery. But they have a della Francesca look to them. *Luca, are you here?*

Appropriately, Santa Maria del Calcinaio marks the end of the Cortona trail. Luca had a hand in hiring Francesco di Giorgio Martini, the architect for this monumental beauty that has anchored the view below the town walls since the church's completion in 1513. Driving up from the valley, rounding the bend, suddenly the grand dome appears. I feel exhilarated, as though I've been given a big *ciao, bella* from the Renaissance. The name, St. Mary of the Lime Pit, comes from the area where shoemakers tanned their hides with local lime. The exact story of construction is lost but involved an ox who genuflected before an image of the Virgin in a niche. Miracles ensued, and the mighty church was built on the spot. The precious image is now on the altar. Here, Luca left us his *Immaculate Conception with Six Prophets and Two Donors.* Below God and the Virgin, six prophets hold open their books and scrolls, all inscribed with Latin scripture about the immaculate conception. I was glad I had my binoculars with me because the light is dim and the painting not in good condition. A pity.

This work is dated 1523–1524 in *Luca Signorelli*. Since Luca died in 1523, were the last touches put on by his nephew? I am shocked that the painting is not identified in the church. There is a lurid old postcard for sale that assigns it to "school of Signorelli." Kanter and Henry's book asserts that this was Signorelli's last painting.

When I learned that, I had to give up believing the local lore about his death. From Vasari, everyone around Cortona knows the story of Luca dying two weeks after a fall while painting at Il Palazzone, the Passerini villa just up the hill. My friend Lyndall, widow of the last Passerini owner, lives in the tower. The family figures in Italian history since the twelfth century, so a Signorelli can be taken for granted in such a palazzo. She flicked on lights and we passed through several rooms painted by local Signorelli pupil Tommaso Bernabei (known as Il Papacello). His grotesque-style frescoes depict episodes from Roman history, including defeat at the hands of Hannibal at Lake Trasimeno. This fascinates especially because he gives us a Renaissance view of Cortona. Then we came to the dim little altar with the Signorellis, his *Baptism of Christ* and the Sibyl with Latin inscriptions. No one ever bothered to strip the side walls even though Faith, Hope, and Charity are said to wait below the whitewash. "He fell right here, toppled off the scaffolding," Lyndall said as she pointed. And that was the closest I'd ever felt to his physical presence.

But the super-sleuths date his Palazzone work to 1522 and 1523, a year before the Calcinaio *Immaculate Conception*. Did he fall, maybe twist his ankle? Isn't there usually a drop of truth in a legend? I'll guess he limped back into town in early evening, probably had a jug of wine and played a few hands of *briscola* with neighbors in the piazza.

∽

To CONTINUE THE Signorelli Trail, allow two days for this loop. Cross the Val di Chiana to Foiano and Lucignano, recross the valley to Castiglion Fiorentino. Proceed to Arezzo, then to Sansepolcro, Città di Castello, Umbertide, and Perugia.

This is prime roaming land. Take the unpaved turns toward a bell tower, or a tiny town with one bar where you are sure to meet someone as indigenous as a summer wheatfield, or—great luck—you may find, as I did, a ruined rectory (cutlery still in a drawer) and collapsed church with fresco remnants and stones with iron rings you can lift to look down onto heaps of mildewed holy bones. The wreck may be for sale and you can sink in your life savings and years of your life. Such unexpected turns tempt fate.

Foiano, a market town in the fertile Val di Chiana, is known for *bistecca,* the enormous steaks from the really enormous white *chianina,* cows. The town should be better known for its piazzas, friendly citizens, the oldest *carnevale* festival in Italy, a trove of della Robbias, and, in the Chiesa della Collegiata, a great Signorelli. I don't think he left anyone out of his *Incoronazione della Vergine, con i santi Giuseppe, Maria Maddalena, Martino, Leonardo, Antonio da Padova, Benedetto, Girolamo, Giovanni Evangelista e Michele, quattro angeli e un committente; Coronation of the Virgin with Saints Joseph, Mary Magdalene, Martin, Leonard, Anthony of Padua, Benedict, Jerome, John the Baptist and Michael, Four Angels and a Donor.* The saints, foregrounded and turned away from the celestial vision, kneel in prayer. San Martino looks resplendent in the embroidered mantle that he halved with a beggar, and he sits in high contrast to San Benedetto, who's semi-nude with his rock of penance before him. These are memorable faces, the smallest of which, the donor, is supposed to be a self-portrait of Signorelli in old age. The cultural director of Foiano told me unequivocably that this is Signorelli's last painting. Henry and Kanter disagree, placing it at March 1522 to June 1523. I wonder if, during that last period of his life, Luca might have been working on three paintings at once. Who knows where he brushed his last stroke.

Lucignano has one of the most enchanting town plans of any hill town, an elliptical form with concentric radiating streets. Because of the winding narrow passageways, it's easy to imagine life there centuries ago. I am fond of the striped facade of San Francesco, with its ashen blue door. Inside, I like to visit Sant'Agatha who is holding her two breasts like cupcakes on a plate in one hand and the pincers that removed them in the other. Here also is a painting of death on horseback, riding hell-for-leather, full tilt, his white hair blown back, his bow drawn with the arrow aimed at an unsuspecting couple.

Next door in the Town Hall, a fabulous Luca awaits, *San Francesco che riceve le stimmate, Saint Francis Receiving the Stigmata.* This painting fascinates me because of its lost context. Francis and a companion are kneeling while the angel—or Christ—flies down in exuberant coral robes. The color catches my eye because the lunette-shaped painting is said to have topped an *armadio,* armoire, that held the venerated *Albero della Vita, Tree of Life,* a striking six-foot-tall reliquary preserved in the next room. The tree branches are made of gilded copper, silver, and gold, and are adorned with coral, rock-crystal medallions, and miniatures. The tree is crowned by Christ on the cross, and just above is the curious figure of a pelican in a nest. A pelican? The bird, who pecks its own breast to feed its young, symbolizes selfless devotion to family.

Castiglion Fiorentino suffers from proximity to Cortona, which has such a plethora of art treasures. But Castiglion Fiorentino has solid virtues—an intact medieval village perched above the undulant Val di Chio, where groves produce optimal olive oil. Inside the walls, cart-wide streets lead to one of those balcony-of-the-world lookouts framed through an impressive loggia designed by Vasari. The untouristy town tastes of the "real" Tuscany. Fortunately, Luca stopped in around 1505, leaving at the Collegiata di San Giuliano a *Lamentation Over the Dead Christ.*

Could *this* body of Christ be modeled on his own dead son Antonio, who died of the plague in 1502? Vasari connected the drawing Luca made of his son to the *Lamentation* in Cortona, but according to Kanter, the Cortona painting was completed a few months before Antonio died. Perhaps Vasari confused it with a later work. Whatever the truth, Luca's Christs often look like local boys. This one must have been at least inspired by Antonio's body. It's interesting, too, that the *Virgin of the Misericordia* here may be the only remaining painting by the unfortunate son, Antonio Signorelli.

Arezzo, capital of our province, sponsors a huge monthly antiques market. Vendors' stands sprawl from the Vasari arcade, out into the Piazza Grande, and through many narrow streets. When I was given honorary citizenship in Arezzo, the mayor also bestowed on me the title "godmother of the fair." He didn't know how aptly he spoke. I've Christmas-shopped, birthday-shopped, and house-shopped there for all the years I've been in Italy. Almost my entire collection of religious art and artifacts comes from two dealers who pull out their *ex votos* when they see me. Finally restored, Piero della Francesca's *Legend of the True Cross* cycle shines in San Francesco, but now we are pursuing Luca.

Vasari writes about a Cortona procession bringing on their shoulders a commissioned Signorelli painting all the way to

Arezzo. At the age Vasari puts at eighty-one, Luca walked, too. He wanted to oversee the installation. Vasari was then a child just learning to write. He retained a vivid memory of Luca giving him a piece of jasper to wear to prevent nosebleeds and admonishing the father to allow young Giorgio to draw. In the Pinacoteca Comunale we can admire the *Virgin and Child with Saints Donatus, Jerome, Nicholas of Bari, the Prophets David, Ezechiel, Isaiah, and Niccolò Gamurrini.* A host of saints, music-playing angels, and prophets—and even God looking down on all. What music did Luca meditate on as he painted? Look, too, at *Virgin and Child with Saints Francis, Clare, Margaret, Mary Magdalene, and Four Angels.*

In **Sansepolcro,** you might be overwhelmed by Piero della Francesca and not take the ten-minute walk to the small church of San Antonio, where the *Crucifixion with Saints* by Piero's pupil, our Luca Signorelli, hangs over the altar. As in many Renaissance paintings, time collapses on the canvas: In the background Christ is removed from the cross; in the foreground he is crucified and his mother has fainted into the lap of a woman whose red skirt cradles her—while reminding the viewer of blood. Luca slashes the sky behind the head of Christ with a long dark cloud paralleling the bar of the gibbet. Look closely. In one of the two puffy clouds you see the shape of a face. Since there's nothing fanciful in the painting, this must represent God. The painting was a procession standard, two-sided, and the two saints who were once on the other side of the crucifixion are displayed as well.

At **Città di Castello** in the Pinacoteca Comunale, we find *The Martyrdom of Saint Sebastian.* The subject might have been chosen to stop the plague of 1497. Sebastian often was invoked as a protector against the Black Death. He survived the longbow and crossbow enthusiasts who riddled his body. (And if you survive, are you able to claim martyr status?) His heroic recovery may have given hope to those stricken with plague, but it was the association of the plague with the arrow that created his mystique. Throughout these horrific pandemics, the first sign of the disease was described as hitting like an arrow. I also found the death icon of the arrow in a history of the plague in the Ottoman Empire. I've also come across an anonymous medieval painting of a skeleton on horseback shooting arrows at plague victims.

Luca's Sebastian is pilloried with several tormentors ranged below him. Two showcase Luca's fascination with the male body—a man in striped leggings faces us and one shows his back to the viewer. His second-skin gold leggings make his shapely legs and taut buttocks the actual focal point of the painting. If Sebastian had any armed supporter, the archer's rear would have made a prime target. Two other archers are dark-skinned and almost naked, aiming bows, while the well-dressed boys aim crossbows. The dark ones must have been slaves. The background street scene depicts medieval houses, classical buildings, and a glacial landscape based on—who knows—fantasy, or perhaps the Dolomites. From heaven, God looks down from a squashed yellow ovoid, while Sebastian casts his eye upward. Although only six arrows have hit him so far, he would be hard to miss from such proximity.

❧

DOES THE FIRST work of Luca Signorelli remain here, a sacred fresco in the museum? No one knows if this bit of the Virgin's face was painted by Signorelli. The artist almost certainly studied under Piero. In his early career, Luca worked in this Umbrian area for as long as a decade. On his paintings at the National Gallery in Washington, D.C., Luca is identified as Umbrian, though his birthplace, Cortona, sits firmly in Tuscany.

There are other traditionally assigned works of Luca in Città. Because Luca's early years are such a mystery, I like to think his hand created some of these.

The *Virgin and Child with Saints Francis, Bonaventure, Louis of Toulouse, Anthony of Padua, Cecilia, Clare, Catherine, and Elisabeth of Hungary*—what a crew—previously was omitted from Signorelli's oeuvre, but Kanter affirms it as Luca's. The painting is resplendent in Renaissance fabrics. I love the Virgin's star-scattered dress and the fleur-de-lis cape over Clare's poor dress. The infant Child holding out a crown turns toward St. Cecilia. The women's hands are eloquent; there always must have been a language of gesture in Italy. The six accompanying panels of saints Kanter assigns to the nephew, Francesco Signorelli. Two of those, to me, give off the perfume of Signorelli.

At **Umbertide,** Luca's *Deposition from the Cross* remains on the altar at Santa Croce, as he intended, bestowing its mellow golds, ochres, and browns on all who come to visit. In front of this painting, I always think of the smooth Italian word *ambrato,* ambered. The intimate details of this scene startle me. A holy woman holds out her hand to catch blood dripping from Jesus's feet. Two robust men on ladders detach his arms from the cross as he slumps forward. The three predella scenes recall Piero della Francesca's treatment of the Holy Cross themes in Arezzo's San Francesco, but Luca's realism shows how far he moved from the precepts of his former teacher.

Luca was paid around seventy florins for this fine work. How did he spend those gold coins? Vials of ground lapis lazuli for the blue of a Madonna's dress, a stone roof for his studio, a brace of woodcocks for a feast, and lambskin slippers to wear in front of the fire?

The **Perugia** altarpiece in the city's Museo Diocesano has great charm and impact. The Virgin reads a book while the

Child holding a lily looks down at the pages. Below her, an angel strums a lute. He is seated on a dais with glasses of wild-flowers on either side of him. The four surrounding saints—John the Baptist looks quite wild—resemble cutouts pasted on the canvas. They would appear almost Byzantine if they were not so active and expressive. There's another Signorelli *Virgin and Child* with a passel of saints in the Perugia's Galleria Nazionale. This one is rare for being in its original frame with the predella scenes intact below.

Capital of Umbria, Perugia draws people from all over the world to its Università per Stranieri, a tough language school for those with the stamina for immersion. Ed's course bumped his Italian to the next level, though the hour commute was agony. The museums house a comprehensive collection of Umbrian art. Perugia has great street life, a marvelous foun-tain, the duomo where the wedding ring of the Virgin resides, pastry and chocolate shops, and good-looking people. You could idle awhile, spend a few days (or a year) exploring Um-bria, especially Assisi, Spello, Spoleto, and the ceramic centers, Deruta and Gualdo Tadino.

The contiguous trail ends in Perugia.

⌇

BUT, please, pursue Luca further:

Devote a half day to the great **Abbadia Monte Oliveto Maggiore** near Asciano, and less than twenty miles south of Siena. The Signorelli and Sodoma frescoes, painted on cloister walls surrounding a courtyard of lemon trees, highlight the life and miracles of San Benedetto, St. Benedict. Several scenes involve falling rafters and stones and monks miraculously saved from death by the good Benedetto. (Very appealing sub-ject matter for this serial restorer. He should be the patron of builders.) One involves a bucket brigade putting out a fire.

The most touching fresco, *How Saint Benedict Reproved the Monks for Eating Outside the Monastery,* appeals to me not for it's didactic purpose but for the homey interior scene of a meal being served by two graceful women—surely a minestrone, a savory leg of lamb, field greens, and plums. Benedetto must have been, well, *a saint*—sweet, helpful, steady—because his miracles were not show-stoppers. His were everyday, even mundane, not flashy instant cures or water-into-wine dramas.

The other half of the day, if you wend your way to **Pienza** you will be startled by this harmonious Renaissance town that smells of pecorino. Shops with open doors lure me toward their cheeses in jackets of hazelnut leaves or ashes. From various outlook spots, you can see grazing all the huddles of sheep that gave the town fame for cheese. I never leave without a hunk of semi-aged pecorino.

The Madonna lost her crown during a restoration of *Madonna della Misericordia with Saints Sebastian and Bernadine.* This painting in San Francesco is worth seeing for the calm Sebastian, standing beside the Virgin, his arrow wounds punctuating his pale body. Mary throws up her hands in a *that's enough* gesture.

Luca loved fabric. Sometimes I flip through Henry and Kanter's *Luca Signorelli* just focusing on the lavish patterns and colors worn by his figures. Catch the wild fabric on her dress in Pienza.

In the wine town of **Montepulciano,** seek out, along with a bottle of Vino Nobile di Montepulciano, Chiesa di Santa Lucia and the simple and regal *Virgin and Child.*

Don't stop now, because his most astounding work, his *sopratutto,* above all, masterpiece is outside Tuscany, in dramatic **Orvieto,** a magnificent town suspended over the countryside on a tufa precipice.

Go to the Duomo and gaze.

Then go to your hotel and read a good book on the cycle.

Then go back and gaze again. Behold the Antichrist! My friend Rena wrote to me, years after seeing the cycle: "The Antichrist floored me. There is a big signboard on the highway near Auburn warning us of The Beast, but I got such an initiation in the nine hours with Signorelli in the chapel that The Beast illustrated by Pentecostals is as nothing."

Maybe, like me, you'll fall in love right there in the Brizio Chapel. Maybe you'll weep a little as the grandeur of Luca's imagination reminds you of how art can stir you toward transformation in your own life.

How to paint the unimaginable? Judgment Day. He cuts loose. There's a wacky, cartoonish element to this estimable cycle. Devils and green bodies, and hellish torture of the damned. Luca's usually restrained, suffering, receptive women are no longer the chronic enablers. They apparently sinned as much as any male, although those who've attained the heavenly grace look beatific again.

As in Milton's *Paradise Lost* and *Paradise Regained,* the heavenly part is less powerful than the riotous orgy of writhing misery. But both aspects are inexhaustible. Ed found the "resurrection of the dead" section so compelling that he used a detail on the cover of one of his books of poems.

This is the moment, to my thinking, that hinges all of Christianity: *You do not die at death. You will be restored to your most perfect body for eternal life.* This places you—you—against a vast backdrop. Without the promise, you're out in the open, on your own; you might as well just invent your own humanist values, live the best life you can, and *Buona notte tutti,* good night, everyone.

Luca's buried skeletons push up through the earth, as though raised by the biotic pull of light. They resume their bodies. Some are completely out and looking good, some are in the process of transformation. We are accustomed to the macrocosmic resurrection of Christ, which hands down the promise to us, but not to the microcosmic sight of resurrected humans.

I've seen Luca's cycle a dozen times and always find new parts to love. John Addington Symonds must have been in Orvieto when he wrote, "To him belongs the credit in an age of ornament and pedantry of having made the human body a language for the utterance of all that is most weighty in the thought of man."

When I visit, the first image I always look at is the self-portrait of the artist, standing with Fra Angelico beside his own creation. He gazes at you. He's a sturdy man. The Signorelli ancestors must have been from northern Italy. He's light. His long blond hair falls in rivulets. A cloth hat sits at an angle, pulled down almost over his eyebrow. So, he consciously tilted his hat. And the well-made coat with stand-up collar and ruched sleeves—he's no fashion slouch. Is he blue-eyed? His right eye looks blue, the left brown. I would like to have a ladder to see up close. He shows himself unretouched—circles under his eyes and the slight beginning of a double chin. A man in his prime. He has completed his masterpiece.

You can come only so close to those you love and never knew, never could have known. I have loved Atatürk, Yeats, Keats, Jeb Stuart, and have felt their presence and distance simultaneously. I've longed for friendship with Colette, Freya Stark, Eudora Welty. Their work draws the lover of words close. Time intervenes with its harsh imperatives. Did Luca walk at night on the Roman road to see the stars? Did his blond hair darken? Did he carry the *bambino* Antonio on his shoulders or keep a falcon or snap a sprig of rosemary for his buttonhole? Was his voice smooth and deep, like a slow pour of newly pressed olive oil? Did he love the bitter taste of wild cherries in June? In November did he pick a frozen grape, bite into icy slivers and fulsome juice? So much we can know from his paintings, but the person remains enigmatic, out of reach. He cleaved the air of the piazza as he crossed and the air closed behind him.

Farther afield, in **Volterra** the *Annunciation* reigns. (Described on page 187.) In this Etruscan city, one of the most evocative in Tuscany, Luca also left *Saint Jerome* and a *Virgin and Child with Saints,* now in the Pinacoteca Civica.

Urbino, Loreto, and **Arcevia** form their own minitrail. See pages 34–47.

AND IF YOU search beyond these suggested sites, you appreciate how ambitious Luca was, how much he accomplished in his long life. I relish the drive and will behind his work. Some of his most moving paintings live in Florence at the Uffizi, I Tatti, Pitti Palace, Galleria Corsini, Galleria Torrigiani, and Museo Horne.

Rome, too, yes, find him. Luca, born in a rural small town, lives all over the world.

Like someone with an ambition to visit all fifty states, I have my list of Luca paintings to visit. There's the half of an Annunciation to see at the Walters in Baltimore, a Virgin in Krakow. Onward to Dublin, Bergamo, Toledo, Ohio, Washington, but only a dream visit to Luca's secular Pan, by all accounts a major work, sadly burned at the end of World War II in Berlin. They're all listed in my Luca notebook, drawing me to travel.

Città di Castello

WHILE ON THE CORTONA-PERUGIA SIGNORELLI Trail, Città di Castello is a prime choice for an overnight stop. I like to take the back roads around Città. From my house in Cortona, we swerve around hills and hollows, along serene fields with crops so green and lush that you want to get out and graze. You traverse the rural, unpopulated, unvisited countryside you dream of finding in Italy. Each carsick curve reveals a verdant vista, a castle floating in the clouds, a ruined tower like an old ink sketch of itself, or a working farm.

En route, I watch for the roadside huts with signs announcing *"Porcini"* and *"Tartufi"* especially around Palazzo del Pero, command central for these elusive morsels. Often the local hunter-gatherers set up impromptu tables in town and display their baskets of porcini, small mounds of fresh black truffles, and rarely the scarcer white truffles, which must come from Piemonte.

The angels in Luca's paintings dine only on this delicacy. At *pranzo,* they put down their lutes and shave the slivers over tagliatelle. As we pass, I can see in Ed's glance visions of chicken with black truffle slices and herbs stuffed under the skin, a creamy risotto absorbing shavings of white truffles, and meaty porcini grilled with a big Fiorentina steak.

Only an hour away, Città di Castello is a top choice of all the fine Umbrian towns. If I were looking for a place to live in Italy now, this would be high on my list. Occasionally, in an Italian town, I intuitively feel *this may be more home than home.* I like its homey dignity, the number of bookstores, and especially the piazza's impressive bell tower with twin clocks, one for the minutes, one for the hours. Sitting outside a café, looking up at those timekeepers, looking around at the choreography of entrances and exits to the piazza, I count as some fine hours. Once I saw two men collide on *motorini,* pick themselves us, straighten their clothes, and embrace. Another day, I saw a man with a prolific mustache reading the paper in dappled shade. From where I was he appeared to be holding a silver fish in his mouth.

Besides the important Pinacoteca, the Museo dell'Opera del Duomo and several churches are on my rounds when I visit. Sometimes it's not the great paintings that grab you. In the Pinacoteca I like to visit *Madonna col Bambino Dormiente, Madonna and Sleeping Baby,* by Vincenzo Chialli. It has the simplicity of an *ex voto.* The Madonna kneels beside the cot of her son, who appears to be around four years old. He's sleeping perfectly. She's obviously up to check on him. We glimpse in the background room her simple bed.

I have never seen this subject painted before, this archetypal scene of the mother who keeps watch and worries and loves. I say to my grandson as I turn off the lamp, "I'll be checking on you." Sometimes he wants to know when. Or he says sleepily, "I'll be checking on you, Franny." On any quest, sometimes the asides have the real news for you.

Getting to know this town is like starting a thousand-piece puzzle; it's best to find the flat edges and construct the outline.

So much complex history simply overwhelms the desire for good background for visiting a town. Papal ownerships, Guelphs, Ghibellines, even Urbino's Duke Federico III da Montefeltro all jerked this fine little city around for centuries. Città di Castello's fragmented past has more pieces than any jigsaw, but the corner pieces, easily placed, are Roman. Originally Tifernum or Tiberinum, the name refers to the Tiber. Colle Plinio, in the vicinity but not definitively located, was the site of Tuscis, where Pliny the Younger built a villa and wrote enchantingly about the garden with his name spelled out in topiary and delicate morsels for guests floated on trays in fountains.

A luminous point in the past occurred when Dr. Maria Montessori gave her first training lectures in 1909. A hundred teachers and a few students participated. She was a guest at Villa Montesca, now a study/conference center and park just outside town. The owners, Baron Leopoldo Franchetti and his American wife, Alice Hallgarten, were enlightened people light-years ahead of their time. Alice not only held a free school in their villa, she established a textile-weaving workshop for local women. The villa's workers lived in exemplary conditions. Their interest in educating local children led to their invitation to Maria Montessori. She spent the summer with them, discussing her methods and writing the book, known to us as *The Montessori Method,* which sent her name out to the world.

Now the town's reputation centers on antiques and a hand-woven textile center (thank you, Alice), as well as being a mecca for reproductions. As we have, many hotel and *agriturismo* owners come to acquire traditional furnishings for their guestrooms.[1] I've brought my sketches to one shop and two weeks later picked up twelve dining room chairs, built and painted exactly as I'd envisioned. I love living with furniture that I've had a chance to design myself. Italy gives many such opportunities to work with artisans. For me this is one of the *primo* advantages of living here.

Città di Castello also is known as the birthplace of the beauty Monica Bellucci and of the artist Alberto Burri, who left his work to the town in two museums, Palazzo Albizzini and Ex-Seccatoi del Tabacco, a former tobacco-drying warehouse. A physician in the Italian army in World War II, Burri began his painting using burlap sacks while he was a prisoner of war in Hereford, Texas. If you've never heard of him, you'll ask why when you visit. He was a forerunner of many of the directions of postwar art.

And then there's Il Postale, a worth-a-journey restaurant in a refitted postal bus garage. Marco and Barbara Bistarelli are young and adventurous. Marco's duck breast with artichokes manages to be both earthy and ethereal. Eating under their care always shows me something new. Who would think to serve cabbage with lobster and a drizzle of hazelnut oil? What would Maria Montessori have ordered? Maybe the *musetto di maiale con salsa amatriciana, sedano e pecorino* would have tempted her: a little pig snout with celery and sheep's cheese and a traditional sauce of tomatoes, garlic, a few red pepper flakes, and pancetta. Amatriciana comes from Amatrice in Lazio, where the recipe originally called for *guanciale,* cheek meat, instead of pancetta. Maria, being an innovator herself, probably would have called out *"Class dismissed!"* at the thought of Il Postale's pear William soufflé with chocolate sauce or the lemon mousse with cubes of mango gel and a fresh celery salsa.

⌒

AMONG THE CHARMS of the upper Tiber valley is Archeologia Arborea. The late Livio dalla Ragione collected rare varieties of fruit trees from abandoned farms, monastery and convent cloisters, and orchards. With his daughter, Isabella, who carries on the work, he started an arboretum in San Lorenzo di Lerchi, just outside town. The trees survive not only as themselves but as a remembrance of an earlier way of life. The Clogmaker's Fig reminds us that the fig wood used to be preferred for making farmer's clogs. When the farmers left the land, the tree almost disappeared. Peasant's Steak Pear speaks for itself.

You can walk the orchard in the warm months, make friends with the Little Convent Apple, Goose Cherry, Giant Fig of the Zoccolanti Friars, Icicle Pear, Small Bloody Peach, Drunken Apple, Ox Muzzle Apple, Pink Stone Apple, Little Fox Pear, and many more. The names seem to contain old tastes: Pink Strawberry Apple, Chestnut Apple, Butter Pear, Lemon Apple, and Cinnamon Pear.

If you adopt a tree, you are entitled to its harvest. The proviso, however, requires you to leave three fruits—one for the sun, one for the earth, and one for the tree itself. This sounds like something St. Francis of Assisi could have written. *Che vita,* what a life, to dwell among these fruit trees.

Perhaps someone brought Luca a basket of dark green figs as he painted the striped leggings on the men in *The Martyrdom of Saint Sebastian.*

◝～◞

Petto d'Anatra Glassato al Caramello
Speziato e Carciofi
Duck Breast with Caramelized Spices and Artichokes

Marco Bistarelli, the chef and co-owner, with his wife, Barbara, of Il Postale, shared their recipe with us. Marco recommends the Anatra Muta for this recipe, what we call the Muscovy Duck, and specifies a female duck.

Serves 4

Salt and pepper
2 duck breasts, about 8 ounces each, skin left on
2 tablespoons extra-virgin olive oil
8 tablespoons butter
3 sprigs of thyme
4 garlic cloves, peeled
Peel and juice of 1 lemon, separated
4 whole fresh artichokes
Handful of fresh parsley, chopped
Dash of white wine (about ¼ cup)
1 cup sugar
20 juniper berries, ground
20 seeds of coriander, ground
20 grains of pink peppercorn, ground
10 whole cumin seeds, ground
Sprinkling of curry
2 fresh chilies, seeded and diced
2 tablespoons balsamic vinegar

Salt and pepper the duck breasts on both sides. Put the oil, butter, thyme, and garlic in a cast-iron pan, sauté 1 minute, then add the lemon peel and duck, skin side down, and cook until the meat reaches a temperature of 125 to 130 degrees F (measured with a cooking thermometer). Remove and keep warm. Reserve the remaining garlic and butter mixture.

Meanwhile, remove all the leaves from the artichokes, spoon out the thistle, and quarter the hearts. Bring a pot of water to a boil and add the lemon juice and artichoke pieces; cook until the artichoke hearts are tender. Submerge the artichokes in a bowl of ice water to stop them from cooking.

To the sauté pan with the garlic-butter mixture added, mix the chopped parsley and white wine, and add the artichokes.

Prepare the spicy sauce by slowly cooking the sugar with the juniper berries, coriander, pink peppercorns, cumin, curry, chilies, and balsamic vinegar until they caramelize slightly.

Reheat the duck in a second sauté pan, adding the spiced caramelized sauce, and let it rest. Cut the duck into slices and place it on a serving dish, spooning over them the artichokes and the sauce.

RISOTTO CON TARTUFI BIANCHI
Risotto with White Truffles

When our friend Fulvio and his wife, Aurora, came to see us in the United States, they brought a gemstone-like white truffle, known as the Alba truffle, the kind found in the Piedmont region of Italy, which we immediately included in our dinner that night. He even brought a truffle slicer. Fulvio had made his Barolo risotto for us before (included in *Bringing Tuscany Home*), so we've adapted his recipe for a truffle risotto.

There are truffles and there are truffles—so beware. We've

had summer truffles that are woody and tasteless, and some in jars are a mere wisp of the real thing.

For all their reputation for being *molto caro,* very expensive, truffles, at least in restaurants in Italy, are used frequently, in season, shaved over pasta.

Serves 4

    6 cups chicken stock
    2 large shallots, finely chopped
    2 tablespoons extra-virgin olive oil
    2 cups carnaroli *rice*
    ½ cup white wine
    ½ cup grated parmigiano
    1 white truffle

Heat the stock and keep it at a simmer. In a separate stockpot, sauté the shallots in the oil for 5 minutes, then add the rice and mix to coat. After 3 minutes, start to gradually ladle in the stock and wine as the rice absorbs the liquid. Keep stirring and ladling in more until the rice is done, al dente. Stir in the grated *parmigiano,* and season to taste. At the table, shave the truffle over the risotto.

August Begins

Salve, caro—

Super-duper crazy-hazy here. Festival ends tonight and has been intense, *magnifico.* Pizza party for twenty today, bocce tournament, darts, swimming. Willie is in *paradiso.* Driving all over Tuscany. Can't count the houseguests. My mind has turned into a *fungo porcino.* My blood has turned into Brunello. Miss you— why did you go? Catch up soon . . . xxxxx F

—EMAIL TO ALBERTO

AUGUST BEGINS CALMLY ENOUGH. MORNING walks to town. In and out before tourist din fills the piazza. The gathering of marjoram, thyme, and sage, tying bunches with string and hanging them to dry. My stack of summer reading diminishing during quiet afternoons. We spend mornings at Bramasole, working on writing projects, cooking, tending the roses, then nights at Fonte for moonlight swims. Ed fires up the grill and we roll out pizzas or slide a *pasta al forno* into the bread oven. Late-summer kitchen darlings are thinly sliced vegetables, any vegetables, layered with lasagne, *parmigiano,* and béchamel. This is so light and, at the same time, rich. The Cardinali and the Callichia families come out on Sunday afternoons to lounge, swim, and cut a watermelon. Aurora brings a plum *crostata*. I make sage shortbread and put out a platter of cheeses, prosecco, water, and a cooler of lemonade. They all arrive with backpacks because the Italians bring several suits to a pool or beach. After each dip, they change into a dry suit. They go through three or four suits, managing to change—years of practice—under a wrapped towel. Watching Claudio maneuver, I think that there are endless cultural differences between us and the Italians, large and small. "Why so many bathing suits?" I ask.

"Wet *costume*?" He grimaces.

Italians also bask in the sun. My dermatologist arms me with SPF 50 sunblock; I've had two suspicious spots burned off, blamed on my days on southern beaches. But here are all these *bronzati* bodies, the older women in bikinis looking quite fine. A paleface, I'm stationed under the umbrella. Ed cavorts in the pool, but I know he has secretly lathered SPF 30 over his face.

When the afternoon cools, we play *bocce* and I'm grudgingly applauded for my "luck." Another cultural point. If they play *bocce* as a birthright, isn't it *wrong* for an American to knock their balls, so to speak?

⟡

THEN ASHLEY AND Willie arrive at the Rome airport. We wait while the customs doors swing open and dazed passengers find the light of day. Face after expectant face, drivers flashing name signs, joyous reunions, people controlled by their mountainous luggage: Finally I spot Ashley's pink sweater, Willie pulling his red and yellow suitcase. He runs into my open arms, almost knocking me backward. *Grazie mille* to the travel gods, they're here. Safe and here. I exhale the long breath I've held since they departed the United States.

We're so excited that Ed misses the "Firenze/Nord" turn and we meander in a backwater of Rome for a half hour. Just what you want to do when you land from a transatlantic flight.

$\backsim$

THE TEMPO QUICKENS; our lulled days are over. Willie runs around the garden, visits every room, naming and therefore reclaiming what he remembers. With no luck, he tries to fit into his rustic highchair, where at six months he had his first taste of pasta with ragù. He finds his bow and arrow, books in Italian, and various soccer balls Italians continue to give him. Ashley locates her sandals, bathrobe, and bathing suit. Their rooms fill with the happy scatter of their summer clothes. As she has each time she's ever entered my house, Ashley says, "I'm hungry." She's delirious to find that Gilda has brought her an eggplant parmigiana and a roast chicken and I've baked a berry crisp and a chocolate cake.

Ashley loves to spend several hours in town every morning, ordering coffee in a couple of bars, sitting in the piazza talking and absorbing *Italy*. Willie, six now, has a standing order for his *merenda,* a ham and cheese *panino* with a *limonata,* lemon soda, at Bar Signorelli. He'd rather be at Fonte with Albano, who lets him help with the pool filter, the locks, the *orto*. He does appreciate the toy-sized trash truck collecting toy-sized trash bags, the street worker raising a cloud of stone dust and Benito opening the old green doors of his Antica Drogheria. The shop closes up so tightly you'd think the Guelphs were about to storm the city and steal the *pappa reale,* artisan honey, pecorino from Pienza, and dried *funghi porcini*.

A moveable feast of friends stops at the table; they visit, share the *Herald Tribune*—a tradition even though more up-to-date news is available on the Internet—and we linger as the protecting shadow recedes and the dog-day sun falls full upon us.

SINCE ASHLEY BUYS all their clothes during her annual visit, we must shop. We drive to special stores we know in Umbertide, Chiassa Superiore, the Prada outlet, pop into the small shops in Camucia—one as chic as any in Florence—and the dreaded Val di Chiana outlet mall, where she finds great tops. She has an unerring instinct for what looks good on her and whizzes through before I've looked at the first rack.

She wants lunch out so she can visit all the *trattorie* during her so-brief two weeks, all the time she could manage this year. We eat *ribollita,* though it's a winter dish, roasted guinea hen, and pots of the ragù she dreams of back in the U.S.

By afternoon, Willie gets to run free at Fonte, play in the pool, and aim with his adored crossbow, a *dangerous* medieval weapon in a miniature version. Ed ratchets down a few decades and they invent fantastical adventures as the arrow is launched toward the target. When we try to get Willie to rest, he insists he does not need a nap. Usually, after a couple of chapters, he drops off because he was up late the night before.

Inevitably, we are going to be out late again and this year he so much wants to be included, not left with a babysitter. We're inclined to take him out. He's here such a short time and I miss him terribly when he leaves. He's interested in everything, more fun than anyone, and his pleasure shines. During their annual visit, I spend my insomniac hours dreaming that we all could live here permanently. By day, I am practical.

AUGUST BECOMES A constant round of dinners. Every Italian on vacation—that's almost the entire population—decides to have a party. Placido threads the spit with pigeons and

chicken. Willie eats two bowls of Fiorella's pasta with tomatoes and basil. We are twelve at their outdoor table. Willie and
Claudia, an eleven-year-old beauty who's been his friend since
he was two, run off to see the falcon and Placido's horse Zucchero, who slid and caused Placido's near-fatal accident. At
Melva and Jim's, we grill steaks and it starts to rain. We grab
everything off the table and run indoors, then it stops and
we take our peach pie outside. At Claudio's camp in the hills,
we dine under a pergola with Edo and Maria's Argentinean
guests. Aurora serves her chocolate torte *and* a birthday cake
for Claudia. At Edo and Maria's summerhouse, they've set up
a salon outside—lamps and rugs, even paintings propped up
on a sideboard. With Edo, expect the unexpected. He mans the
grill, turning out steaks and sausage and hunks of pancetta,
crackly and melting in fat. The wine flows and the night flows
for a long time.

Then the Tuscan Sun Festival begins and August really
heats up, literally and figuratively. This is our sixth festival, so
I know to expect the greatest music and the latest nights. The
concerts begin at nine. Because the festival takes place in the
Teatro Signorelli, the audience is limited to 350. The Teatro, a
nineteenth-century opera house with five tiers of boxes, offers
not only excellent acoustics but an intimate connection with
the musician—every grimace, twinkle in the eye, every flung
drop of sweat. The noisy air-conditioning must be turned off
during the performances, then switched back on during the
interval. Hence, the sweat. Everyone files out for intermission,
passing the watchful eyes of Luca in the form of a white plas-
ter bust. Whether movie, lecture, or concert, intermission is a
must in Italy: No Italian can go for two hours without talking.

Afterward, the musicians and those of us associated with
the festival proceed to dinner in the courtyard of the Etruscan
museum. Sometimes, there's more music at the dinner.

These are heady days. Joshua Bell plays "The Four Seasons" with enough muscle to revive this familiar piece. José Cura's voice wants to push back the walls of the small theater. I watch Willie clap his hands above his head and shout *"Bravo!"* The Bolshoi Ballet performs in the filled-to-seams piazza. Willie squirms, as he does not in concerts. I have to admit, ballet seems . . . *archaic*. Fitting, I think, for my continuous sense of time folding back in the piazza.

We have cooking lessons and lectures in the afternoons, art exhibits, short concerts in the piazza, a fresco workshop, a Renaissance lunch—it's summer camp for grown-ups, with a dash of glam. One night, Robert Redford reads poems that have influenced his life. He's here because his wife, Sibylle Szaggars, has a show of her recent paintings. Since we have a mutual friend, he kisses me on both cheeks when we're introduced and says how much he's been looking forward to meeting me. *Mamma mia*—Robert Redford, oh, how divine he was in *Out of Africa*. He invites us to lunch with several of his friends and I'm seated next to him. We eat *tagliolini al tartufo,* truffle pasta, and talk about books, books, books—Steinbeck, Faulkner, Stegner, and Thomas Wolfe, whose books he read when he made a movie in Asheville, North Carolina. He talks about studying in Italy when he was young and how he's always loved this country. He asks Ashley all about her work. I hear him asking others about themselves and when I later remark on this to Ed, he guesses that "Bob," as we may call him now, probably gets sick of hearing the same set of reactions over and over. "Think of how many people have asked what is his favorite film of all time," he muses. "Imagine how many people have told him where they were when they saw *Butch Cassidy,* or how *The Way We Were* reminds them of themselves."

"Maybe he found a way around how fame isolates you. The

American obsession with celebrity is so sick. He has to deal with that every day of his life." I would hate to be so famous.

"Well, how generous that he tries to connect with others."

All during the week he's here, I see him graciously attentive to those he meets. He must fight hard to remain a "normal" person.

The late-night dinners are exquisite. Enormous candelabra with wavering candles forming wax drip castles on the tablecloth, waiters pouring all the Cortona wines, stars mapped over the courtyard's sky, the entrances of the musicians and singers with the guests clapping and shouting. Then we serve ourselves at the bounteous buffet and settle down with friends at the round tables, reliving the concert and hearing the gossip, for, of course, there are affairs and fits and dramas: *She has a stalker. He has his wife at the villa, the mistress at the hotel. He had a baby with an old girlfriend.* The festival photographer, Henry Fair, holds forth about environmental ruin, jumps up to photograph a diva, allows Willie to take pictures with his camera, jokes far into the night. Barrett, the founder, and a pianist himself, basks in the momentary triumph of the evening, before the niggling details of tomorrow can catch him. Ed, tanned in his beige summer suit, Laura in a stylish Roman sundress, the handsome tenor in black silk, torches casting dramatic chiaroscuro shadows on shoulders and brows, high laughter, laden tables—we are feasting in this ancient *cortile* and we are not so different from those who have done the same in centuries before us. *Luca, were you here, too, raising a glass some long-ago enchanted evening?*

⌒

AT FONTE, WE suddenly are invaded by baby *cinghiale*. Albano and Willie scour the confines where the electric fence previously kept out the beasts. They determine that the *cinghiale* are scooting under the wire. The big hog-mamas, not wanting their noses shocked, wait outside while the *bambini* rampage. With Fabio's help, Albano strings barbed wire under the electric wire, but every morning, Willie leans out the window and gleefully announces, "They came back! There's a *lot* of damage." They rip grass from under the oak tree in their vain search for acorns. Then they claw down in the earth hoping for grubs. We piece back the grass clumps and Albano rolls the lawn flat. What marauders. I get the idea to lay wire fencing over their favored spot. Maybe they'll learn and leave. This enrages them. They tear up more. They learn to tunnel under the wire. Then they discover the roses and add a new level of destruction. Ashley hears them snorting under her window. Albano finds seven asleep under the apple tree. I am sorry to say he bashes one with a shovel. With this bumper crop of boar, the hunters will be happy in September.

Ed chases two at midnight, shouting *"Via, via!"* and I watch him waving the flashlight as he stumbles in the dark. "Out, out!" he shouts. The spectacle of him going full tilt after wild pigs—I've never seen him in a more ridiculous scene. He's incensed when I laugh. They've upturned stone paths. "Do you have a better idea?" he snarls. In the morning he decides on another line of stronger barbed wire and another electrical cord as well.

Coming home late, we spot four of these young Turks stopped in the headlights. Willie is delighted to make their acquaintance. I know he's on the side of these renegades, as I am. Maddening they are, but something in Willie knows to approve their wildness, their midnight raids to get what they want from the real invaders of their hillside.

～✦～

LASAGNE DI VERDURA
Vegetable Lasagna

Pasta sheets, rolled thin, make lasagna an ethereal dish. I could write a book on lasagna. An old favorite, pesto lasagna, has about a hundred calories a bite. Worth every morsel! The cooked pasta is layered with pesto, *bechamella,* and *parmigiano,* topped with coarse bread crumbs. Another beauty—layer the pasta with *bechamella, parmigiano,* and lots of tiny veal meatballs. Some winning combinations for vegetable lasagna: zucchini and tomatoes; eggplant and peppers; roasted asparagus; caramelized onions and chopped parsley; yellow, red, and green bell peppers in separate layers.

Serves 4 to 6

6 sheets of fresh pasta

FOR THE BECHAMELLA SAUCE
4 tablespoons butter
4 tablespoons flour
2 cups milk
3 garlic cloves, minced
1 tablespoon thyme, chopped
½ teaspoon salt
½ teaspoon pepper

FOR THE FILLING
2 tablespoons extra-virgin olive oil or butter
1 minced onion

3 cups fresh vegetables of the season, chopped
Herbs that complement the vegetables

1½ cups parmigiano
Butter and coarse, toasted bread crumbs, for the topping

Preheat oven to 350 degrees F.

Cut pasta sheets to fit a large baking dish. (Some of the middle layers can be in more than one piece.) Lightly oil the dish.

For the *bechamella* sauce: Melt the butter, stir in the flour, and cook together without browning. After 3 or 4 minutes, remove from heat and whisk in the milk all at once. Return to heat, stir, and simmer until the sauce thickens. Add the garlic to the sauce, along with the thyme, salt, and pepper.

For the filling: In a large pan, heat the oil or butter and sauté the onion and chopped fresh vegetables and herbs for 5 to 10 minutes, until almost tender.

Assembly: Cook one sheet of pasta until barely done, remove from the boiling water, and briefly drain on a dishtowel spread on the counter. Place the semi-dry pasta sheet in the lightly oiled baking dish and cover it with a layer of *bechamella* sauce, a layer of vegetables, and a sprinkling of cheese. Continue cooking the next pasta sheet as you prepare each layer. Add a spoon or two of the pasta water to the sauce if you've used too much on the first layers. Top the dish with buttered bread crumbs and more *parmigiano*. Bake, uncovered, for 30 minutes.

∼⁓∼

Torta di Pesche di Melva
Melva's Peach Pie

Melva is certainly one of the most meticulous and joyous cooks I know—what you'll find at her table without fail is exuberance of taste. She brings out plate after plate of wonderful tastes, and her husband, Jim, keeps the glasses full of Tuscan wine. Her antique napkins are big enough to curl up in after dinner and dream soporific dreams.

Melva prefers white peaches for this pie. If the peaches are not sweet enough, adjust the sugar. Here's her recipe:

Serves 6 to 8

> 1 cup flour
> ½ cup white sugar, plus 1 tablespoon
> ¼ teaspoon salt
> ½ cup unsalted butter, very, very (emphasis Melva's) cold
>   and cut into cubes, plus 1 tablespoon butter
> ¼ cup ice water, with ice cubes floating in it
> 5 to 6 cups peaches, sliced
> ½ cup brown sugar
> 1 teaspoon cinnamon
> ½ teaspoon freshly ground nutmeg
> 1 tablespoon flour
> Juice of ½ lemon to prevent discoloration of fruit

Preheat oven to 400 degrees F.

Pulse the flour, sugar, salt, and butter in a food processor until they take the texture of small peas. Transfer to a bowl and add the water, 1 tablespoon at a time, mixing it lightly with a fork, adding a little more until it binds. It should start to stick together, but do not overmix. You don't want it too wet or it will be tough, and if it's too dry it will fall apart, so that's why I like to use my hands. Make a ball, put it in a plastic bag, and flatten it a bit. Chill it for at least 2 hours. You can do it the day before, but not more than that. Then roll it out (see Note), put it in a 9-inch pie pan, cover with plastic wrap, and let it rest for 30 minutes in the refrigerator.

Combine the peaches, brown sugar, cinnamon, nutmeg, flour, and lemon juice, being careful not to mix everything together until you're ready to assemble the pie. Pour the mixture into the piecrust and cover the edges with foil to prevent browning. If you are using one crust, and have excess dough left, you can fold it over the peaches so it looks like a rustic tart. If you use the second crust, roll it out, place on top, crimp edges, and prick holes in the top. Bake for 20 minutes or until you can see the bottom of the crust start to brown a little, then reduce the temperature to 375 degrees F and bake for another 30 minutes.

During the last 10 minutes, remove the foil from the crimped edges.

Let the pie sit out for at least 40 minutes before serving.

NOTE: *Melva sometimes adds chopped pecans (very difficult to find in Italy) to the dough when she rolls it out. The pecans go especially well with the one-crust approach.*

Mangia, Willie, Mangia— Eat, Willie, Eat

LATE IN THE AFTERNOON, WILLIE GOES TO the *orto*. Time to pick dinner. As he runs downhill with two baskets, we follow his red shorts and the sun bouncing off his blond-turning-brown hair. At the gate, three knives lodge in the fence wire. He starts cutting lettuce (thrilled to use the knife), scrambles along the fence picking raspberries, eating them, burrowing his hand among the leaves for tiny strawberries and in the adjacent patch for larger ones. Best always to him is digging potatoes. "There! There! Two, three."

Our own garden-glow feels profound, but his shrieks, as the potatoes roll out from the shovel— strangely clean—or show their yellow skins through the dirt, return us to the louder delight of the discoverer. Earth candy! Pulling up a carrot also provides the eureka moment. Squatting among the frilly greens, he tugs and the carrot erupts from the dirt so suddenly that he almost falls backward. Stubby, gangly, smooth or with little chin hairs, maybe the size of a little finger, none is regular like the ones from the grocery store. Carrots can be taken to the two rabbits, Red Eye and Green Eye, who hover in the back of their cage in near terror when Mr. Blue Eye lifts the lid. Albano has taught Willie to lift the rabbits by their ears. He claims this does not hurt them and keeps them from scratching. Red Eye is white, more docile than black Green Eye, who has mighty claws. They don't seem to appreciate their daily carrots, but Willie persists.

"They don't know how lucky they are," I tell him. "Domenica would have cooked them by now." At the end of summer, she will offer them roasted with fennel, if we want. Which we don't. Rabbit is one thing, *pet* rabbit another.

"Franny has said no," Willie repeats as a little mantra.

We slice off a couple of cucumbers, six tomatoes, tender green beans, some mint, thyme, basil, and a few zucchini still small enough to have the just-opening flower attached. Heaven we have in our baskets, heaven to eat this way. Although Albano was in the military for only two years, he brings a snap-to precision to everything he does. When we started to plot a vegetable garden, he whipped up a porcupine/rabbit/hedgehog-proof wire fence (going almost a foot underground with it) and brought seeds from his own garden. We bought flats of vegetables at the market, tomatoes from a farmer, and scoured the nurseries for yellow raspberries. I wanted *ceci,* chickpeas; Ashley wanted various hot peppers; Ed wanted fennel and chard; we all wanted an endless supply of parsley, basil, celery, onion, and carrots. We'd not had much luck with *melanzane*—the word so much more apt for the plant than "eggplant"—at Bramasole. At Fonte they thrive. Their delicate lavender flower looks transported from a Persian miniature. We gather four for Imam Bayildi (The Priest Fainted). At a restaurant in Naflion, Greece, we loved this intensely flavored roasted mixture piled into its own shell. Why did he faint? Supposedly the dish used so much olive oil that his wife ran through her dowry of twelve huge *orci,* terracotta vats, in as many days. But, more likely, the *melanzane* transcended its own possibilities and sent him into a swoon. We brought the recipe home.

The garden is edenic—neat rows, forked dry branches staked among the beans for them to climb, long bamboo trellises for the tomatoes, a line of robust artichokes and smart little mounded patches for the lettuces, which come and go quickly. We reseed each bed as one patch readies itself for the bowl, so that they're always tender. You have to be a rabbit yourself to keep up with lettuces. If you skip a few days, a whole row turns to limp leather. Some that bolt we let go, just to see how outlandish a lettuce can become.

We were able to show Albano how to lay straw for the strawberries so they stay off the ground and are easier to spot. That red pops out—red as the taffeta dress I wore to the Dixie Ball, the count's Ferrari parked in the piazza, a cardinal's hat, a drop of blood.

Albano has taught us how to plant tomatoes up to their first set of leaves and later how to remove extra shooters. He refrains from watering them too much, which dilutes the flavor. He's shown us how to braid garlic and onions and how to dry and store potatoes. The garden, once started, is not as much work as our prior plots at Bramasole. Because Albano and Ed removed all the weeds and let the soil rest empty for a few months, we weed lightly and have not been plagued with salads mixed with a dozen greeny volunteers.

We wash off the first layer of dirt at the outdoor sink, wash again in the kitchen. Willie, ah, another knife, slices the zucchini and flowers and we sauté them in olive oil, sprinkling torn mint leaves over them. He tails the beans; they steam and are given a douse of lemon juice and some thyme. The beauteous salad perks up with maybe half a cup of herbs, enough oil to make the leaves glisten lightly, and that's it. The potatoes don't need peeling; their skin is thin and taut. Willie precisely quarters them, then they get a brief steam bath, a few shakes of oil, and a lot of parsley. Ashley likes to make her childhood favorite from Julia Child, potatoes dauphinois. Ed prefers them cubed into a bowl, tossed with rosemary and olive oil, then roasted on parchment until they're crisp and crusty. *Che patate!* Is there an ode to the potato? Their mute underground life, their little spotty eyes, their starchy juice, ichor of dark dirt—Keats, Pablo Neruda, how could you overlook them?

I serve the sliced tomatoes and cucumbers separately. When vegetables are this fresh, best to let them sing solos about their own true virtues. Although we may grill sausages or roast a chicken, these summer dinners are all about the plates spread out on the table, full of what's ready to rip right now.

~

WILLIE THOUGHT HE didn't like salad until his *orto* adventures began. The vegetables became personal. He's always liked working in the kitchen right along with whoever's cooking. At two, three, we gave him real jobs: measuring flour, cracking eggs, whisking—even though the cleanup factor multiplied. For Willie, the zucchini's finest hour is the fried flower. Ed showed him how to pick the male blooms, those not attached to developing zucchini. These are suitable for frying. Simply dip them in a thin batter of beer and flour, and fry quickly in hot, hot peanut oil. We like, almost as much, fried sage leaves. Like American southerners, Tuscans will fry anything. We were all enchanted to sample crisp cascades of wisteria and fried fronds of *sambuca,* elderflower, at a friend's house.

For Ed and me, an unexpected bonus of having a grandchild is that we get to cook for him. When he was an infant, Ed began passing coffee beans and strawberries and gorgonzola and fennel seeds under his nose. "Smell this. Doesn't this smell good?" We thought we saw a glimmer of assent in his eyes. "Look," Ed would say as Willie flung his pablum and carrots on the wall, "this is fried calamari and you can have some very soon." We were rewarded with a milky smile. His favorite toy at age one was an old La Pavoni espresso maker that Ed had replaced. Willie loved the pump handle, seeing his face in the stainless steel, filling the tank with water, and toddling toward the electrical outlet with a purposeful look.

As a picky eater since just about that age, I didn't want to see Willie follow my squeamish tastes. I didn't mean to but I passed on my defective palate to my daughter. She will not eat anything that could have had a name, will not eat anything that quivers. I can't face an oyster or the brains and renal organs of any animal. It's a burden for us.

Ed will try anything. Usually he's game when served pots of tripe, songbirds held by their beaks and crunched (bones and all), sea urchins, and internal organs that should never see daylight. I surreptitiously have slipped many morsels of lamb heart and rabbit kidney mousse onto his plate. He looks at me pityingly. "Won't you just try?" The only meal I've seen him balk at was at the Cardinali table when they served veal knuckles. They love this country soul food. Ed struggled to eat the gelatinous, cartilage-riddled, bony hunks. I feigned a *Really not hungry after a huge lunch out.* At their dinner table a couple of weeks later, Fiorella brought out another steamy platter of these knuckles because "Ed had enjoyed them so much."

❧

EATING WITH OUR neighbors, and at other friends' houses, actually gave us the idea to offer Willie the chance to relish meals like Italians. How many times have I seen small children hold out their plate for another helping of calves' liver, bitter greens, pork belly, or lamb kidney? At Antonello's, our electrician who has big casual dinners, we saw five boys head back to the stove for second bowlfuls of snails. Then, in a fine restaurant in the Veneto, I overheard a boy, maybe five, choose the cheese course for his dessert. I'd ordered the chocolate extravaganza myself, even though my white pants were getting hard to zip. The waiter wheeled over the cart and the boy pointed to four cheeses.

We'd go back to the United States and see the dreary "Children's Menu": chicken tenders, hamburgers, pizza, grilled cheese, hot dogs, corn dogs, and, of course, fries. Fries, fries, fries—the horrifying predominance of the French fry in our diet explains a lot. In moderation, a crisp little pile, yes. But *everything* comes with fries. Insane!

I don't think I've ever seen a children's menu in Tuscany. Isn't that a profound cultural cue? Children eat like their families and their families are eating as well as anyone on earth.

⌒

ITALY MAKES WILLIE'S initiation rites easy. Seated among adults and small children, he sees them lapping up whatever is served. The children drink water, never soda. Even in cafés the kids order pear or peach juice in those neat little bottles; colas are for when your tummy is roiling and needs to settle. A mixed carrot, lemon, and orange juice turned out to be a hit.

At the table, there is no discussion among the children about what someone does or does not like, because they like everything Aurora, Fiorella, Lina, Ombretta, Giusi, Silvia, or Donatella serve. The language helps, too. *Coniglio* and *agnello* don't convey the loaded sentiments of Peter Rabbit and Mary's little lamb. While Ashley and I cringe when Domenica discusses her rabbits she will butcher and bone, for Willie—we are amazed—it sounds normal, or maybe abstract. He's yet to witness the bloody transition. Her cages are full of bunnies. Soon, she's pulling a savory pan redolent of thyme and rosemary out of the oven. He's made many stops at Placido's cages and chicken yard on the way to dinner. In the afternoon, a guinea hen is selected; that night the spit turns. When I was a child, I watched Drew, our yard man, wring chickens' necks with a hard snap and the hapless creatures would circle the yard, wings flapping, until they collapsed. Somehow the distance from there to fried chicken and mashed potatoes remained vast.

WILLIE QUICKLY REALIZED that a lot of fun was going on in the kitchen. We gave him his own small but real whisk, wooden spoons, spatulas, a green apron with his name in orange, a set of measuring spoons, and a kitchen scale. Learning to crack and separate eggs resulted in several on the floor. I taught him, as Simca taught me, to break the egg into your palm and let the white run between your fingers.

He whirled the lazy Susan spice rack until the jars flew off. Ed beat whites until he could hold the copper bowl upside down over Willie's head without them sliding out. A big time, as much for us as for Willie. What fun, weighing chocolate, cutting out parchment paper to fit the pan, setting the timer— such solid accomplishments with rewards to follow. I relearned the novelty of a sifter because he loves the soft mountain of flour snowing into the yellow bowl. True to his early training, he holds out the vanilla bean. "Smell this." And the cinnamon and nutmeg. "Eddie, come here. Don't these smell good?" He licks beaters. So do I.

After pancakes, waffles, brownies, cupcakes, and cookies, he learned to make focaccia with Ed. He reveled in kneading and punching down the dough, then pressing his thumb into the surface, dotting it with olives and sun-dried tomatoes. And then eating big squares for a snack, having it sliced for a prosciutto and tomato sandwich for lunch, or lining up thin slices around his plate to eat with soup. He and Ed moved on to pasta, which combined two passions, cooking and machinery. Willie loves the fittings for the hand-cranked pasta maker and the process of turning the handle, feeding out the strands or sheets, then using the ravioli rolling pin.

Often when he comes in the kitchen, he says, "Let's cook something." By now he's chief carrot peeler, lettuce spinner, coffee grinder. Last year, at five, he insisted on making pesto alone. His latest feat is aioli. He can pour slowly and steadily the olive oil into the whirring dry mustard, lemon juice, roasted garlic, oil, and egg until it's rich yellow-green and thick for his sandwiches.

~

WHEN I WAS growing up, we had a cook, Willie Bell. My mother, too, was an excellent cook. I never remember being invited to help. Watching Willie, I think how much I would have liked to be involved, as I think most children would. I do remember being told to stay *out* of the way. Big, military-scale maneuvers were under way. The bridge club was coming, my father had invited forty for lunch in the yard, or a party for a bride was imminent. I watched and, I suppose, learned by osmosis, because when I married at twenty-two, I seemed to already know how to at least get dinner on the table.

In Mother's kitchen, my spot was on the counter by the fridge. *Don't kick that cabinet door.* Willie Bell always seemed to be grinding meat with a gadget that screwed tight onto the counter lip. I thought to myself, *I never will touch raw meat.* She made sausage patties, and ground ham for a dish she made with pimientos and olives in a loaf pan.

My mother made frozen fruit salad and Chicken Divan and Black Bottom Pie for her luncheons. My father hunted quail and dove in the fall. An early memory (three?), clear as a photograph, is of him standing in the doorway holding open his brown hunting coat. All the tiny inside pockets were filled with dead birds with drooped heads. At the sink, Willie Bell already worked over a pile of doves, plucking them with a little plonking sound as she jerked at the feathers. Their smooth mauve bodies were thrown in a mound beside me. Later the cream-smothered doves and quail appeared at the table with cheese grits and Willie's supreme biscuits—crunchy on the outside, soft within. I liked the peppery quail but never would eat dove because of the creepy color of their stripped bodies.

From our Georgia kitchen issued forth lemony pound cake, country captain chicken, corn soufflé, caramel cake, tarragon green beans, deviled crab, pecan pie, vegetable croquettes, guinea hen, Sally Lunn, country hams, grapefruit aspic, chocolate icebox cake, pan-roasted duck (beware of biting buckshot deep in the flesh), date pudding, brown sugar muffins, watermelon rind pickles, fried chicken, Brunswick stew, ladyfinger peas, peach pickles, butterbeans, squash casserole, fruit cobblers, ambrosia, cheese straws, lemon cheesecake, icebox cookies, date bars, jetties, roasted pecans, and peach ice cream. I sat on the churn and Willie Bell cranked the handle.

To my ears, this is a mesmerizing litany, a splendid inheritance. If there's a fire at my house, I'll run for the cabinet where I keep the notebook of my mother's recipes. That scrawled, stained, sometimes baffling collection—no method is included, ever—is far more precious than the diamond she slipped off her finger and gave me when I went off to college. The red cover and some of the pages are burned around the edges from when I set it on the stove and lit the wrong burner. Somehow, this gives it a fragile feel: something snatched and treasured from the consuming fire of the past.

Growing up with such fresh, made-from-scratch food, how did I turn out to be a picky eater? What a brat I must have been.

I used to grade the meal, announcing to my mother that she and Willie Bell got an A, B, or C. Why did they laugh instead of sending me to my room? I didn't like breakfast and, if I was served an egg, I cajoled Willie Bell into eating the white as I sopped the runny yolk onto my toast. As the third girl, I usually was ignored at the table. No one ever said, "Try this," or, "Clean that plate." I hid my book in my lap and constantly looked down to read. Most of what I still won't eat is, I notice, what's missing from my mother's recipes. We were inland people. No fish. Fried catfish was served locally but I didn't like the name *catfish,* or the whiskery look that inspired it. Finny items on a menu still give me the most trouble. I can appreciate flounder and halibut, but they don't tempt me. Having visited several hatcheries, I won't eat any farm-raised fish. They swim in poop their whole lives. I'm saved in seafood restaurants by crab, shrimp (wild-caught only), sea bass, sole, and lobster. Although we lived in a rural area where the pig and cow thrived, I never met sweetbreads, veal cheeks, liver, or anything involving nether regions, inner organs, or feet. Willie Bell loved a good gizzard dinner. Needless to say, the word put me off. Later, as an aspiring cook taking Simca's course in France, I was horrified to see her demonstrate how to amputate a chicken's feet and cook them in a soup.

Willie sometimes balks, too. He won't eat the crust of bread. He says he does not like broccoli, though he eats it. When he says, "I don't like rice," we answer, "What's not to like, sir?" He tried clams, and I thought he fought back tears. When he comes to Italy, we establish a 15 New Tastes Prize and through the weeks he enthusiastically lists his new conquests—cheeses, truffle bruschetta, limoncello (a sip), red currants, farro, squid ink risotto, quince preserves, *salume,* pumpkin ravioli, and black figs. For his prize, he gets to pick out a new book. Our reward is his engagement at the table. He has joined the conversation that has been taking place on this hillside for centuries.

~ ✍ ~

AGLIO ARROSTO
Roasted Garlic

Albano is a master grower of garlic. After he pulls up the drying garlic bulbs, he'll spend a morning braiding, and by noon he'll present us with three or four white plaits that will last us through the summer and fall. These garlics don't have the bitter taste that older garlic can get, mainly from the sprout in the center. You can remove the sprout by slicing the clove and lifting out the greeny sprout.

With some chopped nuts mixed in, roasted garlic is an easy *crostino*. Or, spread on bread and serve with any meat that has juices to dip into. And with bruschetta, pop it into your soup bowl.

Look for dense, good-sized heads of garlic.

> 4 *(or more) whole heads of garlic*
> *Olive oil*
> *Salt*

Preheat the oven to 450 degrees F.

Gently remove the papery outer skin of the garlic bulb and slice off the very top, exposing the cloves. Place each in a square of aluminum foil, pour some olive oil on it, and close it tight. Place in a small ovenproof dish.

Roast for 30 to 45 minutes, checking with fork tines after the first 30 minutes.

Let the garlic cool until ready to handle. The roasted bulbs are extremely sticky and there are a variety of ways to remove them from their skins. Take a paring knife and lightly dig out the cloves from the top. Or take a piece of waxed paper, put the garlic head on it root side up, and cover with another piece, then using the heel of your hand, your fingers, a small rolling pin, or a meat pounder, squeeze out the garlic. Scrape it off the waxed paper with a knife and into a glass container with a lid. Otherwise, and this seems best to me, you can separate the cloves gently and have your guests or yourself squeeze out the garlic onto a piece of bread, adding salt to taste.

⌒ ৽ ⌒

IMAM BAYILDI: THE PRIEST FAINTED
Stuffed or Filled Eggplant

Ed says that as with *stew,* the word *stuffed* is unfortunate when applied to food. We feel *stuffed* after Thanksgiving dinner's *stuffed* turkey (let's hope absent of *stuffed shirts* and other forms of *stuffiness*) and retire to the *overstuffed* sofa. We *stuff* our gym clothes in our gym bag as we leave the gym. We watch the gluttonous *stuff their faces* with hot dogs. We catch a cold and our nose is *stuffed up.* We get our *stuffing* knocked out of us in fifth grade. Some of us have the right *stuff* and some of us have the wrong. *Pieno* and *ripieno,* on the other hand, point to the idea of *fill, filled, full*—you're *full* to the brim, but that's a good thing. At least you're not *stuffed.*

Serves 4 to 6

2 large or 4 medium eggplants
4 tablespoons extra-virgin olive oil
1 large onion, chopped
4 garlic cloves, minced
½ cup parsley, chopped

5 fresh or canned tomatoes, chopped
2 tablespoons tomato paste
½ teaspoon salt
½ teaspoon pepper
¼ cup parmigiano

Preheat oven to 375 degrees F.

Cut each eggplant in two lengthwise. Being careful not to rip the skin, scoop out the white part, and chop, reserving the shells. Heat the oil in a sauté pan and add the onion, cooking until it softens, about 4 minutes. Add the garlic and continue cooking for another 2 minutes. Then add the eggplant, parsley, tomatoes, tomato paste, salt, and pepper, and cook for 5 to 7 minutes. In the meantime, place the shells on an oiled sheet pan. Fill them with the eggplant mixture, and sprinkle *parmigiano* on top. Bake for about 20 to 25 minutes. If the eggplants are large, you can halve them.

Pollo con Carciofi, Pomodori, e Ceci
Chicken with Artichokes,
Sun-Dried Tomatoes, and Chickpeas

Chickpeas are a late love of ours. Just a taste of chickpea fritters, Sicilian street food, and we were fans. Now we roast them for snacks, serve them with herbs and tomatoes as a cold salad, and adore them with this super-fast chicken dinner in one pot. Soak chickpeas overnight and simmer them in light stock with onion, celery, carrot, and garlic. Cooking them yourself yields a much better texture than you'll find in the overly soft and viscous canned chickpeas. Artichokes partner so well with *ceci*. Although fresh artichokes are a primary passion, in this recipe I opt for the convenience of canned or frozen ones.

Serves 4

> *5 tablespoons extra-virgin olive oil*
> *1 whole chicken, cut in 8 pieces, seasoned with salt and*
>   *pepper*
> *½ cup red wine*
> *¼ cup chopped Italian parsley*
> *¼ cup thyme or marjoram leaves*
> *2 cups chickpeas, cooked*
> *1 can of artichokes, drained*
> *½ cup sun-dried tomatoes*
> *1 medium onion, chopped and sautéed*

Preheat oven to 350 degrees F.

Heat the oil in a flameproof and ovenproof casserole. Sauté the chicken for 3 to 5 minutes per side in the oil. Do in batches if necessary. Add wine and transfer to a baking dish.

Mix the remaining ingredients, pour over the chicken, and bake, covered, for 30 to 45 minutes, depending on the size of the pieces, turning the chicken once.

FOCACCIA

What better place to focus on some focaccia than the *focolare,* Italian for hearth or fireplace, which could very well be the root of this ubiquitous bread. Willie and Ed make it often. It has a simplicity of preparation, a small number of ingredients, and everybody likes it. During the *vendemmia,* grape harvest, focaccia is baked for breakfast with small sugared grapes.

> *2 packages dry yeast*
> *2 cups warm water*
> *4 to 5 cups all-purpose flour*
> *1 or 2 tablespoons olive oil, plus more for bowl*
> *Coarse sea salt*
> *Rosemary, minced*

Preheat oven to 400 degrees F.

Combine the yeast and water in a large bowl and let stand for about 10 minutes. Then add 4 cups of flour to the bowl and mix well. On a floured surface, knead the dough for 10 to 15 minutes, adding flour as needed, until the dough is uniformly elastic. Oil a large bowl, add the dough, and turn to coat all sides with the oil, then cover with a tea towel and put in a warm place for 1 hour.

Punch down the dough—it should have about doubled— then spread it with your fingers onto a parchment-lined sheet pan. Cover with a tea towel and let it rise again for about 45 minutes.

With your fingertips, dimple the dough all over. Sprinkle with the 1 or 2 tablespoons of oil and then the coarse salt and minced rosemary.

Bake in a hot oven for 20 to 25 minutes, then slide off the sheet pan onto a cooling rack.

Slice into 1-inch strips for snacks or 3-inch squares for sandwiches.

MAIONESE ALL'AGLIO
Aioli—Garlic Mayonnaise

Aioli turns a sandwich into an event. A dab on asparagus, a dip for French fries or crudités, the binder for shrimp or chicken salads, a sauce for artichokes—aioli bumps it all up a notch. Since most people don't bother to make their own mayonnaise, it's fun to take a jar to hosts. By the way, you can make aioli in five minutes max.

Makes 1 cup

½ teaspoon dry mustard
1 egg plus 1 egg yolk
2 tablespoons lemon juice
3 garlic cloves
½ teaspoon salt
1 cup extra-virgin olive oil

Put the mustard, whole egg and egg yolk, lemon juice, garlic, salt, and ¼ cup of the oil in the food processor and process for 30 seconds. Then with the processor running, slowly, slowly pour in the remaining oil in a thin, steady stream, and process until emulsified.

Since the Etruscans

SINCE THE ETRUSCANS, AND MAYBE BEFORE, food in this hill town has been the daily focus of 99 percent of the population. Those tomb frescoes show people feasting even after death. They shimmy among the olive trees. And so it continues. Local people take their daily walk on the road below our house. Often, bits of conversation float up. We hear *ravioli, porcini, ricotta, noce, grappa, cinghiale, ciliege*. Often arguments ensue: "Lapo makes the best pecorino." "No, it's Carla." "What shit you speak!" "Carla's sheep graze on *insalata di campo*." "Hah! She has rats in her barn."

On and on. Where you eat well, where you don't. Who's stealing cantaloupes out of the fields, who raises rabbits on bread and greens, and who raises them on bought *mangimi*. Pruning the roses, clipping the hedge, we hear these *passeggiata* discussions constantly. We used to say, *Do they think of nothing but food?* Now we've joined them.

Our time here has exactly paralleled the rise in food and wine consciousness within Tuscany. When Ed and I first visited the local *trattorie* in 1990, the waiters offered two wines—*bianco* or *nero*. The menus could have been printed at a central office, because they were all the same. This was fine with us—we loved wild boar with pappardelle, hearty *ribollita,* grilled sausages, and the hefty *bistecca* with oil and rosemary. After a while, we began to seek out the one or two specialties of each trattoria: the marinated zucchini at one, the spinach gnocchi at another, the superb veal roast at our local restaurant that also catered for the Pope. Cheese was cheese: *parmigiano* or pecorino, and maybe a taleggio at the grocery store.

Fast-forward to the present and you find an amped-up culinary scene, an exploded wine appreciation, and an expansion of knowledge around artisan foods of all kinds. *Astounding.* For so long, Tuscany did not change; now change is coming rapidly. In our town of 2,500 within the ancient walls, you easily find of an evening, not just a Brunello tasting, but an esoteric evening with Arnaldo pairing the wines of Friuli with cheeses aged in caves, or bringing forth whole dinners built around *lardo di Colonnata.* The authentic Tuscan food still reigns, but chefs also have come to town (okay, maybe from only five miles away) who devote themselves to taking local ingredients and creatively upping the ante. This is a fine state of affairs: the baby basking in the bathwater. Old traditions stay intact and the new coexist. The same philosophy that would enable Luca to be able to find his house in Cortona today.

I brought Marcella Hazan and a few other books from California, where we'd long reveled in the grassroots food revolution that eventually transformed American restaurants and contributed to that greatest of changes, the revival of farmers' markets across the country. I'd studied with Simca and later cooked my way through the books she wrote with Julia Child. I loved Paula Wolfert's *Couscous and Other Good Food from Morocco* and Diana Kennedy's tome on regional Mexican food. I took classes in Chinese cooking at extended ed.

In my family's southern home, we were already talking about what was for dinner while at lunch. Southern food, America's greatest culinary tradition, in some ways represents the polar opposite to Mediterranean food. Tuscans like to fry, too, but southerners will fry *anything* not moving. Ever had a fried dill pickle? And we used lard, bacon grease, lots of butter. The delicious desserts are loaded with sugar. Vegetables used to be cooked to death with a slab of salt pork. Just thinking about the southern table I pulled my chair up to makes my cholesterol level jump. But there are other strong, positive similarities between my mother's kitchen in Georgia and my own *cucina* in Italy: local, high-quality meat, farm vegetables and eggs, chickens that have roamed, fruit picked off the tree, especially peaches to eat over the sink because they're drippy with juice. Like my Italian neighbors, we didn't eat processed food, except for potato chips, mayonnaise when Willie Bell didn't have time to make it, and the ubiquitous canned cream of mushroom soup, that binding ingredient of both green bean casserole topped with fried onion rings, and the family heirloom, squash and cheddar casserole. My mother didn't favor the popular jewel-colored Jell-O salads that appeared at our church's dinner-on-the-grounds; she preferred spicy tomato aspic in a ring mold and a delicate gelled chicken salad in a charlotte mold. Those I would not eat, once I heard that gelatin came from horse hooves. Today I would love to find that delicate nut-and-celery-studded chicken on my refrigerator shelf.

Tenet number one of the Mediterranean diet crosses easily into the southern kitchen: When ingredients are good, you don't have to torture them into complex recipes. One, two, or three flavors, bold and fresh.

Writing this, I'm hungry. I'm missing that table set with embroidered organdy mats and my mother's blue and white Spode. The air-conditioner labored in the dining room window and when Willie Bell swung through the kitchen door, bearing her cornmeal-stuffed chicken, a blast of hot air whooshed in. After everything was cleared, Willie Bell sat down at the kitchen table for her own noon meal. I sometimes sat with her. I'd have another biscuit or a glass of her pineapple tea. My parents went to their afternoon naps. My sisters disappeared into their room to play records and curl their hair. The yellow kitchen in memory is always one hundred degrees, with a fan stirring a little air from the corner. Willie still had the dishes to do. This was long ago, another era, and in so many ways a wrong one. But I dearly loved her.

⁓

When I began to be invited into Tuscan homes, began to ask my neighbors how they made cabbage soup, or *tortellini in brodo,* or *pappa al pomodoro,* I often thought of Willie Bell and my mother, launching into their day. I wished they could come with me to visit Tuscan friends in their kitchens.

Very quickly, I stored my cookbooks. They began to seem fussy. During those first years, I realized that none of my Italian friends used them at all, except sometimes for baking. Baking, other than bread, doesn't occupy much of a Tuscan cook's time. If a dessert other than cheese and fruit is called for, most just throw together a fruit *crostata,* which they know by heart.

How stunned Willie Bell and my mother would have been to take their seats at the Cardinali table, to sample fresh fava beans with pecorino, Fiorella's pasta with *funghi in bianco,* a white sauce with porcini, and a falling-apart osso buco underlined with a few threads of local saffron. I think they would have felt right at home, as I have. Still, they might want to offer their hosts a southern dessert. I made that mistake. What a treat, I thought, my grandmother's coconut pie or my mother's chocolate fudge cake. The current American sugar consumption level of 137 pounds per person per year was probably even higher in the South when I grew up. Plain to see, by what they left on the plate, my Italian friends couldn't take more than a few tastes of the sugar-stunned desserts. I have retooled myself over the years and compromise with fruit tarts made with half the usual amount of sugar. But sometimes when expat friends come to dine, we celebrate our sweet heritage of walnut buttercream cake or profiteroles.

I've learned the most from Giusi, Fiorella, and Gilda. I've eaten at the best restaurants in New York and San Francisco, the ones with all the hype and the food shows and the books. After dinners at the di Palma house and the Cardinali house, I can't worship at those urban temples. These two home cooks have a depth of information on ingredients, a vast—*vast!*—range of dishes they serve, and an inborn aptitude for knowing what's ripe next week, what's ripe today. Years of cooking with them and with many others revealed to me the unprinted, unresearched side of the Mediterranean diet.

Why is the food so good? What secrets do they harbor? So much about olive oil. We began pressing our oil as soon as we cleared the land that had been abandoned for thirty years. Picking olives immediately connects you with the ancient cycle of the seasons. The brand-new greeny oil was a revelation. Even buying expensive oil in the United States, we realized, was only a shadow of the real thing glowing like liquid emeralds in the demijohn.[1] Our salads became paradigms. We made every bruschetta imaginable. As we began to try to duplicate Giusi's eggplant parmigiana, her *arista,* pork loin, even her plain green beans, we fell short. Then we watched closely. Whereas we drizzled the olive oil into the pan, she flipped off the spout and poured. She used three times what we did.

As I recounted in *Bringing Tuscany Home,* we became curious and began to ask friends how much oil they used per week. The average for a small family or couple turned out to be about a liter a week. We'd had things backward. While we meted out the olive oil in our California kitchen, we poured the wine freely. After a dinner for eight, we'd haul about that many bottles out to the recycle bin.

In Italy, back in the *nero* and *bianco* days, I recall seeing the *carabinieri* at lunch, pouring water into their wine. Even now, with farm wine, I still see that occasionally. Among our friends, we began to notice that after a party there would be only two or three empty bottles, and equally that many, or more, of water bottles. And the wine drinking commenced when the food was served. Only a few friends thought to offer a glass before dinner. We got it! Wine is for food, a part of the balancing act that comprises the Italian *cena*.

Olive oil, in the Mediterranean, is not only an ingredient; it's a libation, a holy substance that connects you to the earth and promotes a sense of belonging in time.

Time turns out to be the major ingredient of Tuscan dining. *Ritmo,* rhythm: Time is stretched by the pace of the dinner, which arrives in four or five distinct courses. This makes a tremendous difference, this balance, this dance of courses, this symphonic development—or maybe it's a series of arias. *Antipasto, primo, secondo, dolce*. Each is savored.

The American way: a light first course and an enormous main course with the plate filled. Perhaps a salad after. Then a rather stupendous dessert. What differs here in Italia is that courses are equal. Moderation is assumed. What else? The amount of meat. I never knew a rabbit or chicken could be cut in so many pieces. Even big grilled steaks are usually cut for two or three. So the quantity of meat consumed is quite small. The famous six-hour dinners, even eight, are stretched and stretched by the arrival of cheese, the *dolce,* the bowl of clementines or grapes, then the after-dinner grappa or *diges-*

tivo. Each movement of the symphony is nicely defined and serves to punctuate what's going on at the table.

"You never grow old at the table," Tuscans say. The grinding wheel of time stops at the dining room door, leaving those who pass the pasta bowl suspended in the aromas of rising steam. And it seems true.

At the call *"A tavola!,"* to the table, you flush with pleasure; you are coming into a celebratory ambience. Something wonderful is about to happen. Food is natural, eaten with gusto. It must affect your digestion if you think the first quality of pasta is that it's fattening. If the word "sin" is attached to dessert. I've never heard of a dish referred to as "your protein" or "a carb," and there's no dreary talk at all about glutens, portion control, fat content, or calories. Eating in Italy made me aware of how tortured the relationship to food is in my country. After a long Tuscan dinner, I feel not only the gift of exceptional company, food, and wine, but also an inexplicable sense of well-being, of revival. Dinner invigorates the spirit as it nourishes the body.

The last secret revealed to me is that "seasonal" means more in the Tuscan countryside than my passing up strawberries from Chile in winter, a chef's credo on the menu, or appearing at the Saturday farmers' market. The time for the gathering of wild asparagus segues into the two weeks for crunchy green almonds. Then we'll be picking wild cherries and young nettles and borage. Our neighbors get up before dawn to gather snails from the stone walls. We're all hunter-gatherers, we're foragers. Want to see the dentist? He's out picking his olives. The carpenter? Gone hunting. Here's the polar opposite of selecting green peppers coated with wax, soft apples plastered with stickers. No prewashed lettuce compares to raunchy wild field greens. The porcini and chestnut gathering in fall signals the beginning of long winter dinners by the fire. This foraging—not only does it yield the delicious gifts from the land—the practice brings with it a deep-rooted connection to the earth. On even the tiniest plot behind, beside, in front of an Italian house, someone tends tomatoes, basil, zucchini, lettuces, and garlic.

Maybe you've accepted an invitation to a Tuscan dinner, a long table under a grape pergola. The plates don't necessarily match and the wine is poured into tumblers. The table is laden with garden-fresh food, bread baked this morning, and wine that tastes of the Tuscan sun. This dinner never will be only dinner. Often it seems to me that a pact exists among the guests: Everyone will shine; everyone will ensure that others are cosseted, flattered, that they will laugh. The intimate society of diners creates this bond over and over. You are crowded together because the table seats only twenty and twenty-five have arrived. Friends play musical chairs throughout the evening so they get to visit with everyone. They may sing or play cards, get up to dance, even smoke those awful stubby cigars. The butcher may leap on the table and begin reciting Dante. Someone may fire a shotgun into the air. A dog will graze among the legs. Someone may shout out a proposal of marriage.

You never know what will happen in the course of a big night under the stars in Tuscany. You may even find yourself belting out "Unchained Melody" into a karaoke mike, as I did. When the ordinary leaps beyond ordinary, you follow. This table, at my neighbor's house, is set for the best life has to offer.

So, Willie. The long table. Shoes off. Fork poised. Pull up the extra chair for the stranger. Always, the garden. A basket by the back door. Let the butterflies and lizards and neighborhood cats have the run of the house. Windows open, heart and mind open. Fall into the round of giving melons, beans, jars of tomatoes. You participate in something larger than yourself. Salt the pasta water. And expect to be surprised. Always surprised.

Osso Buco

Mario Ponticelli owns Trattoria Etrusca—a few tables inside and a few tables outside. We've eaten what he's served either way. This is his osso buco, and polenta is the natural partner.

Serves 4 to 6

3 pounds osso buco, 4 to 6 pieces
¼ cup extra-virgin olive oil
2 onions, chopped
1 carrot, chopped
1 celery stalk, chopped
3 garlic cloves, minced
1 28-ounce can of tomatoes, chopped
Thyme
Oregano

FOR GREMOLATA
Parsley, chopped
Lemon zest
5 garlic cloves, minced

Preheat the oven to 350 degrees F.

Sauté both sides of the osso buco in the oil, 2 to 3 minutes per side, lightly browning. Remove, then add a little more oil and the chopped vegetables. Cook for 5 minutes, then add the tomatoes, thyme, oregano, and after 3 minutes, the osso buco. Cover and cook 2 hours until tender—actually falling off the bone. Serve the gremolata on top. Italians prize the marrow as much as the meat.

WILLIE BELL'S ICED TEA

Iced tea in the South goes with any meal. Two or three glasses send me on a caffeine high. I make this in Tuscany but must admit I use fruit-herbal teas and no sugar. Still a refresher.

Serves 6 in big glasses

Brew a pot of black tea, about 6 cups—using maybe 6 table-spoons of tea. Cool slightly and pour into a pitcher with ½ cup sugar, stirring until it dissolves. Squeeze in the juice of 2 lemons, then drop the lemons in. Stir in an 8-ounce can of pineapple juice. Serve with several mint sprigs and crushed ice.

Another Willie Bell refresher: Put a big handful of mint sprigs in a pitcher and crush with a pestle or the back of a spoon. Fill with lemonade and serve with crushed ice. She smashed her ice in a pillowcase with a hammer!

A Larger Freedom

WE THROW THE LAST BEST PIZZA PARTY OF THE summer. Chiara brings an orange falcon kite for Willie, and the children run up and down the hills beneath its haphazard flight. Placido and Teddy break my *bocce* winning streak and gloat. They've been humiliated to be beaten by a rookie American. The two bigger boys are cannon-balling the water out of the pool. I'm trying to sing the lyrics to "I'm Yours" so Lina can learn it for the Ferragosto party. The men are playing cards. Chiara, stunning in a green and white bikini, stretches out in the low rays.

When the sun falls behind the chestnut grove, Ashley and I bring out platters of antipasti and everyone gathers at two linked tables. Inside the *forno,* the fast flames look almost liquid. Ed shoves aside the coals, and Domenica, Ivan, and I begin to turn out the pizzas. The children don't linger. Claudia takes Willie's hand and they're back in the water, riding a raft as if it were a horse. I pass the salad as the margherita arrives, followed by anchovy and caper, then a sequence of other thin-crusted pizzas.

Dessert is the famous snowball meringues (cream-filled clouds) from the town bakery, Ivan's dense chocolate cake, and a watermelon I've cooled in the bathtub. I take out the limoncello from the freezer and the grappa, turn up the guitar music of Ottmar Liebert on the way outside. Everyone is laughing— some joke I missed. So much laughter. I will always be amazed.

When I gather Willie up for bed, he seems exhausted. "Franny," he says, "I want to stay here forever." He smells of melon, grass, pool water.

"I know, sweetie. But you have to go back to Rocco. He's in his run right now thinking, 'Where's Willie?' And soon you have school—first grade!—and your friends . . ."

"But . . . I like living *here*. It's different."

"Yes, you're so right, my love." He visited for the first time when he was six weeks old. I thought even then he was unusually alert and happy when propped on cushions under the lime trees or wheeled to the piazza, where he was greeted as "baby Jesus" because of his blond hair. (*All* babies are worshipped in Italy.) At two, he cried when he had to leave. At that age, can you sense the spirit of a place? This boy, I must stay mindful, is experiencing the mystery of childhood that will endure his entire life. I count to twenty in Italian, then back down, tickling his back, and before I get to zero, he's asleep.

⁓

No one should travel in August, but we always forget. The four of us take the train to Florence and wander about in the heat and throngs. Ashley looks in a few shops, but it's too stifling hot to contemplate winter. The summer clothes look like the leftovers they are.

We take a taxi to La Specola, the natural history museum that displays one of each animal, fish, fowl collected in some dim past. We're enthralled, even though the taxidermists' black stitches show and there's dust on the noses of the tigers. We've come for the wax models of human bodies made for medical students at the beginning of the nineteenth century. Ed and I have been before and thought Willie would be interested. We're the only ones here. I'm struck by the framed anatomical drawings, which I don't remember. The intricate and exact livers and spleens seem to have a faint backwash of diluted blood. Willie is most interested in the spiderwebs of veins on the écorchéd model showing the vascular system. When I point out the splayed woman with twins inside, he says, "Gross."

We feel splayed ourselves by the heat. We go back to the hotel for rest, air-conditioning, showers. Before dinner, there is a consummate moment. On the rooftop terrace, we order drinks just as a copper sheen of light hits all the rooftops and domes around us. The four of us linger in that radiance and I try to make indelible in memory the faces of the three I love best with the city of Florence behind them.

The hit of the trip is the History of Science museum. Who would not be wide-eyed to see the lenses of Galileo? With them he found four moons of Jupiter. With his new, improved telescope he determined that the Milky Way was made of stars. Less enthralling—a bit of one of his fingers is also on view. Looking at the artistic design, lustrous woods, embossed metals of the astrolabes, medical tools, and clocks, you realize that science and art were once complementary. Those Medici patrons wanted not only useful globes, compasses, microscopes, balance scales, and barometers, but works of art. So much invention was lavished around the skill of telling time. Water clocks, hourglasses, and best of all the sundials and meridian lines. "What's this?" "How does this work?" Willie asks a hundred times. Italy is completely fabulous for children.

Last year he loved the Boboli Gardens and walking along the Arno and the confectionary Duomo. Next year—San Marco's monastery and a climb to the top of Giotto's bell tower. Equally miraculous—to be in Florence with a child. He stares at the sidewalk artists re-creating masterpieces in chalk, points at muskrats along the shore of the Arno, loves the names of pasta, designs on drains, the variety of motorcycles, gelato displayed with a fan of pineapple, a split coconut, a crescent of watermelon. And so we marvel too.

~

ONE REASON WILLIE is fascinated with the sundials is that he has just learned to tell time. His frequent bulletins on the correct time of day remind me that this vacation has flown. For the last few days in Cortona, we scale back activities just to spend hours swimming, talking, picking the remaining sunflowers and strawberries, and drawing. He's hoping the blackberries will ripen before he leaves, but they are still hard and pink. We pick Genovese basil and he makes the pesto himself, as he did last year. We cook potatoes with rosemary. I teach him to roast whole heads of garlic, then spread the hot garlic on bread, something he devours, squeezing out the pulp "like toothpaste." He and Ed read and take off from the page into other imaginary realms where they are skunks or horses and there are dangers to be escaped. They swim at night; they check on our water tanks and cistern. At least one irrigation outlet is always sending up a geyser.

I never love Italy more than when Willie is here. Everything good about living here magnifies. Everything just ordinary takes on the aura of his interest. Which theologian said that religion should feel like a larger freedom? I like the idea and connect it with love as well. Having this boy in my life offers many large gifts and the best is an expansive sense of largesse. Maybe freedom comes when you can feel your best self way out in the open.

⌒

AUGUST 15, ASSUMPTION—the day the Virgin Mary was whooshed into heaven. We celebrate this greatest holiday of the year by gathering with friends to eat *bistecca* together. The town has a Sagra della Bistecca, with an enormous grill set up in the park and droves of people lining up. Considering the crowd, the food is remarkably good.

Our friends Ombretta and Piero, like hundreds of others, have their own private *sagra*. The party on their terrace above their olive grove ends with dancing. Ashley makes sure every year that her vacation includes this evening with many of our friends, including Claudio, the handsome *carabinieri* marshal who's also a good dancer. Everybody brings a steak and Placido presides as grill master. There are platters of *salumi,* ripe tomatoes, baskets of bread, wine—that's it. Piero brings out his karaoke equipment and Lina, who has a big, great voice, sings. As the evening progresses, several of us take a turn, including me. I'm especially looking forward to this year's party because Lina will sing my favorite song of the summer.

At seven we set off to meet Melva and Jim for a pre-party glass of prosecco at Bar Torreone. Leaden clouds are gathering. As we sit under umbrellas, a few drops fall. Luca moves us inside just as the clouds tilt and all the rain that has not fallen in August spills as though from a giant dishpan. The hot street turns into a torrent and starts to steam. Lightning careens around the sky and the thunder rattles our backbones. "Is it raining there?" Ed calls Placido.

"No, I'm lighting the fire."

We settle back and chat with our friends' American guests

and other people in the bar. In ten minutes, Placido calls back. Canceled. The storm quickly crossed the valley and Ombretta scooped up the place settings. She's drenched, the fire is out, no sign of letup.

You don't just stroll into a restaurant on Ferragosto. They're jammed. We call Riccardo and Silvia. We know Il Falconiere is booked, but maybe their newly reopened Locanda del Mulino outside Cortona has space. Yes, they can seat the eight of us, even join us for dessert. We dash out into the storm and soon are welcomed at the cozy inn. No one will be singing "I'm Yours," but the goose sauce for the pasta is rich, the steak just fine. Willie gets to order potatoes cooked in the ashes, which appeals to him. The creek out back—dry this morning—is roiling past.

We're all, I suspect, flashing on the evening we missed, Ashley especially because she loves to dance. Riccardo and Silvia appear after dinner and we share the excitement of opening their first champagne-method prosecco. Riccardo shows Ed how to hold the bottle and slash down with a special sword, lopping off the cork, the top of the bottle, and letting out the yeast. Spectacular. Let's hope the spilling bubbles wash away any bits of glass. Theirs is the first champagne ever made from Sangiovese grapes. It's rosy amber in the glass and spritzy and spicy to the taste. A treat to be with the Baracchis for this inauguration, as we were for the first vertical tasting of their Arditos.

In Tuscany, it seems, if something is taken away, something else is always given.

The Ferragosto party will be tomorrow night instead. Too bad for us. We leave early for Rome.

On this day before Ashley and Willie fly home, we take the two-hour train ride and check into a small hotel that is new to us. Our usual haunts are full. Plain but pleasant, our rooms have step-out balconies with ailing plants and the requisite rooftop views. The terrace across the way is derelict except for garlands of purple morning glories swooping down from the railing. "Morning Glories on a Roman Balcony" I paint in my mind. Nothing else in nature, not the grape, the iris, Venetian velvet, or the amethyst goes as deeply into purple as these flowers with their white star hearts. The color is so intense, so saturated with itself that tears come to my eyes.

I come to Rome for color. I love the recently repainted buildings in chalky blue, yellow the shade of winter light, and champagne with a spoonful of peach juice. Someone discovered that lighter colors preceded Rome's characteristic sienna, ochre, and ingot gold.

We walk past the jarring white building by the American architect Richard Meier, built to house the august monument to peace built by Augustus. What an awesome responsibility. While the classic modern building would be a handsome museum in Pittsburgh or Minneapolis, the hard edges look at odds with the mellow *centro storico* surroundings. Although the materials are elegant and the lines sure and well integrated, essentially this building has an already-dated, generic impression. I've seen it before in many places.[1]

Don't mess with Rome! Many contemporary projects are planned. This makes me nervous. Who *is* up to encasing Augustus's Ara Pacis? Maybe building a simple glass box could have made a statement and still would have left Rome alone.

The fountain out front could be at an upscale branch bank, but at least it's providing some relief for the backpack-laden tourists who are wading. Willie would like to join them. Instead, he counts it as number three in his cataloging of fountains spotted. By lunchtime, he's up to ten, including the three in the Piazza Navona.

Roma, the day after Ferragosto—did the Apocalypse

happen and we missed it? I know many restaurants close now, know the Romans go on vacation, but who could think that the streets would be *empty* of traffic, so many shops shuttered, even the bars closed? Suddenly the buildings are prominent, also the trees, river, and sky. There are tourists in big clumps at the major sites but otherwise, turn down any enticing street and it's yours. Serene blue plumbago blooms on windowsills in front of closed curtains. Gone fishing. Along the Tiber, the drying leaves of the sycamores rustle with a hint of fall and the light falls in golden bars. Inside the Pantheon I get to see Willie look up at the great round opening from the classical world. When we were here in March, Alberto laid down on the floor under that heavenly aperture, arms and legs out like the da Vinci drawing. If one of us did that today, we'd be trampled. "Agrippa," we tell Willie, "a very important builder a long, long time ago." When we near the Trevi fountain, Ed puts his hands over Willie's eyes until he's right in front. The expression on his face! Elation unadorned, pure and plain. Many coins are tossed. This makes eighteen fountains for the afternoon and after this, no reason to go on. We walk to Campo de Fiori, which enfolds the memory of Field of Flowers, and then are lost for half an hour as we search for Pierluigi, one of the few restaurants remaining open in late August. We should have called—all tables are booked. But in the Italian way, a table is brought out and we are seated in the stately piazza, where we have a fine dinner on a perfect Roman evening. The waiter asks Ashley, "Would the young man like pasta with tomato sauce?"

Willie considers and replies, "I'll have the grilled sea bass, please." Oh, yes! Our gustatory training is working.

We each have something pulled out of the sea and drink a summer white from the Alto Adige.

We taxi back, all exhausted, fall into our beds, and in the morning we are off to the airport, and they are gone, gone, gone. On the way to Fiumicino, when I pointed out a stand of ruins, Willie closed his eyes and said, "I can't see any more. If I see any more, I will miss Rome too much." A response any passionate traveler recognizes.

~

WE'RE JUST TWO now in Trastevere on a quiet Sunday morning, the cobble streets shining from a light rain, a cat asleep on the hood of a Cinquecento, fragile grandmother-handkerchief scent of oleander, intimate churches in neighborhood piazzas, seven bright T-shirts strung on a line with the same blue, blue sky above that Agrippa saw when he gazed through the open eye of the Pantheon. I feel a bit lost, lonely. Love, I know, spares you nothing. Always the motions within a family involve a giving, a taking away, an abundance, a loss. And the small departures accent the future day when the big green wave sweeps you under and those left pick up and go on.

At a bookstall—why would this be open when all else is closed?—I find an old brown book stamped in gold: *Venice* by Augustus J. C. Hare. The little volume distracts me with its woodcuts and quoted poetry, classical references and the Victorian approach to travel—leisurely, erudite, practical. Listed inside are his many books on Italy, France, Spain. I do love a traveling man. Or woman. Vernon Lee, for one. Back at the hotel, I read her book *The Spirit of Rome,* published in 1906, which reads like a journal but with a writer's passion for language and image. I like her description of coming upon the little corpse of a kingfisher: "sky blue breast, greenish turquoise ruff, and glossy dark back, lying in state, as dead birds do." Her writing about Rome affects me like quick, vibrant watercolors. She describes the old olives in the hills as "pruned square, but of full dense foliage, not smoke-like but the color of old dark silver." I love descriptive writing when it *takes you there*. She can be slapdash and elliptical, but often I come upon paragraphs so wise that I copy them in my notebook:

> I feel very much the grandeur of Rome; not in the sense of the heroic or tragic; but grandeur in the sense of splendid rhetoric. The great size of most things, the huge pilasters and columns of churches, the huge stretches of palace, the profusion of water, the stature of the people, their great beards and heads of hair, their lazy drawl—all this tends to the grand, the emphatic. It is not a grandeur of effort and far-fetchedness like that of Jesuit Spain, still less of achievement and restrained force like that of Tuscany. It is a splendid wide-mouthed rhetoric; with a meaning certainly but with no restriction of things to mere meaning.

I second that. Rome constantly outdoes itself. I like her choice of "rhetoric," in the sense of effective speaking or writing. As though Rome were a revelatory book to read, which it is.

This is the first time I've been back in Rome since I read Vernon Lee. Often as I meander, I wish for the companionship of dead writers who've given me an intensely personal view of a place. I envision her as she appeared in John Singer Sargent's portrait—wire-rim glasses, eyes as dark as black olives, severe and professorial except for the partially open mouth, which gives her a tentative quality. Her book about Rome is all observer; she's not there except as the eye. But there's the gift: We see as she saw. And now and then a door swings open and you see what you've always known but never put into words:

> I find that the pleasure I derive from churches is mainly due to their being the most inhabited things in the world: inhabited by generation after generation, each bringing its something grand or paltry like its feelings, sometimes things stolen from previous generations like the rites themselves with their Pagan and Hebrew color; bringing something, sticking in something, regardless of crowding (as life is ever regardless of other life): tombs, pictures, silver hearts and votive pictures of accidents and illnesses, paper flowers, marbled woodwork, pews, hangings. And each generation also wearing something away, the bricks and marble discs into unevenness, the columns into polish, effacing with their tread the egotism of the effigies, reducing them to that mere film, mere outline of rigid feet, cushioned head and folded hands . . .[2]

❧

IN ALBERTO'S HONOR, we visit the Caravaggios in the Palazzo Barberini. He loves Caravaggio's light and shadow, his force driving through his brushes directly onto the canvas. These two are unusual. A powerful, subtle Judith lopping off the head of Holofernes, who looks scary and very real. Then there's the most mysterious painting of Caravaggio's I've seen, shadowy Narcissus gazing into a dark pool.

❧

ALMOST AS FINE, for dinner a plate of tiny veal meatballs with artichokes and caramelized cherry tomatoes, served with two crisp slabs of grilled polenta. And a waiter named Pasquale who brings over morsels to taste and insists on selecting the wine. A warm night in Rome and everyone left in the deserted city dines outside. I feel that I've lived here for a thousand years.

~

Roma non fu fatta in un giorno, the verbs reinforcing the remote past. Though not built in a day, though not knowable in a lifetime, Rome can be absorbed in a few hours: buildings, ruins, streets, the sound of bells, colors imprinting forever inside the mind of the blissful observer. Of the great cities, Rome has the biggest heart. In this end-of-August silence, I can hear it beating.

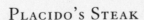

Purée di Cannellini con Gamberi e Pomodori
Purée of Cannellini Beans with Prawns and Cherry Tomatoes

Villa La Massa, one of the premier hotels in Italy, is located just outside Florence. Head chef Andrea Quagliarella gave me this one. The unusual pairing reminds me of the southern classic shrimp and grits.

Serves 6

1 pound cannellini beans
20 prawns, shelled, cooked, and seasoned
12 shrimp, shelled, cooked, and seasoned
2 ripe tomatoes, chopped
Extra-virgin olive oil
1 small bunch of fresh thyme, coarsely chopped
Salt and pepper

Soak the beans in water overnight, bring them to a boil in abundant salted water, then simmer for about 2 hours. Purée with enough cooking water to form a light cream and pour into soup plates. Add the prawns and shrimp with some chopped tomatoes already mixed with oil and thyme. Add some more extra-virgin olive oil and fresh ground pepper.

Placido's Steak

Placido, known from childhood as "Plari," is a grill master. Whether it's porcini, slabs of pancetta, guinea hens, pigeons, or little birds—he times by instinct and smell and also remains perfectly at ease. He mans the grill at Ombretta and Piero's annual Ferragosto party, where Lina sings as he cooks and everyone dances on the terrace. We all come to the *festa* with steaks in hand.

First, we go to Claudio's, the *macelleria* right inside one of the Cortona gates, and ask for the same kind of steak that Plari buys for himself. Antonella, all dressed up behind the counter, selects a hefty piece and whacks at it a bit. We walk out with gargantuan steaks from those famous, huge white cows called *Chianina*. Tuscans like their steak *al sangue,* bloody, so grilling time here is approximate. After the steak is lifted from its oil bath, you can dip in slices of bread and grill them for quick *bruschette.*

Serves 1 or 2

> *1 big thick T-bone steak*
> *Extra-virgin olive oil*
> *Salt and pepper*
> *Rosemary, minced*
> *1 garlic clove, minced (optional—Placido does not use it)*

Cut gashes in the strip of fat on the outside of the steak so that it doesn't curl up in the heat. Prepare a pan large enough to hold the steak. Add oil, salt, pepper, rosemary, and garlic.

Place the steak on the hot grill. Do not touch it for at least 2 minutes. Turn over and cook for another 2 minutes. Bathe the steak in the oil bath on both sides, sprinkling more salt and pepper. Serve warm.

100 Jars of Summer Sun

"IT'S BEEN DRY OTHER YEARS, TOO — *PORCA miseria*. Why are they so rambunctious this year—sniffling out the damp roots under my oaks?"

"Hunting season has just been extended for this fall—there's a population explosion."

"One came eye to eye with me while I was in the pool. He leaned down and took a slurp."

On the third Sunday of each month, an antiques market takes place in Piazza Signorelli. Everyone comes to mingle and look at bells, books, tools, and baskets. But this late-August morning, hardly any-one examines the andirons and old postcards of Capri. They are talking boar.

I'd like to look at the vintage cooking utensils, but no. Even Walter, our elegant architect, has had an invasion. Over his shoulder, I see a man aiming an imaginary rifle.

"Put out a bag of corn every night for three nights. On the third night, when there's a crowd, shoot them," Riccardo advises.

"Shoot—are you mad? You can kill a *person* in Italy easier than killing a boar off season."

Paolo makes the gesture of crossed wrists, signifying imprisonment.

Ed recounts our saga. The irrigation comes on at dawn and shortly thereafter, a battalion invades.

Rob tells us, "I slept outside on a cot for three nights and they stayed away. On the fourth night, I slept very soundly and woke up at dawn. The ground all around me was ripped away." They'd frolicked around him, chomping his new lawn, possibly nosing his toes. The head of the *Cinghiale squadra* mumbles as he moves away, "Go sleep with your wife instead. Unless you want a tusk up your ass."

In the afternoon, we walk the fence at Fonte, noting scuffle marks where they've squeaked under. Ed decides to build a wire fence behind the electrical and barbed wires. This war against the *cinghiale* is beginning to seem Sisyphean. I pick up windfall apples and sling them into the woods, hoping to slake their thirst.

⁓

THE APPLE TREE branches bend under the weight of the fruit. When we bought Fonte, the tree was tangled with vines and full of dead branches. Beppe and Armando pruned and cleaned for a day and now it repays with lavish crops of old-style, small apples, hard, tart and sweet. Boars love the taste and so do I. They'd probably gobble up my late-summer rustic tart with an unformed crust. Just roll the pastry out, slide onto a cookie sheet, pile in sliced, lightly sugared apples and chopped walnuts. Dot with butter, and fold the edges of the pastry around the fruit. Bake in a 350 degree F oven until the pastry looks toasty. So very delicious dabbed on top with a mixture of sweetened mascarpone and whipping cream.

Ed will be pleased tonight with the tart. All day he and Albano have been digging holes in search of a leaking tube. So far no luck. The wet spot extends for fifty feet and doesn't seem wetter in any one place than another. Ed called the plumber and he answered from the beach at Rimini. A bad leak can take down a hillside. We've had enough of that.

On such days, I feel too ashamed to loll by the pool reading and feel that I should be as industrious as they. I decide to make Ed's favorite pasta for dinner and to set the outdoor table out-of-mind around the corner from the wet spot. We'll face the chestnuts and the view of Cortona instead. I start in the *orto* with a basket of *ciliegini,* little cherry tomatoes, some of which are splitting on the vine. I eat as I pick, understanding with each burst of quintessential flavor, that, yes, tomatoes are a fruit.

I wish Willie were here to help make *pici.* It's the best pasta to make with a child—or an adult. As I measure the flour and crack the egg, I think of how much he'd love to thrust his fingers into the gooey mix.

Ed has the ambition to try every pasta in Italy. Our local mom-and-pop-sized grocery store carries fifty-something shapes of dried pasta. The Bottega della Pasta Fresca, just inside the Porta Colonia gate, turns out wheels and Mexican hats and pillows and snail shells. The number of different pastas in all of Italy must approach infinity. On every trip we collect a new *orecchiette,* the ear-shaped pasta that is so delicious with broccoli heads, or packages of *conchiglioni,* giant conch shells for stuffing with shrimp, or *strozzapreti,* the "priest strangler," which once was fed to priests at Sunday dinner so that they were too full to eat much of the expensive meat served after the pasta course. I developed a passion for *fregula*—almost like Israeli couscous, only more delicate—in Sardegna.

We like the fanciful figurative language of pasta. The names bring a smile as you drop the box into your basket. Dinner is already getting off to a good start. *Farfalle,* butterflies, remind us of our garden, swarming with white and purple wings all summer. The sounds in *fusilli* twist like the curly pasta. *Mezze maniche,* half sleeves, look exactly like sections of a sleeve for a fat little arm. Hail is much feared locally because it can destroy the olive flowers at a critical moment. But a Tuscan pasta has been christened *grandinine,* tiny hail balls. *Occhi di pernice,* the miniature rings used in soups, resemble the eyes of a partridge. Lilies, stars, cock's combs, radiators, elbows— good nouns of everyday life seem to adhere to pasta.

Despite our fascination with names and shapes, Ed's progress toward eating all the pastas in Italy is distinctly hampered. After scanning a trattoria menu, he often says, as though it were a discovery, "I think I'll have the *pici*."

And I usually respond, "Yes, that sounds good."

Pici qualifies as the most robust of Tuscan pastas. No one seems to know the meaning of the name, though the De Mauro unabridged dictionary says the word came into the language in 1891. I think in these Tuscan hills *pici* has been around for eons, as essential as gnarly olive roots and bunches of grapes drying for *vin santo* in the rafters. Especially in the Siena and Arezzo provinces of Tuscany, *pici* appears on almost every menu.

In correct Italian, one says PEE-chee, but our local dialect slushes *-ci* sounds into *-s* sounds. Around Cortona, you hear PEE-she, just as you hear *cappushino,* instead of *cappuccino.* *Pici,* a plural like *spaghetti,* has no *picio,* singular, in the dictionary, though people in these parts offer a *picio* to a baby or pick up a dropped one from the floor.

Usually not included in cookbooks or seen on American menus, *pici* is the pasta closest to the Tuscan heart. Only the simple, down-home *tortelloni in brodo* comes close. We've had *tortelloni in brodo* every Christmas we've spent at our neighbors' bountiful table. It's quadruple the size of *tortellini,* those little meat- or cheese-stuffed nubbins of pasta whose shape was inspired by the navel of Venus. Fiorella's herb and chicken *tortelloni* float in the hearty broth of an old hen, a dish that warms everyone at the holiday table. The plump squares are substantially stuffed, not just with a spoonful like ravioli.

I cover my pasta mound with a dishcloth for its brief rest, and take my glass of tea outside to watch the work. "I'm making *pici*," I call to Ed.

He gives me a thumbs-up. "Soul food." This late in the summer, he's as tan as an Italian. I remember a friend's description, *the muscular poet*. His workouts with kettle bells have pumped up his biceps even more. Shirt off, sweating, he flashes a smile and goes back to wielding the shovel. I'm happy that we're having dinner alone. The greengage tablecloth, a few white roses, candlelight, and the moon—with the background music of snorting boar.

I like to make my strands of *pici* at least a foot long and about as thick as spaghetti enlarged three times, so that the bite is chewy and substantial. I've seen it almost pencil-thick, coated with goose sauce. Most of dried *pici*, available in every *gastronomia*, is quite scrawny by local standards. Although the dried variety works well, fresh is definitely best. A good bowl of *pici* brings you to the ample bosom of the *signora* who invented it when the larder was almost bare. *Pici* emerged from *cucina povera*, the poor kitchen, source of countless inventions in the repertoire of Italian cuisine. Surely the first *pici* maker had fieldworkers to feed at the end of winter when the *prosciutto* and *salumi* were gone. The thick shape of this pasta makes it seem like meat. It stokes the energy of wheat gatherers and olive pickers, as well as those now climbing steep streets in order to see a painting by Signorelli.

Some foods, as Proust with his madeleines knew, are memory foods. Like biscuits for southerners, tortillas for Mexicans, tagines for Moroccans, and, who knows, perhaps haggis for Scots, *pici* by now catapults me back to happy associations.

I didn't know how deeply the local people felt about *pici* until I went into Maria and Vitalia's fresh pasta shop on Liberation Day, Italy's memorial to the end of World War II. I looked in the kitchen where Maria was lifting off the long ropes of pasta as they extruded from the machine. A small line formed at the counter. "We've sold one hundred and eighty kilos [almost 400 pounds] of *pici* this morning," Vitalia told us. I ordered our five hundred grams, plus a few of the borage-stuffed ravioli. Later in the morning, we saw Vitalia in his white coat crossing the piazza, tray aloft, making his deliveries for the one o'clock *pranzo* rush. A scene from a Balthus painting, a visitor might observe, but locally, it's just *normale*. By one o'clock, rich aromas of chefs' special sauces drifted from the doorways and we rushed into Santino Cenci's Trattoria Toscano, suddenly starving.

Every day Santino offers a homey specialty, such as veal shank, beef stew, or *polpettone,* his version of meatloaf that banishes forever my old dorm-food associations with that dish. He makes terrific *pici* with the classic duck sauce. I've never seen it elsewhere, but he makes a leek sauce as well. Santino always comes out to say hello and make sure everyone is eating well. "Do Americans order *pici*?" I asked him.

"Yes—always the duck. There's not a *picio* left on the plate." Ah, there's the singular again, which doesn't legally exist. Obviously, the local wines go well with *pici*. Cortona's hills are attracting big attention among winemakers recently. Of course, this area always had wine—from someone's Uncle Anselmo's to the prestigious vineyards Avigonesi and Poliziano, between here and Montepulciano. Now we have several DOC wines and everywhere a new awareness of wines not stored in the family cantina demijohn. With my *pici* on Liberation Day, however, I told Santino's son, Massimo, "I don't want to drink any wine. Only water. I have work to do." He rolled his eyes and threw up his hands. In a few minutes he brought over two glasses of wine anyway and we drank them.

At nearby Trattoria Dardano, home away from home for us, Paolo's mother and grandmother epitomize *casalinga,* home-style cooking. Their intense *pici* sauce is the basic *contadina* tomato sauce that has spent an afternoon on the back burner. During hunting season, Ed prefers the hare or boar sauce. We've known Paolo, now in his late twenties, since he was Willie's age and already happily helping bus plates for his parents. He's putting his own touches on the family business. He loves to hear people guess the ingredients of his special *digestivo,* which arrives as a gift after dinner. Following the model of *limoncello,* Paolo invented a concentrated, malachite-green elixir made from bay leaves. Potent and perfumy, this little shot feels as though it could cure anything from migraine to palsy.

On Piazza Signorelli, Taverna Pane e Vino serves *pici alle molliche,* also a simple recipe: anchovies, coarse, crunchy bread crumbs, and a hint of hot peppers. Ed is wild for that. Pane e Vino, owned by Debora and Arnaldo, attracts a young clientele from all over the region, drawn by the simple food and the inspired wine list, the best in town. With this *pici,* we always drink a Tenuta Sette Ponti Crognolo, from a polestar vineyard right up in the rural Val d'Arno area north of Arezzo. While there, Ed said, "Why don't we start making *pici?*" He has already made the flat, wide *pappardelle* for wild boar sauce, and flat sheets for lasagne and cannelloni. As we left, he took out his phone. "Let's call Silvia."

Silvia uses ingredients from her own gardens and nearby farms and interprets them with freshness and verve. She's the only chef I know who manages to make *pici* light, with her sauce of cherry tomatoes, fava beans, and a few dabs of pesto thinned with olive oil. Silvia, a beauty who dazzles us with a sense of style that permeates every aspect of her life, comes from a local family of women who can flat-out cook. For decades, her mother owned Locanda del Mulino, a small inn on a stream, with a cozy restaurant where the tablecloths were angled layers of checked fabrics in cheerful colors. She recently turned the inn over to Silvia and Riccardo, who promptly remodeled the rooms and brought their own inimitable style to the restaurant, while keeping the cooks. The back terrace, overlooking a rushing stream, became one of the best spots on earth for a bowl of *pici* on a summer evening.

Silvia's aunt owns Fontelunga, a complex of farmhouses for rent, with dinner served in her own home. Needless to say, *pici* is on the menu, sometimes with goose sauce, along with farro soup, splendid guinea hens on the spit, veal roasts, and cheeses from a local shepherd.

∽

"Will you teach us to make *pici*?" Ed asked Silvia. Before we could set a date, Riccardo was on the line, too, planning a feast after the lesson. "Bring friends," he insisted. "We'll have three kinds of *pici,* then a leg of lamb roasted in a crust . . ."

A serene kitchen is a good sign of a fine meal. At Il Falconiere, the kitchen is blue-and-white tile, traditional *cotto* floor, a wall of copper pots, and gleaming, spotless counters with baskets of pristine vegetables. *Pici,* I soon learned, is easy to make. One of Silvia's assistants, Ulive, formed the flour into a volcano shape, worked an egg into the well, and added enough water to make the dough pliable and not sticky. She formed a dome and covered it for a nap. This is the part of pasta and bread making that I love. There—done, the satisfying soft loaf resting under a white towel.

We moved to the stove. The kitchen filled with robust aromas of garlic, duck pieces cooked with celery, carrots, onion, and handfuls of basil torn into quartered cherry tomatoes. Three sauces going at once. For the *pici all'aglione,* with garlic, toasted bread crumbs, *parmigiano* or pecorino, and liberal olive oil, Silvia simmered the chopped garlic in milk, then threw away the milk. The bread crumbs she stirred into the garlic were quite fine. "And the pecorino?" I asked.

"The cheese is stirred into the just-drained pasta," Silvia explained, "*before* the sauce is added—this makes the cheese cling to the pasta instead of melting into the sauce."

I jotted this *truc* in my notebook.

When the pasta dough had rested, Ulive cut a slice off the loaf and quickly rolled it out. She then cut the flattened circle into strands with a knife. This is where the fun began. She and Silvia showed us how to roll each piece until it was a yard long. Ulive worked on the board, pulling to lengthen as she rolled. Silvia preferred to roll in the air, letting gravity extend the length. Memories of making snakes with Play-Doh! We had fun looping the strands onto a tray, noticing how their *pici* achieved more uniformity than ours. Inevitably, some break. The result is a distinctly homemade product, with a sense of excitement from the actual creation of something only experienced previously through machines or the hands of others. "I love this!" I tell Ed. "It's fun, like crafts at camp—knitting potholders or gluing together trivets with wine corks." We're big proponents of the Slow Food movement. Making *pici* by hand is so nicely slow. The motion is meditative and the result soul-stirring.

Dinner in the garden after our lesson lasted five hours. The arched iron rose pergolas framed the night views of the valley and at the end of the garden came the musical sound of water falling into the ancient cistern. Dining here, I always sense the presence of Riccardo's ancestor, the seventeenth-century poet who raised falcons. Each of the three *pici* was served separately, with just-right wines to match. With the lightest, the *pici* with cherry tomatoes, the newest fava beans, and pecorino, we drank a Capanelle Chardonnay. With the piquant garlic *pici,* we had a red wine from over in the coastal Maremma area of Tuscany, a Morellino di Scansano made by Moris Farms. Ed and I often drink Moris Farms' Avvoltore and are happy to try their Morellino. With the duck-sauced *pici,* Riccardo poured his own poetic estate wine, Rosso Smeriglio Baracchi 2001. The duck sauce was *magnifico.* After the duck was sautéed with the vegetables, ground veal and pork were added, along with fresh tomato sauce. The simmered result was incomparably rich and savory. I resolved to take the time to peel my tomatoes from then on.

As promised, the dinner proceeded to three-month-old lamb, butterflied and spread with herbs, then wrapped and baked in bread dough. With this pièce de résistance, Riccardo honored us with the unveiling of his big-lipped, mellow-voiced Baracchi Ardito 2001. This was an exciting moment. We were there the spring he planted the vines, when the grapes were picked, and when the juice went into barrels. Now the wine pours. We rejoiced that such a blissful wine came from the hills spreading out below us, then rising to the noble profile of Cortona in the distance.

❦

THE MOTION OF rolling the strands in the air feels fundamental, like spinning yarn from wool. Good, I've made too much. Thinking back on all the fun and warmth around eating *pici,* I also think forward to lunch tomorrow. Reheated, the strands will have absorbed more of my fresh garlic and tomato sauce. Maybe I'll dab on some *robiola* cheese to melt into the tastes. For now, loops are arranged like necklaces on a cookie sheet.

My apple tart waits on top of the stove. Table set, wine selected, roses plopped into a pewter jug: immortal joys.

⁓

AT THE END of August, this high up, the garden peaks. At Domenica's house, her outdoor kitchen becomes a tomato factory. We pick as many as we can haul from our *orto* and search cabinets for all the empty jars from last year. Only our tops have to be replaced every year. All the hardware stores sell the equipment for this ritual. I've always wanted one of those outdoor burners with the aluminum pot that's big enough to bathe in. For our purposes, the stove works well.

The process is deeply familiar. My mother and Willie Bell devoted a day at the height of Georgia peach season to making their special Pickled Peaches, sterilizing the jars on the outdoor fireplace in a black iron pot. The entire yard filled with the scents of peaches and cloves, and, in turn, when the peaches appeared alongside the Thanksgiving turkey or the Christmas quail platters, the dining room filled with a summer morning.

Putting up tomatoes couldn't be simpler, but still it's a lot of work. After the jars are sterilized in a big vat, you pack in the tomatoes and top with a few leaves of basil. Then you cap the jars and lower them into a boiling bath for one hour, Domenica lets the water cool, then with tongs lifts the jars onto the counter. The lids must whoosh down in the center, then you know they're airtight and will last for more than a year. While a hundred or so suffice for us, the pantries of Gilda, Domenica, Giusi, and Fiorella are jammed by now with three or four hundred jars. Aren't we fortunate that the Americas gave Italians the tomato?

For us, there's no greater satisfaction in the kitchen than rows of jars of tomatoes lined up, ready to pop open. They're wonderful gifts to expat friends who don't devote their Augusts to this lovely slavery. It's fun to say to family members visiting while we're gone, "Use all the tomatoes you want." When one of us is alone for dinner, these jars offer a quick soup or pasta sauce with all the comfort of a real meal without time spent in the kitchen. Gilda and I save bits of cloth all year so we have bright patterns to cut into squares, place over the lids, and tie with raffia or ribbon. Gilda also puts up roasted peppers, sausages, and cherries. Ivan makes quince, fig, and squash preserves. Fiorella even puts up jars of eggplant.

~

Tom'ato palooka parallels another seasonal passion. Now we snip wild fennel flowers, dry them on screens for a couple of days, then shred them of their stems and store the fragrant flecks in small jars. People on their walks carry small bags for yellow fennel flowers they can reach above the roadsides. How many ankles have been broken in mad leaps over ditches in hot pursuit of this delicate flower? Everyone knows that a gentle scattering transforms pork roasts and potatoes. The green-gold color and the mysterious antique scent remind me of medieval herbal cures and love potions. I think there's some mythic attraction to fennel, perhaps because we first received fire when Prometheus ferried coals inside a fennel stalk. Baked fennel is superb. A little eponymous sprinkling doesn't hurt that dish at all.

While cutting the fennel flowers, I pull an apple off the tree. Via my scented hands I learn that fennel and apple dance to the same tune. A pan of apples is baking in the oven and the added scent of fennel smells right.

For the *contadini,* St. John the Baptist's day (June 24) is when you stomp down the garlic spears to stop the energy from going into the aboveground shoots; St. Filbert's Day

(August 22) is when you gather the hazelnuts. Probably a mnemonic from when people were more tied to the church calendar than to their electronic agendas, the association of a farm task with a saint, speaks to a drastically different state of mind. I enjoy the image that arises. John up in my *orto* stamping down the garlic with his boots, Filbert reaching over the hydrangeas to pick up the hazelnuts in their frilly shells. Today should be championed by someone—maybe the local Santa Margherita—as fennel picking day.

THE FRONT WINDOWS of Bramasole we keep closed at night now because the air has changed from balmy summer sweetness to chill-tinged breezes. We leave open the small back window of our bedroom almost all year, loving the rush of fresh air and the waves of scent at different seasons—wet spring grasses, plum and apple blossoms, and tonight the spicy fennel flowers. When I'm home in America, I'll call up these seasonal fragrances, fast-frame, along with the cries of night birds.

The most profound scent that wafts through my room is the intense smell of the grasses after a rain at the end of summer. There's something of the brushfire that could have spread but did not, of the parched breath of earth, the ancient smell of old honey in a hive, the sparrow nest Ed brought in, no larger than his hand, fallen from the dog rose by the first fall wind.

Praying for the Queen of Hearts

ED LEFT EARLY ON HIS VESPA TO HELP WITH Riccardo's *vendemmia*. He took the tiny scythe for cutting grapes that we found among the debris when we bought Bramasole. Riccardo uses scissors, but Ed is fond of the worn handle and the old forged sickle blade. He thrives on outdoor work, especially with the camaraderie that grape picking inspires. They move quickly down the rows, and the sun, luscious smells of ripe fruit, rotting smells of already fallen clusters, and the piled crates at just the perfect sugar-content moment dispel the awareness of back-bending labor. The call came early. "We start today. Meet first for a coffee," Riccardo said. "We will be eating early, at twelve." Typical. Any activity is bookended by priority number one, food.

At the end of summer, the intense social whirl slows, spinning out sweet September days with light the color of straw and enough chill by late afternoon to send me to my box of sweaters stored under the bed. The luxury of early fall still seems a prize I've won. When I was teaching, I always left for California at the last minute of summer, practically running to class from the airport. Now, we may linger into this most radiant season. No houseguests, the piazza cleared out, no need to reserve tables for dinner, and the grand heat over—a blissful time. I have a day alone in my study.

With only a shot of caffeine in my coffee, I'm reeling with delusions of grandeur. I riffle through my four project boxes, dreaming of several books I will write, all effortless to plan on a September morning. I like to keep going at once a nonfiction book project, a poetry or novel project, maybe a travel article, plus my business writing for furniture designs.

That's a good way to cook, too. Get three or four pots perking on the stove while rolling out the biscuit dough, chopping the celery, and cleaning out the fridge. Not multitasking, a nasty word that reminds me of driving down the freeway while polishing your nails and talking on the phone, nothing relating. Instead, I like taking advantage of overlaps in activities that connect. I clean the kitchen once; two or three dishes go on the table together. My project boxes offer different places for different rhythms of thought, and the synergy among them yields connections. Sometimes projects finish at the same time.

Work like this feels like play. Play is where we join the gods cavorting on Olympus. From living in Italy and seeing how people live and love, I saw that play is something you don't always know you've lost in daily life. So much energy poured into my job. Leftover time seemed full of a lesser reward: enjoyment. But not play, the exuberant rush of fun that comes so naturally to Italians. At home, many of the activities I planned for fun seemed like summer reruns. Arriving in Italy felt like falling through a trap door into a brighter realm.

Learning from another culture is one of those mysterious

movements of the psyche. I think you learn what you need to unlearn.

~

I HAVE A natural tendency toward tidy priorities. I can't help it. Every pot scrubbed and put away before the dinner is served. A semester's worth of preparation for the first class. The sheets ironed. Misplaced perfectionism takes time. Lots of it. Now I want to jump in off the high dive.

I've occasionally been willing to take a risk when prodded by desire. My big one was plunking down my life savings on this rundown little villa in Tuscany. You hear of people buying houses all over the place now but in 1990, I was in virgin territory, just hoping this was not my own private Donner Pass.

What I experienced was a great big electrical charge to my habits. A grand zap. That act prompted so many other changes. I look back on crucible moments and see how each one burned up something in me and created the ashes from which other plans emerged. Maybe risk is a desperate form of play. You double the stakes and pray that the queen of hearts is dealt to your hand.

How do Italian friends naturally keep the *jouissance* they were born with? I've noticed that they don't talk about priorities. They work but don't become slaves. Always they have time to visit. Early on I learned that in Italian, there is no word for stress; it's a recent import: *lo stress*. Just wasn't a concept. Now *lo stress* exists, but in rural Tuscany work and play are happily still balanced, giving the chance not to just enjoy but to revel in everyday life. Especially the rituals of the table and the piazza. On my first trip to Italy in my twenties, I was having espresso with my husband under those arcades in Bologna. We had just arrived. The café was buzzing, waiters gliding around serving coffee, a musical chairs going on as people visited with one friend, then moved on to another table. The noise level shocked us. The laughter amazed us. The gestures had me secretly practicing in the hotel later. "They are having more fun than we are," I said. We were having fun, too, but not their kind of fun. I have ever since been drawn to that only-Italian quality—I have seen it nowhere else—of taking great satisfaction in the everyday.

I never will completely get over the nagging sense: *I should be doing something.* But my friends and neighbors in Cortona don't have that particular demon. They are doing what they need to do by *being.* People who own so much historical time must feel more comfortable inside time. I see: Time can be a river for floating. Our friends drop in. They call and propose spontaneous excursions. They stay out late having dinner on Wednesday nights. We hardworking Americans instead fight time, wring time out, push up against time, clock ourselves constantly. Italians relish the day. *Carpe diem,* they repeated for so many centuries that they don't have to say it anymore.

"They're playing, you know?" I said to Ed. "They're not force-feeding their days."

❧

WHILE LEARNING ITALIAN, what began to loosen in my skull was the tightly wound spool of *should,* a word I've always found deeply allergic, a word that takes a tremendous toll in time squandered. When my mother said "you should," I was quickly figuring out why I *would not.* "Should" was a word that figured in my leaving my first marriage. But conversely, I'd always applied the word in many guises to myself. You should brush the dog, fluff the pillows, water the plants, clean out the fireplace, get a haircut, replace the cushions the squirrels destroyed. On and on. Then the big one: *You should speak fluently.*

But I had to speak. Before I could speak. Letting loose in language, mistakes and all, finally cut that restraint. The Italians didn't *care* that I bumbled the conditional tense. Better to fail than feel hesitant. Better to let the cushion fluff provide nesting for birds than to experience *lo stress*. Better to have no houseplants. Maybe never mastering the conditional freed me, broke the hold of the *brutto* word *should*.

Isn't it best—to surprise your own life? Beats the bejesus out of my tidy priorities. Hemingway said sometimes he could write better than he could write. If I can extrapolate that— Italians live better than mere living. Even those with little live as though they were put here to flourish and praise.

My flowered project boxes become time capsules. I find menus from Elba, scraps of paper with quotes from Horace, outlines I'll never follow, images detached from their origins, such as:

His imprecise features look as though his face has come unstuck from a gelatin mold and is slightly melting.

And:

A miraculous face—surely she grew not normally but from a bulb deep in earth, issuing forth as if a lily.

Will I ever use those?

~

MATERIAL OFTEN DOES not like to stay in its appropriate box and wants to leap over into another. While slowly writing this memoir, I'm finishing a book of travel narratives. I'm also hunting and gathering for a book about moving back to the South. I've started a magazine article. The South, I find, especially intrudes.

I often consider what my life would have been had I stayed in my hometown, married my first love, who was so beautiful, with eyes green as jasper, black hair cut too short, and a tiny space between his front teeth. With him I could have put down the tap root in the fecund soil of south Georgia. I almost can see it. The one trip to England for Shakespeare and Keats, the blissful vacations at Fernandina Beach where I spent summers as a child, compiling the Methodist Church cookbook, and restoring my grandfather's half-burned house. I deeply admire those who continue to live under the protective veil of deep familiarity. *I have traveled much in Fitzgerald.* The scenario is vividly imaginable/unimaginable. There I might have written seven southern novels by now, become an eccentric, caused a few scandals. There would still be those who said, "Got your daddy's lips. I'd know you anywhere."

At sixteen, I was, way down in the swamps, already dreaming of old-world avenues with chestnuts in bloom, wavy colored reflections in the Grand Canal, and most of all the dry Attic air of Greece, where even the wind might seem to blow ancient sighs of the Oracle.

In my high-school senior notebook I wrote only one sentence from the required reading of *The Old Man and the Sea*:

I have seen the lions on the beach at evening.

The colors of the sand and the light glancing off the water and the tawny animals cuffing each other and tumbling—the whole image rose in my mind, as though I actually had seen those lions pacing the tide line in Africa.

Instead of staying where I belonged, I took the first thing smoking on the runway out of Georgia. My grandfather said I could go to college anywhere I wanted as long as it was not north of the Mason-Dixon line. I had an unexplainable longing to escape. Is there a genetic marker for that? I made it to Virginia.

In college I heard a speech by Ramsey Clark, then attorney general. He talked about the passionate, active life and concluded that when he died, he wanted to be exhausted. "Just throw me on the scrap heap," he said. Amen, I thought. *A way to double* life, I thought. When I move on to glory (let's assume), I hope I will have lived twice the years actually granted to me.

❧

I LET THIS southern interlude into my pages today because the force to *go* probably landed me in Italy, in this study where I lean out the window drinking light, this unlikely place for a south Georgia girl who spent high school reading about The War between the States.

Could I as well be in the front bedroom at Daddy Jack's house, my desk in front of the fireplace, the flower-sprigged wallpaper, my papers spread on the blanket chest, and Aunt Hazel's iron bulldog to keep me company? How—ever—to understand one's choices? One thing leads to another, my mother would say with resignation. Maybe it's that simple. Mr. Ramsey Clark, yes, writing and reading sustain me, pleasures to keep for an entire life, as politics did yours. As for exhaustion, wait—I'm not tired yet.

❧

MY STUDY SEEMS like a visible expression of mind: the jar from Greece where I keep pens; the wall cabinet Antonio made, lined with old photos of Italians; a row of inks I rarely use but think I'm going to; the walnut desk—long enough—that Fabrizio found for me; books stacked on the deep sill—and I must move them when it rains because the window leaks—the stuffed bookcase Ann Cornelisen gave me when she left Italy for good and never wrote a book again. One window looks south, the other east, always magnets causing me to look out. The small room is pale yellow with a border Eugenio painted under the beams, of the wild potato vine that crawls over our hills and the birds and butterflies that visit the garden, sometimes flying in one window and out the other, as though this room were part of the trees and sky, and maybe it is. This study, this house and garden, this town and landscape have given me books to write. I wish I could do justice to the place. In a life, though, whether you meet your aspirations or only strive, the important thing is the passionate interest, that true-north needle keeping you focused. I'm not the tortured kind of writer who forces herself to the computer and cranks out a certain number of words a day. Since age nine, when I found out that you didn't have to be dead to be a writer, I always thought writing books was the best life I could imagine—joyful and exciting. I was right.

Later, when I toyed with architecture as a profession, I still intended to write. But then I had to admit that I was not going to get beyond the quadratic equation in math. My interest, I told myself loftily, was in the integrity of buildings, how they interacted with their surroundings and people—not with the intricacies of structures, the vents and insulation and conduits. Especially since those aspects required advanced math. Now I would just like to write a book about buildings I admire.

Writing *is* play. You choose a subject and set out to learn and think as much as you can about it. Then you get to let your imagination loose in the arena. My project boxes remind me of the cigar boxes I used to collect and stack in my toy cabinet. One held pieces of pretty broken glass. In others I collected postcards, paper dolls, crayons, and shells. In this grown-up playroom I like to layer a lot of possibilities that may spark energy and combust among themselves. Maybe one idea hybridizes into an unexpected chain of thoughts.

I used to quote Ezra Pound's dictum to my students: *Make it new.* He meant this as a push toward the creative, a push *away* from what's known, accepted, expected. To fall into grooves already well worn may be comfortable, but it's hard to rise over the edges of what you've fallen into. To poets, he was admonishing them to abandon the old forms and rhymes, to find their voices in something fresh. As a life philosophy, *make it new* challenges the day. As a writer, he knew his business.

~

IN MY HERB garden, I made a table out of a slab of marble I found in the weeds when we moved in. This table under a pear tree became my sanctuary, my outdoor study. I balance a bowl of pasta with arugula pesto on my notebook and climb the steps to the first terrace level. One stone is loose and someone could stumble if it gave way. Oh, yes, the land always has something in mind for us to do.

I flash on the blistering work we did to rebuild the herb garden after the stone wall fell. Aches, sweat, scratches. I developed sciatica and barely could get out of bed. Still, we loved the work; we were living in the world of the project. Drawing the plan, planting the voluptuous Eden roses to climb the wall, watching bees ricochet among the new plants, lying in the grass at night watching falling stars, chasing fireflies, driving back from the nursery in the hot Fiat with scents of herbs filling the car. We made this room outside.

As indoors and outdoors became seamless, I got back the thrilling feeling I had in the long twilights of a Georgia summer when all the neighborhood children played kick the cans in the alleys and hide-and-seek among the bridal wreath bushes and old matriach gardenias. When the mothers began to call, often we pretended not to hear. We were on the cusp of night in soft southern air, held in that air as though we belonged to the place itself and not the lighted houses with mothers outlined in the doorways.

Instead of being surrounded by bookshelves inside, I'm

within a softer surround: tarragon, rue, lemon balm, mints, lavender, santolina, roses, and the afternoon ahead with no more to do than watch the lambent rays streak the valley below. A dangling olive branch brushes my neck. Did my mother's spirit flash by?

Just as I open my book, I hear *"C'è nessuno?"* Anyone home? Chiara comes in the gate, smiling up at me. She's holding a colander and because it is September, I know she is bringing blackberries. *Carpe diem. Carpe lucem.* Seize the day. Seize the light.

Permission for the New

THE BUTCHER GAVE ME A HUNK OF PROSCIUTTO bone. When I brought it home Gilda laughed. "This goes back, way back," she said. "My grandmother used to cook these. You only find it"— she gestured toward the mountains—"in remote places." She soaked it for two days in water to release the salt, stripped off the meat, added tomato and cannellini beans, then put the pot on to simmer. Last night we were astonished to taste the intense meat, and the thick rough stew infused with a dense, rich, *confit* taste. Some flavors evoke memory and emotion. This dish recalled the *contadini* who always used what they had. It tasted as though it had been prepared with a ladle of time added to the pot. Ancient wisdom: Scrape the bone for every shred of flavor. And, simultaneously, it was a big new treat to us.

~

IN JUST THIS way, what's old becomes new again.

Walter comes to the door this morning with long rolls of architectural drawings under his arm. As usual, he's impeccable in a light brown suede jacket, just pressed pants, and polished shoes. Looking at him inspires confidence that any project he supervises will exceed specs; the attention to detail will drive builders mad. But fortunately, Rosanno, one builder he often selects, may be as particular as he. Together, they'd be the ones to deliver Bramasole into its next stage of life. He's smiling and shaking his head in disbelief. "Great news. The comune has approved everything. *Tutto. Veremente un miracolo.*" Everything. Truly a miracle.

He comes inside and, first things first, Ed makes espresso. Walter spreads out the drawings, awed over all the approvals of usually difficult requests. They've even approved a two-car garage into the hillside because seventy years ago Bramasole was a house for the owner and for the farm tenant. Any garage used to be impossible, then one per house was allowed as long as it could be concealed. Two is a coup. "Look, the back terrace. The doubling of the living room. The pool out on the point, only they want you to move it over two meters."

We did not expect a decision so soon. Over the six months since application, the value of our portfolio of investments has nose-dived in the American recession. "The timing is now a problem," Ed starts.

Walter has anticipated as much and waves his arm. "My friends, don't worry. We have three years to complete the work. And extensions are possible. Just spend time thinking, planning, even looking for special materials. You're going to want an old fireplace in stone, stone door surrounds and wooden doors; don't worry."

We chat about his daughter graduating from law school, his mother's illness. He's determined now to move into his dream villa. Then he's answering his phone and must rush.

We stare at each other. All the ambitious possibilities for Bramasole's transformation spread and curl across the table.

For most of the summer, we didn't talk about the Great Remodel. Occasionally, when Ed checked our plummeting investment balance, he'd curse and say we shouldn't spend *anything*.

As I put on the pasta water for lunch and Ed starts the salad, we both speak at once, "You know, I'm not so sure . . ." We laugh.

We've both been thinking to ourselves, mulling through these weeks, and quietly came to the same conclusion. Bramasole is what it is, as Fulvio told us. Changing it, even for such great luxive improvements as Walter and we envisioned, might mean we'd lose our deepest psychological connection with the house. I'm fearful of wedding the patinas of its history to updated surfaces and structures, even carefully executed works. Redone, it would be brilliant but not as intriguing and mysterious. We fear it would be cored of its *anima,* soul.

"But the roof," I begin. Just this morning I heard the owl stomping in the attic over my head. Trickle marks of rain down the pale yellow walls don't classify as charming patina.

"Agreed. We must replace the roof," Ed says. "Rosanno says it's dangerous up there."

"Well, over two hundred years—the beams underneath must be twigs. Rosanno said they'd use as much of the old tile as possible."

"Yes, and we have another stash, remember, from the side of Fonte that had collapsed." We, like all Tuscans in old houses, keep our piles of stone, brick, and tile. You never know when they may be useful.

"And Ed, the terrace door. We've just got to do some maintenance things even though they're not exciting."

"The screens."

"Oh, I forgot. The humidity problem." Since the living

room walls dried by June and I swabbed them with two coats of whitewash, I'd blocked out the moldy smell of spring, the white-sprouted wall, and the dehumidifier toiling away.

We stare at the plans. Just what we've mentioned sounds scary, given the economy. What if it plunges further?

I take the plates to the table, pushing aside the neat and inspired plans. "Let's wait six months to decide on how and when we'll get into all this."

"Even if we hadn't lost a *sacco di soldi,* I think we would have come to the same decision. It seems right." Ed serves the salad. He has made a ton. We're going back to the United States soon and he wants to graze completely through the *orto* lettuces before we go. "The *time.* All the meetings over every little doorknob. The trips to the bank. I'm over the whole remodeling venture. I need a remodel myself."

"And it's just not long since Fonte and the fallen walls. We need to focus on our own lives." I'm dreaming already of traveling for my southern book and of a garden plan I've revealed to no one. Time has been on my mind all year. I'm dreaming of free-running hours.

"We're used to the small kitchen. I'm attached to the platters all around the room. Just grab one when you need to."

"Not everything has to be perfect."

"When was it ever?"

"It's been close enough."

"Yes," I admit. We've been lucky to live in this dreamcatcher, quirky house. "Remember that dream I had? When that stern dean tried to make me choose between my arm and Bramasole?"

"Yes, you couldn't."

"Now I can. I'd choose my arm, thank you very much. A slow sifting of priorities, I guess."

"Well, I knew you would go for the arm, even if you didn't."

"Remember that Auden poem we used to love:

Although I love you, you will have to leap;
Our dream of safety has to disappear."

"Yes—'Leap Before You Look,' or is it 'Look Before You Leap'?"

"Actually, it *is* leap first—reminds me of swinging out over the river on a vine and there's that moment just before you start to swing back. That's the moment to drop, the only moment. Just as your hands let go, before you fall and the river catches you, the exhilaration . . ."

"So, you're saying?"

"Let's do what has to be done but beyond that, let's swing out over the river and let go. Just see how we can open up to what's new. Faith."

"*Va bene.* Maybe I'll start writing novels on the walls like William Faulkner. Maybe that would be more fun than a temperature-controlled wine cellar."

"You did really want that, didn't you?"

"*Non ne vale la pena.*" Not worth the pain. "And we've been here almost twenty years. *Twenty years!* Longer than either of us has lived anywhere, except where we grew up."

"Well, I did fantasize about the spacious dining room. But now I don't care. I love this oval table with the pale ring where someone put down a hot dish. And when we eat inside, eight is plenty at a time. Let's ex out that desire for more."

"Yes, to hell with it! Not that I'm not furious that our economy has tanked but, I don't know, maybe it signals a time to regroup. Re-examine."

"Like it or not." And I do not. But somehow we do like

taking more control and deciding that simplicity offers a chance to leap.

∽

WITH THE DECISION made, both of us feel a fresh energy in being at Bramasole. I rearrange all six bookcases jammed with books we've accumulated in our almost twenty years here. Travel and reference in my study, fiction in a bedroom, art in the living room, poetry in Ed's study, nonfiction in our room, and children's books and miscellaneous in the hall.

Ed paints the kitchen door. Gilda waxes the *cotto* floors and we faithfully clip the dead roses. As I begin to pack to go home, I also reorder the cantina (no field mice this year) and Ed throws out junk in the *limonaia*. I'm going to look for new chairs for the living room. The springs of our white pair ping when you lean back and threaten to burst out. A flying spark from the fireplace burned a hole in the seat of one. Ed suggests that we paint our bedroom blue. I throw out three boxes of old clothes and convert the nineteen-year-old towels to kitchen rags. We both clear our desks, a semi-monumental task. Next spring I will add more old roses to the garden.

"What's for dinner?" Ed asks as he bundles the recycling. There's just enough left of Gilda's prosciutto bone creation. What a dish! And Ed will open an Ardito from our stash under the stairs.

∽

WE READY THE house for its time alone, when we are happily back with our family and friends in North Carolina, when we will hold the image of Bramasole serenely looking South, reflecting winter light, assuming a solitary dignity as it has for 220 years and as it will long after we are simply among those who have for a time loved the life on this hillside.

∽

THE MORNING BEFORE we leave for four months, I walk into town with my notebook. In the bar, I silently nod to Luca's portrait and take my coffee outside. Before I can open my notebook, Claudio joins me, then Sheryl, who's shopping early for the imminent arrival of guests, then Ed pulls up on his Vespa and orders a coffee. Eta and Marco, just opening their doors, come out to chat. Taut Jacqueline plops down like a puppet whose strings have been relaxed. Placido is here, talking to Lucio.

We're all here, in the piazza on a bright September morning. The pigeons are too excitable today and keep toddling toward our table and swooping low. I see the mayor look out his medieval window. He has stopped smoking and must pace. Delivery men step fast to haul goods into shops before they must clear their trucks out of the piazza. Jim walks up with his paper and takes his place. Alessandra stops with her dog, then moves on toward her shop under the Teatro. Angela—"pride of Cortona"—passes with her big smile and outspoken breasts. Massimo brings more cappuccinos, and suddenly a low helicopter crosses the sky above the town hall. I recall the Fellini scene, where the crucifix dangles over Rome. In the spring, I daydreamed that the airlifted Placido was waving down at all of us.

The helicopter pulls up from the scene, leaving us below, around a table in the piazza, up and up until we are indistinguishable from others visiting at tables, then up higher until we are specks, and the town spreads along the hillside, narrow streets, domes, bell towers, and rooftops left in a broad swath of green and stone and tile that could be framed and called *A View of Cortona.*

Envoi—
For Song

VENUS CATCHES IN A FLAT BUBBLE OF THE OLD glass in my bedroom window. For a moment, the spangling planet seems trapped. The blue light splits, pulsates: deep-sea fish eye flashing, quartz crystal I scooped from a stream in Alabama, ice cube splintering under a pick. A fox begins to yap in the olive grove. I lie on my side watching Venus traverse from middle pane to top, cross to the right, sliding over other imperfections in the glass, then out of sight. The night before I leave here, I don't sleep. I dwell—my sisters say, "You dwell on things"—on the unnatural act of flying in a silver bullet seven miles above the earth.

One hour, two? At a glance, how fixed the stars seem—but how quickly this handful of light moves across the window. I've never comprehended the basics: birth, random suffering, death, the momentum of earth wobbling on its axis. *"Swiftly tilting planet,"* a poet called it.[1] I do understand the natural state of two feet on the ground.

The snappy fox, Venus in the glass, and me, thirsty, sleepless, hot—a chance triangulation. I shift my mind back through space, beyond this sparkling darling named for love. A spider, traveling as she goes: my mind raveling farther than my imagination, farther than lenses can see, out into the gray abyss where one waits to be born. (I smile in the dark, remembering when I asked Willie at four where he was before he was born and he replied, "I think Phoenix.") Out there, free-fall for centuries. Touch nothing until the universe curves.

Does it turn back on itself, bringing time back? Inside the globe of my skull, gliding too far, vertiginously, and that plane I'll board, with its false world inside, as though hurtling through black space were a normal act. Is the universe—at some megadistance—shaped like the bones of the cranium? Am I lying in the canaliculi of a colossal mind? Or lying on soft sheets in my earthly iron bed with a boat painted on a tin disk above my head?

Oh, yes, it's the earth that moves around an axis I used to think was real, like a skewer through a tomato, and we ride on this ball suspended in space only by a concatenation of whirling magnetic forces which, according to a smart-mouth friend, add up to God. Any other god, says he, is firmly in the realm of *Jack and the Beanstalk* and cows jumping over the moon. I twirled my lemonade straw and asked, "What made the universe?" The inverse square law, he proclaimed, though right now I don't remember what equals what.

The fox simply calls out in the night. I would like to feel my hand around the shape of his foxy little head, raised in a silvery cry, his feet tensing in earth wet from afternoon rain, his rusty fur smelling of the lair. Soaked grasses, fallen sunflowers, earthworms, black holes, meteors, constellations like lions and a crown of laurel. This bed by the window, traction of fox paws, traction of Venus. Water from the well in a silver cup.

Then the first bird's piercing notes. The black sky, overlaid with a bridal veil of stars, shows no faint ray at the brink of the hills nor a subtle lightening of the eastern sky. But this *merlo,* this blackbird, knows. How, I wonder.

A House Flying

1. Anneli Rufus recounts much lively lore in her *Magnificant Corpses*. Caroline Walker Bynum's work is extraordinary, especially *Holy Feast and Holy Fast* and *The Resurrection of the Body*.

2. A study for that fresco is owned by the Getty in Los Angeles, while the Gatti hangs at the Metropolitan Museum in New York.

Orto and Oven

1. There are also succulent little clams called *dateri* in Sicily. This points to the importance and ascendancy of Arab cuisine in the area. The desert dates provide the metaphor; note that the dates were *not* called tomato and clam!

Gite al Mare

1. The designation Blue Banner, awarded by the European Foundation for Environmental Education, goes to clean, environmentally well-managed beaches with high water quality. The Marche's current Blue Banner beaches are, from north to south, Gabicce Mare, Pesaro, Fano, Senigallia, Sirolo, Numana, Porto Recanati, Civitanova Marche, Porto San Giorgio, Grottammare, and San Benedetto del Tronto.

Amici

1. This and other quests came to us through reading *Timeless Cities: An Architect's Reflections on Renaissance Italy* by David Mayernik. During a February week in Rome, this book took Ed, Alberto, and me deeper and deeper into the city. The author connects the portico of the mausoleum of Augustus to dimensions of the Pantheon portico. He traces various architectural programs throughout history and gives the reader a way to "read the whole city as a comprehensible story." Most important to us is Mayernik's explanation of Roman architectural structure as places to store memories of ideas, i.e., mnemonics such as ancient rhetoricians constructed to aid their remembrance of texts before print. Whole routes of building programs recalled to the ancients places where Romulus and Remus were born, where St. Paul stopped, or where some historical meeting occurred. The buildings were meant to connect with cultural memory. This, for me, is a book to read and read again.

The Signorelli Trail

1. *Luca Signorelli: The Complete Paintings,* Tom Henry and Laurence Kanter. This great tome is invaluable, since it represents the most recent and authoritative information on many facets of Signorelli's work. For many facts used in this chapter, I read conflicting information from several authors and Internet sources. I relied on Henry and Kanter for the definitive word. As new research takes place, attributions are subject to expansion or modification, but for now, I think, this is the best information available.

Città di Castello

1. *Agriturismo* signifies a country bed and breakfast where actual farming takes place. For example, Giusi, who worked at Bramasole for years and is our close friend, converted a sheep pen on her husband's family farm into a guesthouse, now rented through Classic Tuscan Homes. Such felicitous accommodations exist all over Italy and are a special way to travel. You're in touch with a family, usually

with a traditional way of life, and you experience a highly personal Tuscany. Many Internet sites and several books list *agriturismo* accommodations. A great value, as well as a pleasure.

SINCE THE ETRUSCANS

1. In *Bringing Tuscany Home* I wrote more extensively about olive oil. It's bothersome—maddening!—that so much misinformation continues to circulate. Recently I saw an article in a respected food magazine recommending that you keep your oil in a plastic container. Please! The smell of plastic enters oil in less than two days. We bring our oil home from the mill in huge plastic jugs and transfer it immediately into stainless steel containers called *fustini*. As we leave the mill, the owner always reminds us, "Get the oil out of that plastic as soon as you can." Buy the youngest oil you can find and store it in a cool, dark cupboard. At home in America, we have a *fustino* for the loose oil we ship home in metal containers. We store the bottles we bring back in the wine fridge. The constant 57 degrees and dark location keep the oil in *primo* condition. A bottle of oil left in bright light will start to go "off" in a week. Carefully stored unopened bottles can last three or four years, even longer. The oil doesn't really expire on a sell-by date. It simply loses its kick very slowly. Tuscans save any oil from last year or the year before and use it for roasting and basting, using the new oil right away for vegetables and salads. The sell-by date on bottles *is* important because one, fresher is better, and two, the oil probably has been exposed to light. See other information in *Bringing Tuscany Home*. If you are traveling in Italy, you can pick up a *fustino* at a hardware store. They come in several sizes and have a spout at the bottom for refilling your bottles.

A LARGER FREEDOM

1. I'm mixed on installing contemporary architecture into such particular areas long defined as themselves. Theoretically, the idea is exciting but in reality, landing an anachronism into such a setting rearranges everything. That's the point—but a point well taken? Does the new building redefine, invigorate, or creatively juxtapose

the venerable neighbors? New York seems somehow able to absorb contemporary architecture; the on-going pace of the city takes in all styles. The dirty glass pyramid—now twenty years old—outside the Louvre dismayed me when it landed there and still does. It distracts from the somber heavy weight of the past embodied in the Louvre standing gloomily on its own. I was shocked in Toronto when I saw the Royal Ontario Museum. Out in a field on its own, okay, although I imagine it still would look like a contemporary building that had somehow been dropped from a height and sheared into crash angles. Where it stands, it does not so much wake up the neighborhood with a splash of cold water in the face as put the rest of the area on hold while it tries its best to shock.

Theoretically, such drastic interventions work, but where? I'm looking. I like the atrium designed by Sir Norman Foster at the old patent office in Washington. It neither obscures nor competes with the adjacent structures but instead bridges, shields, and provides a new and welcome interior space. There's a sense of *enlightening*.

2. Vernon Lee wrote more than forty books, at least one on beauty. She was known as a writer of supernatural stories, but what I admire is her acute sense of place, as in *The Spirit of Rome*. She was English by parentage, born in France, but loved Italy and chose to live here for half a century. If intrigued, read *Vernon Lee: A Literary Biography* by Vineta Colby. *The Spirit of Rome* is available online through Project Gutenberg Canada Ebook.

Envoi

1. "The Morning Song of Senlin" by Conrad Aiken. A part toward the end often flashes through my mind: *It is morning,* Senlin says, *I ascend from darkness / And depart on the winds of space for I know not where.*

Cruttwell, Maud. *Luca Signorelli*. London: George Bell and Sons, 1899.

Gilbert, Creighton E. *How Fra Angelico and Luca Signorelli Saw the End of the World*. University Park, Pennsylvania: The Pennsylvania State University Press, 2002.

Henry, Tom, and Laurence Kanter. *Luca Signorelli: The Complete Paintings*. New York: Rizzoli, 2002.

Mayernik, David. *Timeless Cities: An Architect's Reflections on Renaissance Italy*. Cambridge, Massachusetts: Westview Press, 2003.

Vasari, Giorgio; translated by Gaston du C. de Vere. *Lives of the Most Excellent Painters, Sculptors, and Architects*. New York: Modern Library Classics, 2006.

ABOUT THE AUTHOR

In addition to her Tuscany memoirs, *Under the Tuscan Sun* and *Bella Tuscany,* Frances Mayes is the author of the travel memoir *A Year in the World;* the illustrated books *In Tuscany* and *Bringing Tuscany Home; Swan,* a novel; *The Discovery of Poetry,* a text for readers; and five books of poetry. She divides her time between homes in Italy and North Carolina.